Return to Murmansk

Return to Murmansk

Henry Swain

Seafarer Books
London

© Seafarer Books 1996

First published by Seafarer Books
10 Malden Road London NW5 3HR

ISBN 085036 452 3 Hbk
ISBN 085036 453 1 Pbk

Typesetting by Computerset, Harmondsworth, Middlesex
Printed in Finland by WSOY

Foreword

Why should anyone want to take a yacht to North Russia – to sail into the high Arctic, the rock-strewn inshore passage up the Norwegian coast, past the North Cape and hundreds of miles of bleak headlands of the Norwegian north coast? Henry Swain sailed his 34ft *Callisto* along this route, to Murmansk. Forty-five years earlier Henry had sailed as an Able Seaman in a warship bound for the same port. Escorting merchant ships taking supplies to Russia, was one of the more hazardous tasks undertaken by the Royal and Merchant Navies in the Second World War. Henry writes frankly about his fears and worries of those days and about the good and the less good things that happened to him then. This book tells about how he came to terms with those experiences in his own particular way.

Return to Murmansk gives a vivid account of life on the Lower Deck in a small escort ship on the Russian convoy run. Conversations and encounters with messmates are faithfully recalled to illuminate life in such uncomfortable and occasionally frightening circumstances. The book gives a similarly vivid account of conversations and encounters on board *Callisto* – occasionally also uncomfortable and frightening, perhaps more than it need have been because of the associations in his own mind between the two journeys.

So why did I write a foreword for his book? Firstly and obviously because he asked me to, secondly because we are both yachtsmen and thirdly because we were involved in different wars at opposite ends of the world.

But fourthly and most importantly for me, the reader may well be struck by the open way Henry tells us about his fears and their longer term consequences. This is not an easy subject for anyone to write about, but I expect that sailors of all sorts can benefit from his candour – as much to discover that they are not alone in their fears as anything else – but also to be reminded that the usual and most effective way for us all of dealing with them is to face them squarely and then get on with what still has to be done.

Admiral Sir John Woodward, R.N.

Author's Note

I am grateful to friends who helped me to sail and write. In particular I would like to thank:

David Turner	My friend and advisor
Sandy Simpson	Administrator and secretary
Roy Sowden	Joint owner of yacht *Callisto* and Principal of Dukeries Complex, Nottinghamshire
Moira Johnston	Literary advisor
Dick Squires MBE	Chairman, North Russia Club
Nicholas Luker	Department of Slavonic Studies, The University of Nottingham
Nikolai Berezhnoi	Mayor of Murmansk
Sergei Polosov	Secretary, Murmansk Section Soviet War Veterans Committee
Natasha Galliayva	English teacher, School 51 Murmansk
Marilyn Angles	Secretarial Services

H.S.

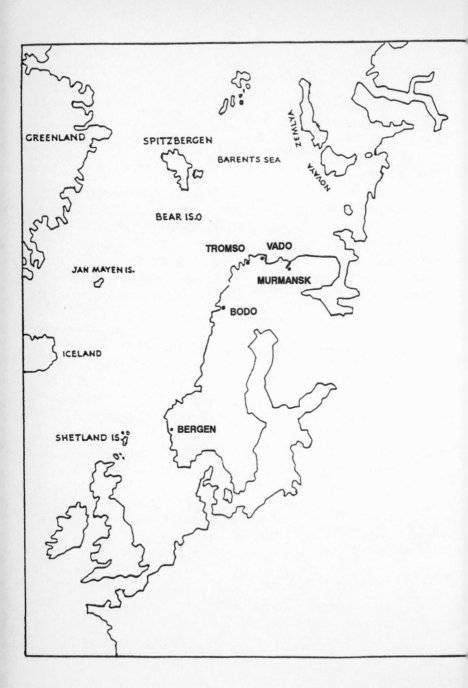

GREENLAND

SPITZBERGEN

BARENTS SEA

ZEMLYA

NOVAYA

BEAR IS.

TROMSO   VADO

JAN MAYEN IS.

MURMANSK

BODO

ICELAND

BERGEN

SHETLAND IS.

Chapter One

I couldn't see anything beyond the yacht. Visibility was less than 200 yards. The shores of the fjord which were close on either side of us might just as well not have been there. We were in an isolated world enclosed by the relentlessly falling rain.

'Keep on 340,' I said to Tom Nunn who was steering, looking half drowned in his oilskins.

'340 degrees,' he repeated. He glanced away from the compass looking ahead into the opaque wall of the rain. 'When do you expect to see the next mark?'

'Beacon in 5 minutes if you keep on this course. Leave it to starboard.'

My compass course was an act of faith – a faint line drawn on the chart showing the direction we had to steer. If you couldn't see anything around you you had to believe in it. The Decca Navigator fixed in front of the chart table could give us our exact position but at the moment it was emitting a bleeping noise and the display said 'position suspect'. It was having its own electronic problems which it sometimes did when you needed it most.

We had left Bergen an hour ago and in the absence of wind were motoring slowly along Herdlefjord. Our 34 foot yacht *Callisto* was heading north. We were at the beginning of a voyage towards the arctic port of Murmansk 1500 miles away in distant Russia. It wasn't a good start.

I stared into the rain. I could feel a cold rivulet of water inside my oilskins. My glasses were perfectly useless in this weather and I put them in my pocket.

Anne Swain, who shared the forenoon watch with Tom, was a huddled figure sitting beside him in the cockpit. Rain was pouring off her oilskin hood and her face was wet. She gave me a thin smile. I think she believed in me. The two other members of the crew now not on watch were sensibly below in the saloon keeping dry.

Earlier, in Bergen, I had wondered whether I should postpone sailing until the weather cleared. It would have been prudent seamanship but bad psychology. It was going to need a lot of determination to sail a small yacht to Russia. I had to demonstrate to the crew from the start that we were not going to be deterred by adverse conditions. A delay because of a gale could have been acceptable but if you were careful rain and poor visibility, though uncomfortable and nerve racking, were not a hazard. One other consideration had influenced my decision. Bergen, by all reports, was one of the wettest places in Europe. The only way to get out of the rain was to get out of Bergen.

'I think I can see it,' Tom said, 'close on the starboard bow.' He sounded relieved. Unlike Anne he knew enough about navigation to appreciate the fragility of the pencilled lines on the chart. As we approached it we could see the yellow and black stripes on the beacon and the top mark showing that it was located west of a rock or shoal.

'I'll need a new course to steer,' Tom said.

I went below and looked at the chart. I dried my glasses in a half wet handkerchief and layed off a new course with the parallel rule for the next beacon a mile away. My oilskins dripped pools of water on the chart. I went back up the ladder into the rain.

'Steer 350,' I said, trying to sound confident, 'twelve minutes.' There was no tide running. With the motor at medium revs that would be the time it would take us to cover a mile.

The three of us sat disconsolate in the cockpit enduring but alert in the falling rain. Nobody said anything. There was just the sound of the motor and the sloshing of our bow wave. Tom was intent on the compass and the view over our bow. Anne and I kept a lookout for other ships. The sea lanes near Bergen were fairly busy; in this visibility any ship would be close to us by the time we saw it. I looked for comfort at the radar reflector half way up our mast. Big ships with the magic eye could perhaps see us before we saw them but I preferred to rely on our own vigilance.

I told myself there was no danger. With our good Norwegian charts and our accurate compasses we could feel our way along the fjords. But I wasn't enjoying myself. I was feeling cold and damp. For some reason my mouth was dry.

After half an hour and two beacons later Tom suddenly said, 'I think it's beginning to clear. I can see the shore.'

The rain was getting lighter and the low grey clouds had acquired a silvery luminosity. Gradually the downpour stopped. Tom pushed back the hood of his oilskin. Astern the clouds were still thick over Bergen but ahead in the north we could see a thin line of blue sky.

'That was nasty,' Tom said. '*Callisto*'s first test.' We could see the lighthouses and beacons plainly now. He grinned behind his black beard. The water was still dripping off his oilskins.

We were where I expected we were. The abstractions on the chart had become real land and water confirming our position. For all my long experience of sailing I had never lost my wonder of navigating by the simple geometry of dead reckoning. With only three pieces of information – compass direction, tidal stream and distance run you could pilot any ship from a known position to another shown on the chart. You could do this in the blackest night or the thickest fog and the technology was a thousand years old. The now unneeded Decca was just beginning to produce some meaningful figures.

In a few minutes the sun began to shine through thinning clouds. Anne stood up and looked around her with disbelief. It was our first clear view of the Norwegian coast. The sea was smooth silver. On our port side were the green islands with meadows and houses along the shore, their painted timber walls shining in the sunshine. To the east was the great white mass of the famous Norwegian mountains with the snow line quite low. It was early June and after the rain there was a freshness in the air. *Callisto* had sailed out of blindness into a bright world of light and colour. I took off my oilskin jacket and sat down in the cockpit. I felt the tension running out of me. We had cleared Bergen, we were on our way to Russia and we had suddenly been favoured with the gift of vision. We could see where we were going and the deck was beginning to dry.

Everything was going to depend on good charts. I had been worried about charts in Bergen. I couldn't remember much else about the city. We had arrived there yesterday afternoon in the overnight Newcastle Ferry. *Callisto* was lying alongside the Fish Quay, a short distance from the ferry terminal. My partner, Roy Sowden, joint owner of the yacht, had left her with full tank of diesel and water ready to sail in the morning. It was raining and I was obsessed by the need to buy Norwegian charts. The charms of Bergen were wasted on me. I had intended to buy the charts before sailing next day when the shops opened but I was dismayed to find that Monday 4th June was a public holiday. No shops open, no charts. I had the alternative of sailing with the small scale Admiralty charts or delaying our start. The pilot books I had read hadn't mentioned public holidays. In this state of indecision I fell into conversation with the skipper of the Norwegian yacht tied up alongside us. He had come from the north and was heading for Oslo.

'I'm moving house,' he said, 'I've had enough of the arctic.'

4

In answer to his question I told him rather miserably that I was sailing towards Tromso but I had only British charts.

'They won't do,' he said, thought for a moment, and then said, 'Would you like to buy mine? You can have them for half price. I paid nine Kroner each for them. They will get you nearly to the Lofoten Islands.'

After that, even in the rain, Bergen had seemed a marvellous city.

Tom handed over the tiller to Anne. She steered carefully. She had not sailed very much and she had her eyes fixed on the compass holding the course Tom had given her. I could see her knuckles white as she gripped the tiller. In a few days she would be able to steer with only an occasional glance at the compass using the features of the land to keep an accurate course. When she had offered to join the crew she had said that she had no great ambitions to be a sailor, but she would do the cooking and stand her watches. She is a senior member of a successful architectural practice: I hoped she would not mind being told what to do all the time by Tom who was much younger.

Now we were well clear of the rain and Bergen I could leave Tom to sail the yacht through the fjord. He was dividing his time between going below to the chart table and standing in the cockpit staring through binoculars at lighthouses and beacons. He is my nephew and has often sailed with me. I know him to be an experienced and careful navigator. Sometimes he let the binoculars hang loosely on the lanyard round his neck and looked all around at the surface of the shining sea. He was hoping to see the blue ruffle on the water that would indicate a breeze. He would like enough wind to sail by so that we could silence the endless clattering of the motor.

I had been examining the small scale Admiralty charts of the Norwegian coast on and off for many weeks. Norway is a vast archipelago. Hundreds of islands, connected to each other and to the mainland by bridges and ferries, shelter the coast from the North Atlantic. Most of the time in our passage north we would be threading our way through narrow sounds and fjords. This sea lane is called the skjaergard or inner leads. It is the great all weather highway of Norway by which every town and settlement is connected by the fast ships of the Coastal Express. Tom was now using the new large scale Norwegian charts.

'I'm getting the feel of this,' he said. 'It isn't navigation at all: it's pilotage. It is going to be like entering harbour all the time. It's well enough marked but it'll be hard work.' He spoke as if he had given the matter a lot of thought.

We both looked at a lighthouse white in the sun on our port bow. It had a circular conical roof like a Chinaman's hat. Tom sighed, 'They all look alike, though.' Tom looked serious but his eyes were glittering. Sailing these strange waters was a new challenge. Other members of our crews sometimes found him rather reserved and dour and, when we were in harbour, he went ashore by himself. I particularly wanted him on this trip.

He went below to make up the log book on the hour – distance travelled, barometric pressure, wind force and direction and Decca co-ordinates.

'Alter course to 335,' he said to Anne as he came up into the cockpit.

I wasn't checking his course. As skipper you have to walk a narrow path between your overall responsibility for the safety of the yacht and proper delegation to the crew. I had sailed in too many yachts where the skipper had fussed over me. I thought cautiously that I had got it about right. On the one hand no-one had ever got me into serious trouble, and on the other, I had never had difficulty in getting crews to sail with me.

Tom relieved Anne at the helm.

'Well done, Anne,' I said. I wished Tom had said it though.

I left them to it and went below. I glanced at the chart and then sat down on the port berth in the comfort of the saloon. Leaning back against the cushions, relaxed at last after the excitement of leaving Bergen, I had an attack of nerves.

I think it was the difficult departure from Bergen that rattled me. In fact it had all gone quite well but surely this new blue sky was deceitful. Who was I, an ordinary coastal sailor, to dare to set out on such a voyage? I had read stories of British yachts with tough crews sailing to Spitzbergen, Norway and Greenland but none had crossed the Barents Sea to Russia.

Why couldn't I have stayed at home? I had recently given up the rather difficult job of being County Architect of Nottinghamshire and now with free time on my hands for the first time in my life I had chosen to do something even more difficult.

I was also affected by my tiredness. Getting permission to enter the Soviet port of Murmansk had been a nightmare. I had spent £300 in phone calls and telexes and my correspondence file was an inch thick. I had spent hours each week refreshing my very shaky knowledge of the Russian language. I had had help from many friends and in the end had been successful. But it had all been exhausting and I had only received the visas for my crew and me three days before the ferry crossing from Newcastle. I felt as if I had completed a hard cruise already instead of starting one.

Now before me the days stretched endlessly. Did I know enough? Was I strong enough for what lay ahead? Was my crew tough enough? It was eight hundred miles to Tromso in the high arctic and beyond that the horrors that I had seen on my school atlas. It was geography not navigation that had frightened me. North Cape was the end of the world, the most northerly point of Europe. On the map it looked quite close to the North Pole. Beyond this grim headland was the Barents Sea and the tundra of north Norway and Russia. At the top right hand corner of the map was Murmansk. If we ever got there what would it be like to sail our small yacht into a huge naval and commercial harbour in a very foreign land? In truth, fretting in the saloon, I couldn't make up my mind whether this was an ordinary summer coastal cruise or some kind of foolhardy expedition.

The scene in the saloon was in marked contrast to my own anxieties. Sunbeams rocked gently lighting the soft upholstery and the pale hardwood. We were using the traditional four hour watch system which I had got used to during my service in the Royal Navy. Ashley Pritchard and Kate Marsden were off duty in the forenoon. They were sprawled on the cushions reading. Ashley's sailing smock was a joyful red and there were coppery glints in Kate's dark hair. They would have plenty of time for sight seeing when they took over for the afternoon watch. In the meantime they were relaxing contentedly as if we were setting off for a day's sail from Whitby to Scarborough. I had advised everybody to get as much rest as possible when they were off watch but I didn't seem to be able to take my own advice. I found myself resenting this sense of domestic calm. The crew seemed to have a blind faith in *Callisto*'s ability to pick her way through an eight hundred mile labyrinth of islands and skerries on an unknown coast. I suppose I should have been flattered: instead I felt lonely and oppressed by the atmosphere of casual indifference in the saloon. I badly needed to light my pipe so I went back on deck.

I immediately felt better. The yacht was now the centre of a great bowl of silver and blue – a summer day in Norway. The sunlight was strengthening and it was quite warm in the cockpit. Tom had handed the tiller back to Anne and was taking routine compass bearings on a distant merchant ship. Big ships travel three times faster than our modest five knots and in the narrow channels they have right of way. We had the mains'l set as we always do when motoring: it makes us more conspicuous as well as steadying us. When Tom was satisfied that the ship would pass us well clear on the starboard side he put the prismatic compass in his pocket and gazed at the slowly passing shoreline.

After a minute he said, 'Have you noticed the way houses are built right on the water's edge? You never see that at home. No tide.'

'And no really rough seas,' I said. It was like sailing on Windermere.

The neat timber houses among the trees seemed to be saying, 'This isn't the tideswept rough coast of Britain that you're used to. If you can manage that you can manage this.' As an architect I can read the messages that buildings send.

Tom again relieved Anne at the tiller. She went below to begin preparations for lunch. I was still restless so I edged my way along the side deck to the bow inspecting each part of the rigging and deck equipment. *Callisto* was in perfect order from her sharp stem slicing into the smooth water to the Red Ensign fluttering on her stern. Chromium and stainless steel winches and shackles and white glassfibre deck shone in the sun. The small Norwegian courtesy flag flew from the yardarm on her mast. I could fuss about her if I wanted to but there was nothing that needed attention. Roy and I had gone over every inch of her during March in Whitby as we do each season. We had changed the engine oil and filters, dismantled and greased winches and hatches and renewed any running rigging that showed the slightest sign of wear. We had cleaned and repainted her underwater hull. There had been no need for special preparation for the long cruise to Russia.

As I stood on the foredeck looking aft at the white wake extending astern, I reflected that she had already been well tested. Roy and his crew had sailed the yacht from Whitby, via Stonehaven to Bergen in four days – a difficult crossing of the North Sea. When I had boarded her yesterday I had found that Roy had written in the log book, 'Hope *Callisto* brings you as much enjoyment as we have had bringing her to Norway.'

Callisto was going to do her part in getting us to Murmansk: the problem was going to be me.

I was alone on watch in the cockpit from 8 p.m. until midnight. I connected the autohelm to the tiller which allowed me to visit the chart table. We had had a light breeze during the afternoon which had let us turn off the motor for two hours. For a while we enjoyed peace and quiet. The only sound was the hiss of the bow wave as the yacht heeled to the wind. The breeze had died soon after five o'clock and once again we were motoring through the stillness of narrow sounds. The sun was shining low in the north-west and sometimes we ran through the shadow of the islands.

The crew were below having supper. The continuous noise of the motor cut me off from their conversation. I was glad to be by myself. Privacy is one of the things you don't get in a small yacht making a long passage but I like some space around me. My one-man evening watch was my formula for getting away from the others for a while each day. The sound of laughter coming up the companion ladder suggested that the others quite liked the idea too.

The big island of Maloy was on the port side. We were already sixty miles north of Bergen and there were few houses. Inspite of the land all around us we seemed to be in a world of our own. I was experiencing some anxiety about the weather. During the night we should be leaving the sheltered waters of the skjaergard and would for a while be in the open Atlantic rounding the peninsula of Stattlandet. This was one of the few places where we should be on an exposed coast.

Earlier I had called up Alesund coastal radio on the VHF for a weather forecast. They answered in English but were inclined to cross examine us. Who were we? They had no record of us. What was our call sign? What was our telephone charge number? It was very different from calling up Whitby coast guards. In the end I gathered that the weather would be continuing fine with a light breeze. They were helpful but I would need to learn more about Norwegian radio stations. Quite unjustifiably I felt we were a small foreign yacht bothering them. I was inclined to sulk.

When Tom came up into the cockpit with my supper he enquired, 'Have you stopped worrying about weather?'

'Yes,' I said doubtfully, 'but I've never sailed without the BBC shipping forecasts. They don't tell you much about it here.'

Tom said confidently, 'A bloke I talked to in Bergen said it would be okay, like this for several days. He had seen it on television. You're worrying too much, Henry, this isn't the UK. I don't suppose the weather changes all that fast here. Watch the barometer: it's perfectly steady.'

He was probably right but I was inclined to reject his easy dismissal of my fears. We were going to sail into the arctic with weather forecasts based on quayside rumour and the barometer. It made me feel as guilty as hell.

'Keep trying with the coastal radios,' Tom added, 'they'll get to know us after a bit.'

I don't like sailing in strong winds and rely on knowledge of the weather to make sure I am in a safe anchorage if gales are predicted. It was quite clear, however, that tonight we should have quiet seas out round Stattlandet.

After Tom had gone below I found I could stop thinking about tomorrow and the day after. There was just this quiet evening and the fascinating task of piloting the yacht through this strange sea that ran through the land. The beacons that I identified on the chart appeared on schedule ahead of us, the autohelm clicked as I adjusted its setting, new vistas of water and shoreline opened before me around each promontory. The fjord was a milky blue and I could see the setting sun lighting up the white summits of the mountains. Alone in the cockpit time, with all its anxieties, seemed to have stopped. There was just an entrancing sense of here and now shared with my beloved yacht and the magic of Norway.

At eleven o'clock the light was beginning to fade and I switched on the navigation lights. Tom came up again. He had been examining the fresh and rather grisly looking chart I had spread on the chart table. It showed a barbed wire entanglement of rocks and reefs marked by red, white and green sectored lights. I could see these pricking out in the twilight ahead of us – a confusion of coloured flashes.

'Why don't you anchor until it gets light?' Tom said, 'You can't expect Ashley to go through that lot on his own.'

I would be handing over the watch to Ashley and Kate at midnight and Ashley had less experience than we had. It was a good point and the chart showed a number of places where we could safely anchor for a few hours.

'Good idea,' I said, 'I'll think about it, now get some sleep. You're on again at four.'

When Ashley and Kate came up at 12 o'clock the sunset was still lighting the sky. I didn't want to stop and anchor. I knew that the crew wouldn't want to start again in a hurry and we were a long way from Tromso. Kate disconnected the autohelm and took the tiller. I went below to the chart table with Ashley and examined the sequence of lights that would guide us through the reefs.

'Some of the lights further north don't seem to be lit,' I said, 'but you can still see the lighthouses.'

Ashley's face was visible in the fading daylight and the faint chart table illumination. He looked confident as he always does. He was 26 years old and a chemical engineer but he seemed to be fitting his professional work around sailing rather than the other way around. When he told me he wanted to come on this long trip I had said, 'What about your career?'

He had replied, 'It won't look too bad on my C.V. if it shows I've sailed to Russia.'

Now he was quietly determined to get there.

Looking at the chart I said, 'You do this bit but I'll stay around for a while.' I hoped he wouldn't feel I lacked faith in him. He nodded; it was going to be tricky.

He drew the ship's course on the chart in pencil and went up into the cockpit.

'Steer 320 degrees,' he told Kate, 'and slow down a bit.' A few minutes later he said, 'Alter course to 340.'

He took bearings on the lights with the prismatic compass and plotted the ship's position on the chart. This went on for half an hour. Then I saw him staring at a beacon through binoculars. It was almost lost against the background of darkening land.

He suddenly said in a taut but calm voice, 'Engine in neutral, Kate. Turn back 180 degrees the way you came. I think that's the wrong beacon.'

With no tide running it was safe to stop.

The wake died away and *Callisto* hung still in the twilight, her engine ticking over slowly. She seemed to be thinking. Ashley and I looked tensely at the chart and counted the flashes of the lights we could see from the cockpit. Some of the lights were moving – probably the navigation lights of fishing boats coming south. No Norwegian familiar with the sectored lights would have the slightest difficulty finding his way through the reefs but we were new to it. After a few minutes I said, rather relieved, 'We're okay. That beacon looks right to me. You're on course.'

Ashley grinned, 'I just wasn't sure.' He said to Kate, 'Put her in gear and get back on 340.' I was grateful to him for erring on the safe side.

After that we ran on with growing confidence. Kate steered silently. If she was worried by the closeness of the rocks which loomed out of the twilight she didn't show it. Perhaps she was reassured by the smooth tranquillity of the night or perhaps, and I hoped this was the real reason, by the obvious care with which the yacht was being piloted through the reefs. Once or twice, however, she did call attention to herself, 'Move over, I can't see the bloody compass.'

I hoped she was enjoying her first night sail: I felt rather responsible for her.

I hadn't known her very long. We had met and talked on occasions in the Theatre Royal Bar in Nottingham. She had been married until quite recently and she told me how she was adapting to life on her own. Later we had talked about sailing and I had said that I hoped to sail to Russia. One evening she had said she wanted to drink cocktails. This had surprised me because she was a serious young woman and was taking a second degree at Loughborough University. I don't think she had ever had a cocktail; perhaps she was looking for new worlds. In the Penthouse Bar, this time with the lights of Nottingham below us and the grand piano playing I said on an impulse, 'Would you like to come in the yacht?' I didn't know what she would say. She was working hard on her thesis and she had never sailed before.

She said, 'I've been wondering when you would invite me.'

We went out for a practice sail from Whitby in April. She turned out to be a fast learner. At one point I made the mistake of explaining latitude and longitude on the Admiralty chart. She gave me a gently withering look, 'I've got a degree in geography,' she said.

Now, this evening, with continual helm orders, she wasn't making any mistakes with her steering. She probably still had an open mind on whether she was going to enjoy this particular new world.

After an hour Ashley said, 'It isn't getting any darker.'

The glow of sunset was merging into the glow of sunrise. The sky was brightening in the north and it was becoming easier to see the beacons. In theory I had known we should be sailing into continuous daylight but I hadn't thought it would be like this on the first night. I gazed in wonder at the brightening sky. It was as though we were already off limits.

At three o'clock when the sun was lighting the high snow we altered course towards the west. We were through the reefs and islands and heading into the open Atlantic. There was no sign of wind and the barometer hadn't moved.

'I'm going below,' I said, 'she's all yours. You can use the autohelm if you want to or give Kate a spell at the tiller.'

I went down into the saloon. Tom was asleep on the starboard berth and I moved quietly so as not to wake him. It was warm and I felt suddenly very tired. I sat down with my elbows on the table and poured myself a glass of whisky. I felt, for the first time, a sense of comfort and relief. Perhaps the worst part of the trip had, after all, been the long campaign in the winter to get permission for the yacht to enter the Soviet Union. The actual sailing might not be too difficult. At last we were really on the way. We had faced the unfamiliar pilotage through the sounds and fjords, and Tom and Ashley were both capable of handling the yacht. There had been little wind and no adventures, but I was content with that. We had not yet been going for 24 hours and by tea time we could be at Alesund.

I took off my jersey and sea boots and lay down in my sleeping bag on the port berth. I felt the yacht beginning to roll gently. She was feeling the slow surge of the ocean which even in calm weather never stops. Before I slept I thought about Murmansk. I dared to think now that we might get there and be the first British yacht to do so. But it wouldn't be the first time for me. I had been there before, forty five years ago. For nearly four years in the second world war the Russian Convoys had run taking supplies to the Soviet Union. The ships had unloaded at Murmansk often after fierce fighting and atrocious weather. What strange impulse was drawing me back? I supposed I could have gone as a tourist but somehow it had seemed important to sail there. As I lay in the warm comfort of the yacht the war time memories of hardship and fear were still vivid.

Chapter Two

I was turning the wheel one or two spokes at a time to keep the ship on an accurate compass course of 220 degrees. In the calm water of the Firth of the Clyde my hands rested lightly on the wheel but I was having to keep a grip on myself. Yesterday the Skipper had told us that we were bound for Russia and at midnight, as the ship began to move down the river, I had had an attack of the shakes. Now in the forenoon carrying out my usual task of steering, I felt less frightened. The familiar routine of the ship had re-asserted itself now that we were again at sea. We could be setting out on a normal Atlantic patrol. My fear was still there but it seemed to be manageable. Through the open door of the wheelhouse I could see the green coast of the Kintyre Peninsula on our starboard side. There was white surf on the beaches and a lighthouse. The high hills were dark against the pale overcast sky. The merchant ships of the convoy were in long columns on the port side but I couldn't see them because the door at that side was closed to keep out the wind. It was 11th March 1945 and still quite cold.

'It's five to ten, Mac.'

MacLaughlan was the leading seaman of the watch and he expected me to remind him of the time. He knew that I watched the clock as well as the compass. He was sitting at the wheelhouse table reading Readers' Digest. He pushed the magazine reluctantly aside and stood up and looked at the clock. Was he checking that I could tell the time? He was in the regular Navy – one of the very few in this ship. To him I must have seemed a sort of civilian – a sailor only for the war. He was satisfied that the hour was nearly up and directed his attention to the seamen sitting on the deck of the wheelhouse.

'Relieve lookouts,' he said briefly. They put out their fags and went up the starboard ladder to the bridge. MacLaughlan was six foot tall and was lean and wary. He was only twenty one like me but he had had a long war. He came from Newcastle and to me seemed a rather desperate fellow but he didn't miss much. He gave me a penetrating look.

'You look pissed off Henry,' he said in his Geordie voice. 'What's worrying you? Didn't you like what the skipper said yesterday?'

He gave me one of his lop-sided smiles. There was the hint of a sneer in that smile. I hadn't liked what the Skipper had told us yesterday. He had said that the 7th Escort group had lost three ships in the Barents Sea on the last convoy and we were joining it as one of the replacements. It had scared me a bit but I wasn't going to admit that to MacLaughlan. He was always needling me because I had a posh voice.

'I'm fed up with steering,' I said. 'Tony and Taff and I have got to drive this thing all the way to Russia in four hour tricks and it's hard work. Everybody else on watch sits around looking at the sea or their instruments waiting for something to happen.'

The giro compass repeater chattered – I was slightly off course. My hands on the wheel automatically corrected. MacLaughlan looked at me as if he didn't believe me; he had seen fear in my eyes. But he let it go. We all had to manage fear –

17

ignoring it, forgetting it, or facing it. Instead he took up my eva-
sive answer to his question. He said, 'We're going to the arctic
and it's going to be bloody cold up there – ice everywhere. It's
not going to be much fun sitting around waiting for something to
happen on the guns or the bridge with your arse freezing. You're
better off in the wheelhouse.'

One of the irritating things about MacLaughlan was that he
was often right. March was the worst month in the arctic with the
ice field furthest south. It would be cold standing watch on the
upper deck; your breath would freeze.

He turned away and put on his long black oilskin and tied
on his regulation uninflated lifebelt with its attached red light.
With his white sea boot stockings turned down over the tops of
his boots and his seaman's cap on he looked the part of the efficient leading seaman of the watch.

Before he left the wheelhouse, I said, 'What do you think
about this trip then, Mac?'

I was curious about this man who had chosen to make a
career in the Royal Navy.

'Same as any other,' he said off-handedly. 'We might get a
run ashore in Murmansk. Change from bloody Liverpool.'

I didn't believe him any more than he believed me.

He went down the wheelhouse ladder to do his hourly
rounds of the upper deck. When he reached the quarter deck, he
would read the dial of the rotating Walker log we towed astern
and report the distance run in the hour to the officer of the watch
when he got to the bridge. I envied him his freedom of movement. He had responsibilities as leading seaman of the watch but
they compared very favourably with my unremitting concentration on the compass, my hands forever moving the spokes of the
wheel and my rooted servitude to the orders from the bridge.

The wheelhouse was directly below the open bridge. The
connecting voice pipe, at the wheelhouse end, opened out into a
shiny copper trumpet shape. It smelt of metal polish and reflected a distorted version of my face. In front of the wheel at which

18

I stood was the magnetic compass and the giro compass repeater was mounted at eye level. The giro pointed true north and this was the compass we used. The magnetic compass was there in case of a giro failure. On my right was the engine room telegraph which, with a loud clang, signalled alterations of speed to the engine room far below us. This was manned by a young ordinary seaman who was the Bosun's Mate of the watch or one of the off-watch look-outs. I had placed a bucket on the deck between the engine room telegraph and the wheel standard so that it wouldn't slide when the ship rolled. This was to be sick in. I wasn't likely to need it after a winter at sea in the North Atlantic but putting it there had become a habit. You couldn't leave the wheel to spew up neatly over the lee side so it was there just in case.

When keeping station on other ships, the officer of the watch was constantly altering the course to steer and the speed of the ship. His voice came down the voice pipe, 'Steer 230 degrees.'

I repeated, 'Steer 230 degrees, sir.'

For this slight alteration I only needed five degrees on the rudder indicator mounted on the wheel standard. A moment later, I shouted up the voice pipe, 'Course 230 degrees.' and heard the answer.

'Very good.'

In two minutes, the voice pipe said, 'Steer 220 degrees, 145 revolutions.' I repeated the order and reported when the ship was on the new course. This would go on until my watch ended at half past twelve.

MacLaughlan didn't get back to the wheelhouse for fifteen minutes.

'I've just seen the canteen manager,' he said, 'and I've changed all my cash for this.'

He pulled out a five pound note from his oilskin pocket. 'I've got this from the sick berth Tiffy.' It was a standard issue condom given to members of the crew going ashore.

' Christ, Mac' I said, 'Isn't it a bit early for a run ashore in Murmansk?'

'It's not for that.'

He undid the condom with practised fingers and slid the rolled up fiver into it, tied a knot and put it into his trouser pocket. He could see my look of wonder. He grinned and said, 'If I go in the sea, the money will be okay.'

A few minutes later, Tony Baynon, one of the three quartermasters, came up the ladder into the wheelhouse. He was carrying a bucket and a broom.

'Buffer told me to sweep up,' he said.

'Bloody needs it too,' said MacLaughlan.

The deck of the wheelhouse was covered with cigarette ends, match stalks and discarded fag packets. People kept going through the wheelhouse – officers, signalmen, the Buffer, all tossing their fag ends onto the deck on their way up to the bridge.

Tony Baynon methodically and rapidly cleaned it all up. He had been steering for four hours this morning until I had relieved him at eight but like everybody else off watch in the ship, he had to turn to in the forenoon. When he had finished he put down his broom and lit a cigarette holding it carefully with the tips of his fingers. He wandered restlessly over to the open door on the starboard side and stared at the coast.

MacLaughlan looked up from the Readers' Digest and gave Tony a disapproving stare, 'You haven't polished the fucking voice pipe' he said.

Tony turned round and said mildly to the leading seaman, 'I can't, Henry's using it.'

This was true. There was now a lot of wheel orders; the ship was altering course to a north west heading rounding the Mull of Kintyre. The last thing I needed was somebody fiddling about me with cotton waste and metal polish. MacLaughlan said nothing and Tony returned to his inspection of the coast.

'There's a village, scattered houses and a castle. It looks civilised,' he said. 'It's too far to see people but I bet they are watching us go past; the convoy must look pretty impressive from the shore.'

He was silent for a moment looking at the land. I could imagine people – farmers, housewives, children – pausing in their work and staring at the great lines of ships on the horizon. Some would notice that the merchant ships were heavily laden and low in the water and conclude that the convoy was not bound for America.

Tony said, 'Lucky sods, I wish to God I was with them.'

The proximity of the everyday world of men and women and the solidity of the land seemed to make the ship seem frail. Tony threw away his cigarette and turned round and grinned at me. 'It looks okay there, Henry' he said. 'Perhaps I'll go to Kintyre after the war; I expect the people are nice.'

He picked up his bucket and broom and went down the ladder.

At twenty eight minutes past twelve, Taffy Jones, the White Watch quartermaster was standing beside me. He had just had his rum and his dinner and was looking cheerful.

'All right, Henry,' he said. 'I'll take her.'

I reported up the voice pipe to the bridge, 'Quartermaster relieved, course 290 degrees, 140 revolutions. Engine half ahead.'

'All yours,' I said. 'The Skipper's on the bridge.'

The wheelhouse was crowded with the seamen of the White Watch being detailed for gun crews and lookouts.

Taff took the wheel, his eyes on the giro compass repeater and his practised hands moving the spokes slowly.

I could go below for dinner but I hesitated for a moment watching the White Watch quartermaster. Did I look as competent as that when I was steering? I doubted it and yet I made no mistakes in the forenoon watch and there were a lot of wheel orders.

After dinner, I went to the upper deck to have a look round. It had been difficult to see much in the forenoon. I climbed the ladders to the deck outside the wheelhouse on the port side. The Mull of Kintyre was still visible to starboard but now I could see

Rathlin Island on the other side of the North Channel. Some of the merchant ships were quite close. Heavily laden and low in the water, they looked enormous with their derricks and high super-structures.

Some of the American ships which I had seen in the harbour had prosaic names like *William Wheelwright, Thomas Donaldson* and *James W Gillis*. The Commodore, the Senior Naval Officer in command of the merchant ships flew his flag on the British freighter *Fort Boise*.

I turned away briefly from the impressive sight of the merchant ships and looked at the ship ahead of us on the starboard bow. She was one of the close escort corvettes; a vessel identical to ours, either Allington Alwick or Bamborough Castle. Her wake was fanning out, involving us. Our wakes interlocked spreading wider and wider. She was rising and subsiding on a fringe of white foam.

Corvettes were the smallest ocean-going warships in the Royal Navy. They were the workhorses of the convoy routes. A Castle class corvette was 252 feet long having a displacement of just over 1,000 tons. The older Flower class corvettes were slightly smaller. Both classes were designed to be built by ship-yards which were not big enough to manage the more effective anti-submarine vessels – frigates, sloops and destroyers. Instead of turbines, corvettes had reciprocating engines which were eas-ily built and easy to maintain. The ships were simple and rugged and built quickly in large numbers. They were a bit small and really too slow for the job but they were cheap and easy to build. The size limitation meant crowding and discomfort for the crew of a hundred men. Even in moderately rough weather, they pitched and rolled violently.

They had a reputation for toughness and people looked at you respectfully when you said you were in a corvette. In spite of all the drawbacks, I was glad to be in a ship like this.

I couldn't see her but I knew that ahead of the convoy was a better anti-submarine ship – HMS *Lapwing*. She was a sloop, a somewhat larger and faster ship than a corvette. She was the senior ship of the close escort group and I was glad she was with us. She had an experienced skipper who was familiar with the Russian run.

The corvette ahead of us seemed small and unimpressive compared with the long column of great merchant ships on our port side. I took another look at the closest one.

She had a deck cargo of freight cars. I remembered seeing her close to in the Clyde and I had noticed that the freight cars had letters of the Russian alphabet stencilled on them. Now here she was really on her way to deliver vehicles, raw materials, machinery and weapons to the Russians and we were close to her guarding her with our watchful and never ceasing radar and asdic pulses. I felt we were doing a good job.

I was fairly keen on the Russians. Since I was a lad of nine, Germans had been marching into and conquering most of the countries of Europe. I had been a schoolboy when their planes destroyed Plymouth, Coventry and a lot of London. One day in the summer of 1941, Hitler attacked Russia with two hundred divisions. I can remember that June morning when my mother woke me drawing wide the curtains of my bedroom windows. In the bright daylight I could see her grave face, 'Germany, Rumania and Finland are invading Russia.'

She, like most people, thought that the Soviet Union would be conquered in a matter of weeks.

I tried to cheer her up. 'Britain's no longer alone now, Mum. We've got an ally,' I said, but this was her second world war and she was tired of it all.

Once again, the dive bombers and the armoured troops had defeated the armies of the Soviet Union, one after another. In a matter of weeks the Germans were within sight of Leningrad and Moscow. Then something happened that had never happened before – they were halted. The much derided Red Army had somehow done the impossible and had stopped the invincible Germans in their tracks. The following year at Stalingrad, the

Germans were decisively defeated and now the German cities of Breslau and Danzig were surrounded and the Russian armoured divisions were within forty miles of Berlin. We were all familiar with the faces of the Russian generals who were leading the attack into Germany – Zhukov, Rokossovski and Koniev. We had their portraits stuck up alongside the pin-up girls in the messdeck.

It wasn't just our ship. Most people in Britain were cheering the Russians on. On my last leave in London, I had noticed that the plinth of Nelson's column had a huge slogan on it:-

USSR

USA

US

U

At the moment the 'U' meant our ship – HMS *Lancaster Castle*.

I began to feel cold sight-seeing on the upper deck. The wind was light but we were steaming at about nine knots into it and after twenty minutes, it began to strike a chill through the two jerseys I was wearing. I should have put on oilskins. I decided to go below. Going down the ladders was a transition from one world to another. Above was the immensity of sea and sky, the lines of ships and the high coasts on both sides – below the claustrophobic domesticity of the seamen's messdeck. The two worlds were really two halves of the same one – the world of a ship at sea but I never really got used to their stark contrast.

The seamen's mess smelt of fuel oil, burnt toast and sweat. The air was hazy with tobacco smoke. The dozen or so seamen who were off watch were either asleep, writing letters to their girls, or talking. The mess tables were cluttered with empty coffee cups, half smoked cigarettes, crusts of bread and magazines. Music from the BBC Forces programme competed with the roar of the air fans and the eternal vibration of the ship's engine. The softness of the men's arms and faces contrasted with the harsh geometry of their surroundings. Everything was steel – its hard unyielding surface defaced with bolts, rivets, and welds. Wherever you looked there were hatch covers, emergency lights, pipes, wheel valves and stopcocks colour coded for fresh water, high pressure steam, oil, compressed air and salt water. Air handling ducts and channel plates for electric wires criss-crossed just above head level. It was likely that the naval architects who had designed our ship had provided detail drawings for the mess deck, but it looked to me as if the chaps who had actually built it had made it up as they went along. The seamen's bare limbs looked somehow frail and vulnerable. I sat on the upholstered locker depressed by the grey familiar scene.

I heard a fragment of conversation that matched my mood, 'The Skipper said the last lot lost three ships; he wasn't talking about Yank freighters – they were our ships – sloops and corvettes.'

Another voice said, 'Christ, three out of nine. I thought we were supposed to be winning the fucking war.'

It seemed others were as apprehensive as I. I had done a Russian convoy before in my previous ship, HMS *Swift*, a fleet destroyer. We had joined a homeward bound convoy in February 1944 off North Cape. We hadn't encountered the enemy but on our way there from the Faeroe Isles, we ran into the most appalling weather. It was my first continuous experience of the North Atlantic and I was sea-sick for five days. I managed to stand my four hour watches but as the ship was working watch on watch, I got desperately tired. On the fifth day, I spewed blood and, weak with hunger, turned in in my hammock for three and a half hours sleep below. I was nineteen and six foot two and I wanted to be a tough sailor and I wet myself. I turned out for my next watch dripping with piss and self disgust and slumped onto the lockers on the port side of the mess. Tears ran down my face. George Whiting, a one badge A.B. from Newcastle who had been through all the war, saw the state I was in, sat down next to me and did something I could never have expected – he put his arm around me. He was a lean, tough Geordie with not much going for him in peace or war and he did the one thing that could help. He said, 'It's the same for all of us Henry on our first trip,' and he hugged me like a woman and went away. Nothing was ever as bad again on that trip. His action had been the deed of a sensitive and generous soul.

I steered in the last dog watch 6.00 – 8.00 p.m. The convoy was heading north through the dusk over a calm grey sea. I would be on watch again at 4 am, in the meantime I had time to read. Reading was, apart from the midday tot of rum, the only escape from the ship. I cleared a space on the mess table and got a book from my locker. It was Boswell's *Tour of the Hebrides*. I rested my elbows on the table and read about Johnson and Boswell's visit to the Isle of Coll. The islands seemed to have more people and prosperity in 1773 than today. For an hour I was out of the ship and out of the war.

At 10 o'clock it was time to sling my hammock. I reluctantly closed the book. Johnson and Boswell's learned conversations ended for the time being. Instead I could hear Gordon Powell, one of the asdic ratings and George Seeley, an Oerlikon gunner, talking quietly in the messdeck of a ship now approaching the same Hebridean Islands.

Gordon Powell was saying, 'I hope we get a run ashore in Murmansk. It would be nice to see some Russians.'

He methodically lit his pipe. He seemed to use a lot of matches. He worked in a bank before he joined the Navy.

George Seeley's hair was dull gold in the electric light. He said, 'It'll be okay if there are Russian women. Do you think there'll be any Gordon?'

He sounded eager. He seemed to have the same sort of priorities as Boswell but with less opportunities.

'Not a hope,' said Gordon Powell. 'We'll probably tie up in some dreary place like Scapa Flow or Lisahally – oil tanks, nissen huts and armed guards.' He looked sad. 'If we do meet any women,' he added, 'you'd better give them a wide berth, George; Russia isn't like Egypt or Malta. I expect they're bloody touchy about them.'

Then he cheered up a bit, 'Still, you never know, we may

26

be lucky. It wouldn't be a bad idea if you saved your cigarettes and nutty.'

Nutty was what we called chocolate. It could be traded for all sorts of things.

Gordon smoked thoughtfully for a minute or two and then knocked his pipe out and stood up, 'I'm turning in,' he said, 'I've got the middle watch.'

I slung my hammock, took off my sea boots, putting them on the side racking with my steel helmet where I knew I could find them in a hurry and swung myself into it. Mull, Skerryvore, Tiree and Coll were somewhere on the starboard bow in the darkness. Drowsily, I thought of Johnson, gale bound on the Isle of Coll. He had said, 'I want to be on the main land and go on with existence. This is a waste of life.'

Gordon Powell had said, 'Oil tanks, nissen huts and armed guards,' and I thought of the dangerous ocean and the endless days ahead. A waste of life.

I steered through the morning watch. After it was over at 8 o'clock I went to the bathroom to wash and shave. It was quite small and crowded with men. The hard electric light was veiled with steam. I couldn't summon energy to fight for a basin. I sat a bit disconsolately on a stool waiting for a bucket to get hot water. There was only one hot tap and a lot of people. The day seemed already to have been going on a long time and there was a lot more of it stretching before me.

A seaman with a missing front tooth was in the bathroom. Oh, God, I thought why had I chosen this minute to be here? He came over to me drying his face with his towel.

'I suppose you're glad we're going to bloody Russia,' he said. It was said accusingly as if it were my fault. I could see his hostile eyes and uneven mouth through the mist of steam. I didn't answer but just stared back at him. He always wanted to provoke a fight. There were plenty of fights on board but they came later. We had only been just over a day at sea. He was the only man in the ship who actively disliked me. I think it was my voice again.

Whilst someone like leading seaman MacLaughlan regarded the way I talked as a strange aberration, this man saw it as a threat. Perhaps to him it represented all the injustices of his underprivileged life. Okay, I could sympathise with that but if he thought for a moment he would have recognised that notwithstanding my accent I was at the present time sharing with him one of the more under-privileged lives on offer. I saw a chance to get a bucket; the crowd in the bathroom was thinning out. I got up and pushed past him.

'Look,' I said, 'you don't like me, so let's leave it like that.'

Even in a ship as small as this it was quite easy to avoid people. I wasn't afraid of a fight but there seemed to be enough enemies already. He let it go and went out of the bathroom.

At 9 o'clock the mess was empty except for Simmonds, the able seaman who was doing duty as cook. It was my turn to be cook as well. He had already washed up the dirty cups and plates and rolled up the oilcloths on the tables. He said, 'Help me square everything up and then you scrub the deck; I'll start on the dinner.'

Simmonds was boss down here, we had elected him to be mess caterer ourselves. He was older than most of us and wore one badge, a chevron on his uniform sleeve – three years good conduct. He wasn't wearing his uniform now but a khaki battledress tunic with the combined operations commando badge on the sleeve. He once showed me a photograph of himself taken when he was a recruit at the beginning of the war. He looked very young then so he wasn't very old now but the photograph was taken before the Malta convoys and before the fighting in the Atlantic.

I liked Simmonds. Being mess caterer was only a small part of his duties and he had no special skill for it but he tried his best to mitigate the appalling feeding arrangements in the ship.

By the time I had scrubbed out, Simmonds had got all his ingredients together. 'I'll make a pot mess for dinner' he said. 'You make a duff for afters.'

CHAPTER TWO

It was quite a difficult job making a pudding for nineteen men especially without a kitchen. I put suet, flour, sugar and currants into a large baking tin and added condensed milk, kneading it to the right consistency. I began to get keen on it and worked on it for quite a while. It was a change from steering. I put flour on the scrubbed mess table and rolled the dough into a long cylinder. Then I wrapped it in a cloth and lashed it with sailmaker's twine using marline hitches. It was exactly like lashing up a small hammock. When it was finished I began to have doubts about it. I remembered my mother or someone talking about having cool light hands for making dough and moving the work as closely as possible to the open kitchen window. My hands had been hot and heavy and there was no window in the messdeck. I looked sadly at the three foot long white sausage lying on the table. It rocked very gently from side to side responding to the movement of the ship. It had deserved a little less effort and rather more skill. I said miserably to Simmonds who was still peeling potatoes, 'I don't think this one's up to standard.'

'What standard?' he said cynically and came over to have a look at it. 'It looks all right to me,' he said, although all he was looking at was the shape of the thing swaddled in its cloth and tied with string. He gave it a prod with his forefinger. 'Feels alright, too.' Then he sighed, 'I wish my missus was doing the cooking.'

I picked it up cradled in my arms and carried it to the two ladders to the maindeck where the galley was situated. I gave it to the ship's cook. He was responsible for the bloody thing from now on.

When I returned below I found that Simmonds had finished preparing the pot mess. He sat down at the table and lit a fag. He said, 'I hate being mess caterer; you can't bloody win.'

He lapsed into gloomy silence, no doubt reflecting on the strange arrangements we had for feeding ourselves.

Just after Simmonds had stubbed out his cigarette we heard the depth charges. The shock wave hit the hull of our ship like a giant sledge hammer. Everything shook. From where we were below the waterline, it sounded rather close. A moment later it was followed by the muffled roar of the explosion born on the air. It sounded a bit further off. We were expecting to hear the alarm buzzers sound action stations but nothing happened. I looked uneasily at Simmonds and he grinned at me.

'I'm going up top to take a look,' he said.

It was as good an excuse as any for getting out of the mess-deck. I didn't think the enemy was out there but if he were, the messdeck low down in the ship was the wrong place to be in. I grabbed my duffel coat and followed Simmonds up the two ladders to the main deck feeling the ship heeling to helm orders. The sea was calm under a pearly grey sky. On our port side the merchant ships were silver against the dark rocky shore of Lewis. To starboard and further off were the magnificent mountains of the mainland with the summits of Stac Pollaidh and Suilven obscured by wisps of cloud.

Outlined against this high coast one of the Flower class corvettes was making a second attack. She looked tough and workmanlike and not beautiful, but she had a pretty name. It was either *Camelia*, *Oxlip* or *Honeysuckle* but I couldn't tell which. Simmonds and I lent on the guardrails and watched her attack with interest. I knew that on her bridge the pinging of the asdic would be heard on the loudspeakers, the returning echo sounding closer and closer as she ran in on the bearing of the target. It would be tense and exciting, like hunting. On the quarterdeck her depth charge crew would have completed reloading after the last attack and be waiting for the firing gong. They would have set the pressure fuses to explode the charges at a predetermined depth. Seen from half a mile away, the corvette's approach to her prey did not, however, look at all dramatic. She had no great bow wave – high speed would have confused her asdic. It all looked rather leisurely as she ran in to attack an apparently empty piece of sea – merely a position shown on her plotting table. When she reached that position her action seemed insignificant too; innocuous looking cylinders rolled in succession over her stern or were tossed sideways by the throwers in slow trajectories and vanished into the water. That seemed to be all but you knew it wasn't. She ran on for long seconds. The sea was silky against a backcloth of remote and peaceful mountains. Suddenly, it erupted astern of her as the depth charges she had dropped exploded together deep below. A great column of water shot into the sky – she was dwarfed by the havoc she had created. Every ship in the convoy would have felt the crack of the shockwave and heard the rumble of the explosion. A thousand tons of water fell back into the sea in a tangled maelstrom. The corvette turned to steam back through the calming water. She looked too small to have committed such monstrous violence.

No wreckage or oil came to the surface and she did not regain asdic contact. We joined her in a search in line abeam with the ships of the convoy leaving us but neither ship picked up the echo. Whatever it was she had attacked had got away or, more likely, hadn't been there in the first place. It could have been a shoal of fish or even an underwater swirl in the currents of the North Minch. It didn't matter – that long underwater shock would have warned any U-boat within miles that the ships of the Escort force of Convoy JW 65 were trigger happy. I could feel the vibration of the screw as the ship increased revolutions to catch up with the convoy.

Simmonds said, 'It could have been a U-boat; they hang about under water near the coasts these days.'

I nodded. The U-boats were no longer capable of the fast surface attacks at night that had previously devastated the convoys. Radar carried by escort vessels and aircraft and radio direction finding had put paid to that, but now all U-boats were fitted with schnorkels. This was an air intake and exhaust device on the surface that allowed them to use their diesel engines whilst submerged. They were now virtually undetectable by radar or eyesight.

'Do you think they'll be waiting for us on the Russian

coast?' I asked.

'Yes,' Simmonds said, 'that's where they were last month.'

He made it sound as if it was some regularly recurring event like payday. It was a depressing thought.

When 'hands to dinner' was piped at noon the mess rum bosun poured out each man's tot in a tea cup. I was not on watch until four in the afternoon and I needed to sleep. The rum would help this. As I drank it slowly I reflected that it would also anaesthetise me sufficiently to enjoy dinner. I could probably even eat my ignorantly contrived duff.

Lying drowsily in my hammock after I had cleared away the dinner, I felt the ship beginning a long steady roll. The mess traps rattled, things started to slide on the deck and on the mess tables, oilskins hung on hooks came to life. We were clearing the Butt of Lewis. We were feeling the restless swell of the Atlantic Ocean which would be with us now for a long time. We were leaving Britain.

Chapter Three

Callisto was sailing on the world's most beautiful coast. Alesund shone in the radiant light like a Greek island city. Entering the small harbour in the early evening of the 5th June was like going indoors. We were hemmed in by the quays and tall gabled buildings, their bright colours reflected in the still water. They echoed back to us the quiet revving of our motor. For a moment the door had closed on the outside world of islands and mountains. We were in a sunny pool which was the middle of a city.

We had left the Atlantic at six in the morning entering Vagsfjorden. All day we had sailed in a light wind or motored through Heroyfjorden and Helmsfjorden. Trees had lined the shores and there were cows in the fields The scattered houses had flag poles with the Norwegian national flag flying. We had watched a Coastal Express ship smartly manoeuvring through a high bridge.

But the bread which we had bought in Bergen from a Texaco filling station – the only place open on Sunday – was already stale. *Callisto* and her crew needed a night in harbour.

Where to moor the ship? I looked for the masts of yachts but there were none. In the thirty six hours from Bergen we had seen no sailing yachts. I had on board a book published by the Norwegian Tourist Board *Gjesthavner i Norge.* It showed a mooring for yachts around the corner in the narrow south end of the harbour. I didn't want to rely too much on this book because rather ominously, it didn't extend north of Trondheim but I was glad to find a small floating pontoon where indicated with a sign saying Gjesthavn. There was a notice that seemed to say that we should pay harbour dues in a nearby shop. There was nobody about, perhaps everybody was having supper.

When you are safely tied up alongside in a new harbour with the mooring lines ashore, sails furled, and the motor switched off, there is always a quiet sense of achievement. Even after such a calm passage I felt a great relief to be in Alesund. Ashley volunteered to cook supper and decreed happy hour. We sat in the sunny cockpit and drank gin and tonic enjoying the sight of a foreign town.

It was hot and I took off my jersey. Kate appeared wearing shorts.

Anne said, 'This place has changed since 1972. It was just warehouses and fishing boats.' She took a small sip of her gin which I didn't think she really liked. 'It's gone up in the world.'

Anne was the only member of the crew who had been to Norway – a cruise in the Coastal Express. The warehouses were all newly painted in yellow, pink and white. Some of them had been converted into apartments and hotels. Smart new buildings had been designed to retain the character of the town, but the fishing boats were still there.

'I suppose it's the oil and the gas,' Anne said sadly. 'They've probably even got traffic jams now.'

From what I could see on the quays and between buildings there were scarcely any cars. Perhaps everybody was still having supper.

Anne went on, 'The town was burnt down in 1904, 10,000

34

people homeless. It was rebuilt in one piece. The book says there's a lot of Art Nouveau detailing, but I can't see any from here.'

Anne had guidebooks and steamer timetables. She was a real tourist. As a sailor I'm inclined to look only at charts and pilot books and hence missed a lot of the interest of the places the yacht visited. Anne may have lacked ambition to master the skills of pilotage and yacht handling but every long distance cruiser needs someone like her on board. When I had planned this cruise in the winter Norway had just been a very long sea route connecting Britain with Russia: Alesund with Anne's help was making me feel it existed as a country in its own right.

Anne may have been worried that Alesund was suffering from too much affluence but I was impressed with it. I had sailed many times in North West Scotland. The Hebrides, remote, windswept and often treeless, had seemed like the end of the world. Here we were nearly four degrees of latitude north of the Isle of Lewis, 240 nautical miles, and the town looked like a large updated version of Dartmouth on a fine day. It may have been the gin but I felt that Norway had gone to my head.

Kate was looking intently at the harbour scene. In our conversations in the bar in Nottingham she had told me about how she had worked her way round the world and visited such unimaginable places as Afghanistan and Thailand. I hoped our first landfall in Norway, only a few hundred miles from home, had not disappointed her. Her eyes seemed to be alive with interest.

After supper Anne, Ashley and Kate went off to climb the steps to the summit of Aksla, the mountain that dominates the town. The guide book said ' . . . there is a bird's-eye view of the whole area which encompasses the sea and islands to the west and the fjords and serried peaks of the Sunnmore Alps to the east.' Kate asked me to come too but I elected to stay in the yacht. I wasn't really tired although I had only had four hours sleep since sailing. My mind seemed too full of new impressions already: I didn't think I could take that view as well. Tom wandered off into the town.

After they had gone I regretted my decision. Kate had wanted me to go with them and I felt rather a spoil-sport. I decided that if I couldn't be a tourist in practice I could be one in theory so I picked up one of Anne's guide books and settled down to read it in the quietness of the saloon. My knowledge of Norway was limited to my reading of the Norse Sagas which were a thousand years out of date and my rather more recent knowledge of Norwegian merchant ships in the war time convoys. Norwegians were good sailors. When a ship of theirs had been torpedoed by U-boats nearly all the crews had survived. With superb discipline they had lowered their boats, hoisted their sails and set course for the nearest land. They had been glad to be rescued, but failing that they would rescue themselves. They had still been Vikings.

The guide book contained interesting facts. There were 4.1 million Norwegians – half the population of London – in a land bigger than Britain. The farmers and fishermen loved solitude: the book said ' .... the townspeople are also fond of solitude, retreating to their weekend cabins where they are loth to be disturbed.'

That explained why nobody in Bergen or Alesund had wandered over to have a look at our yacht and chat to the crew as they would have done in a British port. *Callisto* was our weekend cabin and therefore had to be left alone. Norway had only achieved independence from Sweden in 1905 and people were thin skinned about it. This accounted for all the flag poles with the national flags.

Leaving aside Liberia and Panama, Norway had the fourth biggest fleet of merchant ships in the world. Fishing was still important but their wealth now came from the oil and natural gas coming ashore. They hardly needed this themselves because their own energy came from hydroelectricity. It had brought industry and prosperity in its wake. The guide book didn't say it but it was apparent that the wealth was spread out fairly evenly with universal state education and health services.

36

When the others came back they said they had not been disappointed: the view of the blue sea and islands had been all that the guide book had promised and in addition they had seen *Callisto* in the harbour below them.

Ashley said, 'The restaurant was closed though and there weren't many people about.'

I looked at my watch. 'I'm not surprised, it must have been nearly eleven o'clock when you got there.'

The sun had only just set and it was still daylight. After just over two days in Norway we were still living under our English sky.

Next day we went shopping. Diesel oil and charts were cheap. I bought the nine charts I needed to get us to Tromso at a very good bookshop. Locally produced provisions such as fish, vegetables and bread were expensive but not prohibitive. Anne and Kate bought these in the open air market Kipervik Torget. Nearly everyone spoke English. When they bought gin at the Vinmonopolet – the state liquor store – they needed fistfuls of 10 Kroner notes. A bottle cost more than twenty pounds – happy hour was going to be a little restrained. The Vinmonopolet was civilised and efficient but coming out with the gin made them feel as guilty as if they had been playing the roulette tables at Monte Carlo and losing heavily.

We were lucky that we had brought with us from Britain most of the things we would need. Kate, however, had forgotten her hand cream, and needed a lot of consolation when she found she had to pay for it at Norwegian prices.

On board our new beautifully equipped cruising yacht I felt quite well off. It was a privilege to own such a vessel. Ashore in Alesund I felt so poor that I scarcely dared to look in the shop windows.

'Never mind,' I thought, 'the sea, the sun and the wind are free. We won't spend much time ashore.'

We left Alesund at four o'clock in the afternoon. The mains'l was set in the harbour and we motored between the piers – an unknown ship going on her way. There was a light breeze and we unfurled the big No. 1 Genoa and turned off the motor. The white mountains gradually rose above Alesund as we left it astern and once again we were sailing in the calm blue channels that stretched forever to the north.

Anne and Kate hadn't wanted to leave harbour. We had been there less than 24 hours. Anne said, 'There were three museums I wanted to see.'

We were sitting in the cockpit in the sun. After a night in harbour nobody needed to sleep.

Ashley who wasn't particularly keen on museums said, 'I don't feel there's any real incentive to go ashore in Norway.'

'Why not?' I asked.

'No pubs,' he said. 'If there were any you couldn't afford the beer. It cost £3.50 a glass. Supposing you had to stand a round?'

He was probably thinking of the Mishnish Hotel in Tobermory. We sometimes anchored in the harbour when sailing in North West Scotland and rowed ashore in the dinghy. The bar would be full of ferry crews, local fishermen and yachtsmen talking and drinking. We would stand each other pints and exchange the gossip of the coast.

He said, 'Norway's a nice country but I don't feel we're really in it.' He thought for a minute looking sad. 'We're just alongside it.' Then he cheered up. 'Perhaps it will be different in Russia.'

After that there was silence for a few minutes except for the click of the ratchets as Tom sheeted in the Genoa with a few turns of the big jib winch.

Ashley had reminded me of Russia. I said, 'It's still a hell of a long way to Tromso – 650 miles, then only half way there.'

Tom said, 'Just think about today and the day after.'

It was good advice but I made up my mind to keep going now for a bit, to run off the miles. I would allow myself only to think as far ahead as Tromso where we would be changing crews. We had a dead line to be there by the 23rd June.

My partner, Roy Sowden, had warned me about the distances.

'Why can't we go to Holland,' he had said, 'or somewhere warm like Brittany?'

It was the spring of 1989 and it had been necessary to discuss the cruising programme for the following year. The Dolphin at Whitby overlooks the Esk river. Through the window I could see the fishing boats queueing up waiting for the swing bridge to open. Gulls whirled in the sky. Our home port looked familiar and safe.

Roy had sighed, 'I know you want to sail to Murmansk because you were there in the war but it's a hell of a sail – North Sea, Norway and the Barents Sea.' He took a pencil and did a quick sum on a beer mat. 'Three thousand five hundred miles round trip.'

He addressed himself to his Yorkshire Pudding and minced beef. I still wanted to go.

'*Callisto* can do it,' I said, 'it's mostly ordinary coastal sailing.'

When we had looked for a boat to buy together Roy had persuaded me that a Sadler 34 was the boat for us.

'*Callisto* can go anywhere,' he said defensively. 'I'm not worried about her. On a trip like that it's the crew that will be the problem. Even if we get anyone to come with us it will be rough, long distance sailing and a lot of expensive air fares to godforsaken places.'

I didn't answer this obvious objection but said, 'I don't think any British yacht has ever sailed to Murmansk. It's time somebody went there to see the Russians.'

Roy pushed his empty plate to one side and looked at me steadily. After a minute he gave one of his charming smiles. 'Alright, I'll talk to my crews and see how they feel about it.'

I was content to leave it like that. Although Roy is younger than me he is a more experienced sailor. I would wait for his decision. Through the window I could see the swing bridge slowly opening and the fishing boats revving up their diesels.

A few days later he rang me at home. 'They're crazy,' he said, 'but they all want to come.' Then he went on as if there had been no argument and the trip was now a joint project.

'I've got out a general plan. I'll sail her from Whitby to Bergen in the school spring holiday. You take her north in June and I'll fly there with my crew and sail back in August. I'll put the details in the post.'

'By the way,' he added, 'my friends tell me it is difficult to get permission to sail a yacht into Murmansk: it's a main Soviet fleet base. You had better start working on that fairly soon.'

Before he rang off he said as an afterthought, 'Crews seem to be okay but those distances are going to be hard on you and me.'

Twenty four hours after leaving Alesund we had knocked 120 miles off the distance to Tromso. We were beating against a light wind up wide Trondheimsleia with the island of Hitra on our port side. It lead to Trondheim, the big city that was once the capital of Norway. We would alter course around Hitra and turn off to the north. I was following Tom's suggestion of thinking only one day ahead but it seemed sensible to take advantage of the settled weather and keep going.

Just before midnight we had gone out again into the Atlantic. We left the shelter of the island chain to round the Bud peninsula. The ocean had been as quiet as before. The long swell broke in a thin line of surf faint on the twilight coast. By 4 o'clock we were in bright daylight back in the inner leads. There had been a few rain showers during the day but now the sky was blue with fluffy white clouds. There were many coasters, ferries and fishing boats: Trondheim was a busy port although unseen forty miles inland.

Everything had gone well but when I took over at 8.00 pm for my evening watch we were out of the broad seaway and in the narrow sounds north of Hitra.

After an hour I realised I wasn't enjoying myself very much. The evening sun was shining through a thin veil of clouds and the beacons marking the reefs were quite clear. There were, however, an awful lot of them. I was continually altering course to keep in the channel and the autohelm wasn't working very well. It was holding the compass course setting but hunting ten degrees either side of the mean course. At one point I got out the instruction book and tried numerous adjustments to its responsiveness. Between this and identification of sea marks shown on the chart I was beginning to get into a sweat. I ought to have got one of the others up to help me but they were below relaxing after supper and I was reluctant to break the established watch keeping routine. They would all be standing four hour watches later in the night.

Soon the channel became quite narrow and after looking at the chart to memorise the marks ahead I disconnected the autohelm and took the tiller in my hand. We needed accurate steering at this point.

The mark ahead was a tall brick tower that had once been a manned lighthouse. The chart had shown that we had to pass to the left side of it to keep in clear water. As I got nearer I began to feel uneasy: I could see an occasional white breaker straight ahead. After a few moments a thin necklace of rocks appeared. I left the tiller for a moment and checked again on the chart. The chart was clear – leave it to starboard. Back in the cockpit the rocks were ahead and nearer. Which was reality – a sheet of paper on the chart table or what I could see with my eyes? I could hear the beat of my heart. There could be only one answer in that question, I shoved the throttle back to neutral and the sound of the motor died away. Tom was in the cockpit in a flash. He took one look at the rocks ahead and the tall brick tower on our starboard bow.

'Christ,' he said and dived back down to the chart table.

A second later he was coming up the ladder. 'Alter course to starboard,' he said before he was even in the cockpit. 'You're supposed to pass the other side.'

There was a note of absolute certainty in his voice and I

obeyed without further thought putting the tiller hard over and the motor slowly ahead. I half expected to feel at any moment the sickening shock of the keel hitting rock. Nothing happened. In a few minutes we were back in the channel with the brick tower on our port side.

Tom let out his breath. 'You were rounding the wrong mark,' he said in a tense voice. 'Look,' he pointed astern at a white lighthouse on three legs.

'That's the one that you had to leave to starboard. Didn't you see it?'

I had seen it alright but I had thought it was the one before. I explained this to Tom in a hesitant voice.

'Let's tick the bloody things off on the chart as we pass them. Getting the sequence wrong is the main hazard on this coast.'

Then he looked at me in a more kindly way. 'Weren't you being a bit macho? For godsake call someone up to help if you need to.'

He gave ten minutes concentrated attention to resetting and adjusting the autohelm and went below.

For the last hour until the watch changed at midnight nothing went wrong. I was extremely grateful to Tom for his quick thinking but I was in an agony of hurt pride. I had only made one mistake since leaving Bergen but on this rockstrewn coast that was one mistake too many. I had to say to myself quietly but aloud, 'You were the only casualty: don't lose confidence in yourself.'

I was glad when a fair wind sprang up just before midnight. I payed out the main sheet and silenced the motor. I didn't unfurl the genoa – we seemed to be sailing fast enough without it and there was a clearer view ahead. Ashley and Kate took over the watch. Ashley ticked off the marks on the chart as we passed them in the half light. He wasn't going to make any errors. Kate was a hunched figure steering. I was beginning to feel that my two watch leaders, Tom and Ashley, were better at this close quarters pilotage than I. I ought to have been pleased but some-

42

how the thought depressed me.

I could have gone below and turned in but I wasn't sure what the wind was going to do. It was a fresh breeze and for the first time from the south. I made some soup and handed it up to the cockpit. At about 1.00 am when we ran into more open waters we set the full genoa, more than doubling our sail area. *Callisto* was now sailing fast at seven knots with her big sails dark against the light sky in the north.

Ashley had taken the tiller and he was letting Kate plot our course on the chart and check the beacons and lighthouses with binoculars. The wind was steady enough and the watch seemed a going concern. I left them and went below. It was comfortable in the saloon. I was still suffering from hurt pride but the sound of the bow wave slashing along the hull and one whisky soothed me. I fell asleep quite quickly.

I was awakened just after 4 o'clock by the heeling of the yacht and the sound of the wind. I put on my oilskin jacket and safety harness and went on deck. The wind had increased and was blowing quite hard. Tom who was now on watch had already partly furled the genoa but we were still carrying too much sail. We needed to reef the mains'l.

Reefing is easy in *Callisto*: all the halyards and reefing lines lead aft to the cockpit. It was now broad daylight and the task was quickly done. She ran much more comfortably after that and Anne found the steering was not so heavy.

I went back to my sleeping bag which was still warm. The wind died at around 6.30 a.m. and I was briefly awakened by the motor coming on. This fair wind had been too good to last I thought as I returned to sleep.

Anne told me later what it had been like going on watch at 4 o'clock. She said, 'Tom didn't wake me in time for me to get ready. I went on watch in a hurry, no oilskins, no shoes and no coffee! It was blowing like hell and we were doing seven knots. I had to steer while Tom did heroic things with the sails. I couldn't see the compass because the sun was shining in my eyes.'

She was smiling when she told me but going on watch at 4.00 am is no fun at the best of times and this clearly hadn't been one of them.

'You did very well,' I said consolingly.

'I'll tell you what I felt,' she said. 'I felt as if I ought to have been home in London.'

She finished drinking her breakfast coffee and retired to her cabin to catch up on sleep.

All day we sailed north. The sun shone into the saloon from the open hatch. The sunrays were sliced by the revolving blades of the wind generator mounted on the stern rail. The light flickered like an old movie film.

I decided to make for Rorvik. I knew nothing about it; I was now north of any information I had about facilities for yachts. The map on the back of one of the coloured brochures advertising Norwegian cruises showed that it was a port of call for the Coastal Express. It would be a well marked harbour and surely there would be shops and somewhere to moor overnight. It looked alright on the chart and on an island we should have to pass anyway. It was still less than halfway to Tromso.

I wrote in my diary, 'We are heading for Rorvik and should be there in the early evening. We seem to be in a strangely suspended world of changeless sunshine and endless islands. Watch follows watch, the beacons and lighthouses come up and are passed. The genoa is set and the motor is turned off. The wind fades and the motor is started. Night and day are the same – one long daylight. What happened yesterday? When was yesterday? The only thing that changes is our hourly position creeping north from one chart to the next. We sailed from Bergen on Monday; it is now Friday and we have only stopped once at Alesund.'

I was looking forward to Rorvik.

Chapter Four

I felt a bit nervous as we approached Rorvik: I didn't know what to expect. I could see fishing boats and coastal steamers lying alongside the quays. I took the tiller and throttled back the motor as the crew lowered the mains'l and got fenders out from the cockpit lockers. The chart indicated that there was an inner harbour behind the quays. I wished I had a pilot book which would have told me where a small yacht could lie and what facilities were available. I was, however, beginning to have faith in the Norwegian charts and also confidence in the good sense of the Norwegians. They knew the needs of yachts even if they were rare visitors. I steered *Callisto* hopefully between the high quay walls. Engine in neutral; slow down; give yourself time to think; look around. To my surprise I could see floating pontoons with about fifty boats tied alongside but there was room for us too. 'I'm going alongside over there,' I said, 'port side to.' Ashley and Kate took the mooring lines and stood alertly amidships ready to jump onto the pontoon. The rest of us tied the fenders to the port-side guard rail. I engaged the motor and went in very slowly. It is easy to dent your own or somebody else's boat if you aren't careful and I was half blinded by the low evening sun. I'm not all that confident when motoring at close quarters: *Callisto*'s single propeller makes her do funny things when you put the motor into reverse. I was glad when we were stopped neatly against the pontoon between two other boats. Ashley and Kate secured the mooring lines. Anne went below, turned off the idling motor and put the kettle on. It was a perfectly routine manoeuvre but I felt the usual sense of relief as I tidied up the sheets and halyards in the cockpit before going below. As Ashley came down to the saloon for tea he said, 'It looks like a real yacht harbour. There's a hose pipe on the pontoon.'

Anne said as she poured out tea, 'And Rorvik isn't even in the guide books.'

A few minutes later there was a shout from the pontoon, '*Callisto*, ahoy'. I went on deck. Lohre Einar, the harbour master, greeted us.

'You're alright where you are,' he said, anticipating the first question of a visiting skipper, 'there are showers and a launderette over there.' He pointed to a new building beyond the moorings. 'If there's anything else you want let me know.' Then he added apologetically, 'I'm afraid we have to make a small charge to cover our costs. Post it in the letter box in the shower building when you leave.' It was only three pounds. 'I hope you enjoy your stay in Rorvik.' he said as he left us.

In Bergen and Alesund *Callisto* had been an unknown ship going silently on her way. Here the relaxed friendliness of the harbour master made us feel like welcome guests.

We rested a day and two nights in Rorvik. I hadn't meant to stay so long but events conspired to delay us. Ashley spent all the next day getting a propane adaptor made for our butane gas cooking system. Only propane gas bottles were available in Norway. We wanted diesel and water and the yacht needed a thorough clean up. The crew had time to explore the town.

The town has a population of about 2,000 people. It consists of white and brightly coloured timber buildings, old and new blending comfortably together. The town centre looked immaculate in the clear sunlight. The shops were excellent.

Tom said, 'You can get everything you want here: it's at least as well equipped as Woking'. There was a sense of unhurried calm about it and everything stopped at about 4.00 pm.

Rorvik was the first small Norwegian town we had visited and I got the impression – later reinforced as we sailed further – that the high standard of living was universal. You could slice Norway whichever way you liked – north and south, big city or small settlement, and it was the same all through. As much money had been spent on remote settlements in the north as in Oslo or Bergen – there were the same bridges, the same ferries, libraries, houses and shops, schools, all spread equally through a thousand miles. Norway didn't peter out in the north like Britain.

All the same, it was hard to get beneath the smooth surface of Rorvik. Who were the children in pretty uniforms marching with a band through the town? A sign outside a deserted solicitor's office said, 'Closed for two weeks, gone elk hunting.'

Above all why couldn't you just buy a drink?

Lohre Einar, the harbour master, visited me in the forenoon when the others were ashore. He brought me a list of radio frequencies for weather forecast transmissions in English. We stood on the pontoon by the yacht. He seemed to have time to chat. I wanted to invite him on board but I didn't think it was the sort of thing you did in this country. You probably had to be a close relative.

'Where are you bound for?' he asked.

'Russia,' I said. He nodded but didn't say anything so I amplified my answer. 'I visited Murmansk in the war – Royal Navy.'

He looked interested. 'I was in our navy before serving in merchant ships. I've retired now. I'm not a real harbour master, I just look after the place.'

He gazed at *Callisto*.

'Small boat,' he said but he seemed quite proud of us. We were the only sailing yacht in the harbour. Our tall mast seemed to dominate the motor boats that surrounded us. They were the familiar work horses of the islands, practical and unromantic. *Callisto* with her slim white hull, red ensign at the stern and the Norwegian courtesy flag at the crosstrees looked like an exotic butterfly.

To keep the conversation going I said, 'In the war we operated with a Norwegian ship – the destroyer *Stord*. She came into Scapa whilst our destroyer was there. I think she took part in the action against the German battle cruiser *Scharnhorst* off North Cape.'

'Ah, *Stord*,' he said, 'she was a famous ship.'

After a moment I said, 'We're very impressed with your merchant ships we've seen since Bergen. We haven't seen a foreign flag.'

'It's not as good as it looks,' Lohre said sadly. 'The crews are mostly Philipinos – only the officers are Norwegian.'

Then he cheered up. 'The forecast is for continuous settled weather. You'll have a good trip north.'

After he had gone I sat in the cockpit smoking my pipe and wondering how Ashley was getting on with the propane adaptor. He had been gone for three hours. I had done all my chores and it was nice to be by myself in the sunshine but I was quite glad when Anne returned from a shopping expedition.

'The folk museum was very interesting,' she said. 'Would you like some real coffee?'

She went below to put on the kettle and get out her private supply of freshly ground coffee. Before the trip when I had discussed with her the catering arrangements in the yacht she had said, 'It's all okay by me but I can't stand instant coffee. Do you mind if I bring proper coffee for myself?'

I had envisaged thin glass percolators smashing in the violently heeling yacht. She saw my hesitation. 'I can make it in an ordinary jug with paper filters.' she said.

Anne's coffee had turned out to be better than the stuff we were used to. It was a real privilege to be invited to have a mugful. Everybody looked hopeful when she got out her jug.

We drank coffee in the cockpit. This was the first day we had not been at sea. I was enjoying the peaceful harbour. The deck that I had just washed down was white in the sun. The chromium plated winches sparkled.

'How are you liking this?' I asked. It is difficult to have personal conversation at sea. There are too many people in too small a space. In harbour it is different. People disperse on various missions. There was now a chance to talk individually to the least experienced member of the crew.

Her eyes lit up. 'It's an experience of a lifetime,' she said. 'It's completely different from the cruise in the Coastal Express. We go so much more slowly – we can take everything in.'

She smiled at me. 'It's a sort of crazy adventure but all of you seem to know exactly what you're doing.'

'How do you like being with Tom on watch?'

She looked doubtful. 'That's the bit that worries me,' she said. 'It seems to take me a long time to learn things – steering, jib sheets, chartwork and so on. Tom gets impatient with me. I feel I'm letting him down all the time.'

She looked at me sadly with the big green eyes I have known since she was the young student I met after the war. I was married to her for a while and then we went in different directions. We had remained friends and I appreciated her offer to join us in *Callisto*. She was a good skier but a sailing yacht was an unfamiliar environment and she couldn't expect to learn things as rapidly as the much younger members of the crew.

'Look, Anne,' I said, 'I think you're doing splendidly. You said you were coming for the ride and doing the cooking. You're doing far more than that. You're standing all your watches like everybody else. You are already a useful crew member. Don't worry about Tom's impatience. It's only his manner. In a way it's a compliment. It means he's depending on you. We've got this bloody boat half way to Tromso and you're a card carrying member of her crew.' My pipe had gone out as it always does when I say more than two sentences.

She smiled at me. She seemed somewhat reassured. 'Thanks, Henry,' she said and touched my arm gratefully. I knew this wouldn't be the end of it. Inspite of the good weather and successful pilotage I expected there would be crew problems. There often are in a small vessel making a long passage. In my experience fouled up personal relationships ranked with fog and gales as one of the hazards of sailing.

After lunch Anne went ashore for more sight seeing. I lay down in one of the comfortable saloon berths and went to sleep. I intended to sail as soon as Ashley returned with the gas adaptor and the other members of crew came back from their various missions but there was no hurry. You could sail at any time in this latitude in June. With no darkness there were none of the inevitable tensions of night sailing that I was used to in Britain, navigation lights, radar reflector, aldis lamp, white flares at hand in the cockpit. There would be just the changing of watches and twilight for two or three hours whilst sunset brightened into dawn.

I was awakened by the sound of engines and the clanking of cranes. Two Coastal Express ships had secured on the other side of the quays. They were invisible from the yacht harbour but I could see tourists walking into the town for a short visit and feel a new vibrance in the sleepy air of Rorvik. The arrival of the ferries was a daily event in all the towns and villages of Norway. Here the northbound and southbound ships came almost simultaneously. For half an hour Rorvik was a humming metropolis.

It wasn't until eight in the evening that Ashley returned. The crew were all on board preparing supper prior to sailing.

'I've got it,' he said, handing me the small but vital fitting. He looked triumphant but very tired. 'I've brought my friends to see the yacht,' he said. 'I thought they would like some English tea.' Three people followed him into the saloon. I wanted my

50

supper and I wanted to sail but a visit of Norwegians to the yacht was an occasion which deserved high priority. As Kate put the kettle on Ashley introduced the friends he had acquired in a long day. Robin was the young taxi driver who had driven him to the propane works, his friend was the mechanic who had specially made the fitting and there was a seventeen year old fair haired girl who had somehow got into the act. She seemed to be the mechanic's girlfriend. She was the daughter of a local fish farmer and she was going to Tromso University in the autumn. Obtaining the small metal valve I held in my hand seemed to have required the deployment of a not insignificant proportion of the resources of Rorvik.

They settled in around the saloon table. They didn't seem to be in a hurry and didn't say anything. Kate handed round the tea and decided as hostess to initiate the conversation.

'What's it like living in Rorvik?' she asked.

'It's pretty dull here,' Robin said, 'not much excitement. There's usually a dance on Saturday nights but there isn't one this Saturday. That's why it's so quiet this evening.'

Robin took a cautious sip of his tea. I wished I could have given everybody a glass of Scotch but we had almost run out of it.

'Would you prefer to live somewhere like Bergen or Trondheim?'

Robin thought for a minute. 'No,' he said, 'I've been to Trondheim several times and it's too noisy and crowded. I like a bit more room.'

He looked at his companions and they both nodded. For all its dullness they didn't seem to mind the deprivations of island life. The girl said, 'When I graduate at Tromso I'm coming back to work on the fish farm.'

They fell silent after that gazing around the saloon of the yacht.

'How do you all manage to speak such good English?' I asked.

'We learn it at school,' the girl answered 'and we see a lot

51

of English programmes on television. They don't have sub-titles in Norwegian. Our own programmes aren't up to much.'

There was silence again. They answered questions readily but they didn't feel the need to fill in the gaps in conversation. Could it be a national difference I thought? All the English I knew were embarrassed by silence: they said all sorts of inane things to avoid it. However, we weren't short of questions and were curious about their country.

'We're getting unemployment now,' Robin said 'and we aren't used to it. We've wasted all the money from the off-shore oil. We've paid ourselves too much and raised prices. Now we aren't competitive with other countries.'

They didn't look particularly sad or anxious.

'I like Norway,' I said, 'from the little I've seen of it. Everything looks okay to me.' I hesitated, 'The only silly thing is your drinking laws.' I hoped I hadn't said the wrong thing. Even the pilot book had warned that this was a tricky subject but they nodded their agreement vigorously.

The girl said, 'They cause more problems than they solve. When Norwegians drink now they go on until they become insensible.'

Robin said, 'We have to drive a hundred miles to Trondheim to get a bottle of spirit. All we can get here is very weak beer unless we go to the hotel and then it's too expensive.'

'How do you manage?' Ashley asked.

The girl turned to him and said calmly, 'We make our own of course.'

Ashley looked surprised. 'Isn't that illegal?'

'Yes,' she said, 'but the police don't mind unless you start a factory and start selling the stuff.'

This seemed to be confirming my suspicions that there was something endearingly zany beneath the sensible surface of Norway.

'Why don't the police mind you distilling your own?' I asked.

'Because, of course, the police do it themselves.'

She looked at me in a way that made me feel I ought to have worked that one out. There was another silence whilst I tried to think of the next question. It was broken by the mechanic.

'I remember the day when the Russian factory fishing ship came to Rorvik. It only happened once,' he said and he sighed.

'The Russians wanted long playing records and we had lots of them. They had a big supply of vodka. It was (is this the right English word?) a bonanza!'

Our visitors didn't go until 9.30 and then nobody felt like sailing. As Anne resumed the interrupted preparations for supper she said, 'Coming on board probably made their evening. Not much competition in Rorvik.'

We were grateful to them for all they had told us and for their friendliness and for the help they had given to Ashley.

'I wish we could have offered them a proper drink,' I said regretfully.

'It's not your fault, Henry,' Anne said and added waspishly, 'it's because of their own silly laws.'

We sailed from Rorvik at 9.30 next morning. It was Sunday, a week since leaving Bergen. It was sunny and warm but as usual the wind was light. By eleven forty five we had furled the genoa and resorted to motoring.

I was conscious of the distances we still had to travel. I had studied the charts carefully back in England: I knew the route to the north through the islands – Leka, Vega, Donna, Stott, Tomma and a hundred others. With light winds and only a yacht's auxiliary engine we should have to keep going. If we sailed for a full day and a night and a day we might cover 180 miles. This would take us across the arctic circle and perhaps to Bodo – county town of Nordland. The guide book indicated that we should see some of the wonders of Norway on this leg of the trip, a bonus perhaps, but a side issue as far as I was concerned. I wanted to run off the miles to Russia. I resolved to try for Bodo which would be within striking distance of the Lofoten Islands.

The crew seemed in good heart. Ashley and Kate were on watch and Anne and Tom were clearing up breakfast – an easy task in the calm sheltered water. Nobody demurred when I said we might need to keep going for two days. I thought they were enjoying themselves. Tom was dedicated to the efficient handling of the ship, trying to make use of whatever wind there was. Anne was fascinated by Norway and adapting herself to the strange new world of a small yacht. Ashley, like me, was obsessed by the idea of sailing *Callisto* into Murmansk – a young man, he was pushing out his own frontiers. And Kate? The other beginner – she hadn't told me much but she seemed spellbound by the magnificent scenery and the skill of her watch leader, Ashley, from whom she was learning a great deal. We weren't breaking any records but I supposed when people talked about their holidays it was something to say you had sailed a yacht eight hundred miles from Bergen far into the arctic. They would have wondered why you were sunburnt. And me? At present I was happy sailing on this fine day past the fertile green shores of Helgeland still on schedule for Tromso. It was the future that daunted me – the sea beyond Tromso – North Cape, the Barents Sea and the Soviet Union. I remembered what Roy had said. There would be few problems with the ship or her crews, it was the skippers who would feel the strain.

All that day we sailed when we could and motored when our speed fell below four knots. The seascape scarcely changed – green islands with fields and woods, white villages and the snowy backdrop of the mountains sometimes far away and sometimes close on our starboard side as our track took us nearer to the mainland. It could only change by losing its perfection of green and blue and glittering white. The travel brochures had said it was the most beautiful coast in the world and I was in full agreement. Only a small guilty part of me half regretted the enormous contrasts of the British coast – the low sandy shores of East Anglia, the high rise towers of Sunderland, the smoking chimneys of Teeside and the lonely remoteness of Northumberland.

In the evening we came to one of the sights of Norway. The ship's log book says in Kate's handwriting, '18.30. Saw the mountain with the hole – Trollshatten.' The mountain's real name is Torghatten.

The cruise liners usually altered course here so that the passengers could see right through the hole, but from where we were we could see it quite clearly. Somebody had shot an arrow through the crown of the troll's hat and you could see daylight through it. It was quite impressive but rather a distraction from the task of keeping clear of large merchant ships coming south. The others crowded into the cockpit and took photographs. I didn't bother – half the shops in Norway had postcards of Torghatten.

By seven o'clock we were passing Bronnoysund and I took over the watch an hour later as we headed for Vega.

Sometime during my long solitary watch I became depressed. To begin with I couldn't think why. All was well. The fjords were wider here and there weren't any other ships to worry about. The autohelm clicked reassuringly, an intermittent electronic buzz, heard against the continuous rumble of the motor. The sea was like glass and the sun was veiled by thin cirrus clouds. I wasn't depressed about the high latitudes that lay ahead. Apprehensive, yes, but also excited. It was something else. Perhaps it was a crew problem, I thought, and searched my mind to recall any signs of tension or stress. There had been my conversation with Anne in Rorvik but there seemed to be no other anxieties apart from that. Everyone was getting on well, *Callisto*'s crew was a successful team. After a while the thought slowly came into my mind that one other member of the crew was having personal problems. It was me. I was getting jealous about Kate. The realisation came as a shock. Here was I on the threshold of the arctic, directing a well thought out operation and responsible for a ship and her crew, and I was having feelings like a teenager. I disconnected the autohelm and took the tiller in my hand; perhaps the comforting routine of steering would steady my thoughts.

When I had invited Kate to come on this trip in the Penthouse Bar in Nottingham I had been fooling myself.

'I need another crew member,' I had said. 'I'll be a bit pre-occupied as skipper but the others will look after you.'

It had sounded correct and matter of fact. She had long dark hair like the women Rossetti painted and her eyes sometimes looked green and sometimes blue. She was extremely attractive but I believed that had not weighed with me. I had enjoyed my conversations with her and valued her friendship but she was outside my class. I was too old for her. Now I was confronting the fact that taking charge of a long range cruising yacht was a lot easier than taking charge of myself. I had watched Kate and Ashley, heads together, poring over the chart table, playing chess together and talking through their watches on deck. This was all in the contract. There was nothing I could take exception to and Kate had done all that I had asked. Nevertheless there was a cold knot of loneliness inside me. I felt strangely exiled. Jealousy is a vice which unlike anger diminishes you. I hated myself for it.

The low islands were now casting shadows on the sea as the sun neared the horizon. My watch would soon be over.

I began to feel better. The problem wouldn't go away but I had at least identified it and my depression was lifting. The way you felt about people and the way they responded wasn't a rational process like navigation. Perhaps I could learn to accept the random frailty of human feelings, including my own. You had to learn something on the way to Russia.

The sun had dipped below the northern horizon when I handed over the watch to Tom and Anne at midnight. They were muffled in jerseys, scarves and woolly caps. There was a slight chill in the air. Night was a brief interlude of shadowy daylight.

When I had pointed out the beacons to Tom he said, 'I've got her. Go below, you look tired. Give yourself a glass of Scotch, I think there's a bit in the bottle.' I don't think he liked my one-man watches: he thought I was taking too much on myself. The whisky seemed to knock me out and I slept almost immediately.

At one thirty I was aroused by Anne's voice calling down from the cockpit.

'Sorry to wake you, Henry. It's not an emergency, but you ought to come and see this.'

Nobody woke anyone who was asleep off watch unless they had to. There must be something worthwhile up there. I dragged myself sleepily up the ladder.

'Seven Sisters,' Anne said. She was looking up.

Close on our starboard side was a great wall of snow clad mountains. Their ghostly slopes rose steeply from the pewter coloured sea. They seemed to overhang us. Then I saw what Anne was looking at. Far above, the seven summits were lit by a level blaze of white fire. I gazed in dazzled wonder only half realising that the sun hadn't set up there.

After a minute Anne said doubtfully, 'I hope that was worth being wakened for.'

She was steering and glancing from the compass to the mountains.

'I wouldn't have missed that for anything,' I said thankfully.

The cruise liners usually passed close to the Seven Sisters, one of the sights of Norway, when the passengers were awake, but we had had the privilege of seeing them at night. It would be an unforgettable memory of that long cruise.

We crossed the Arctic Circle at 7.45 that morning. It was Monday 11th June and Ashley and Kate were on watch. Ashley wrote in the remarks column of the log:

'66 degrees 32 minutes North. We have just passed into the land of the midnight sun. I expect we will soon be seeing polar bears, ice caps and eskimos. Well done the good ship *Callisto*.'

It was a childhood vision of the arctic. Maybe we all secretly shared it. We were propelled by an impulse to sail forever north to a place where things were wonderfully different under an eternal sun.

A south west wind came as if to celebrate the occasion. We turned off the motor, unfurled the genoa and eased the mainsheet. We entered the arctic under sail with the wind astern. It was hot in the sunshine.

Last time I crossed the Arctic Circle we were 200 miles off the Norwegian Coast. It had been cold then and the convoy was in range of enemy aircraft.

Chapter Five

I leant on the guardrail aft of the gun where I should not be seen from the bridge and looked about me. The ships of the convoy were shadows moving in the mist. Light rain was coming out of a cold sky and there was some sleet. The wind was light, coming from nowhere, smelling of nothing. It was only after I had been standing still for a while that I felt the chill of its wet fingers. The sea was black with a hint of indigo. Looking down close to the ship's side, I could see streamers of foam turning white and blue.

It was 9.30 in the forenoon on the 14 March 1945 and the convoy was three days out of the Clyde.

I had been splicing an eye in a new four inch circumference flexible steel wire mooring line. It was a task I rather enjoyed and I could work in the fo'c'sle cabouche by myself out of the wind. It was the sort of skilled work peacetime sailors did and for a while I seemed to be out of the war. After an hour and a half I had completed the first tuck with the six strands of the big wire. This was the most difficult bit and it seemed a good idea to knock off for a rest. Outside the cabouche there had been no-one on the fo'c'sle except the two men on watch at the four inch gun. One of them was wearing a telephone headset and the other was reading. They had trained the gun into the wind so that the shield gave them some shelter. The petty officer Ordnance Artificer always grumbled about this practice. He would say fussily, 'They ought to keep the gun trained fore and aft, the young monkeys.'

The mist and rain began to clear. The horizon to the north was a hard dull line and the merchant ships became iron silhouettes. A fleet destroyer on our port bow was turning up high revs on her engines with 30 degrees port rudder, heeling over and making a great bow wave. A Grummon Wildcat fighter from one of the carriers was patrolling overhead. The escort carrier, *Trumpeter*, and the two fleet destroyers *Savage* and *Scourge* had joined from Scapa. It was all very routine and proceeding as ordered. This was the first time that I had really looked at the convoy in its full ocean formation. It covered several square miles of sea. It was like a city – you couldn't see it when you were in it, just the streets. I could only see the nearby ships but I knew that there were twenty four merchant ships forming a compact rectangle in nine columns. I couldn't see *Trumpeter* or the *Campania*, the two escort carriers, but I could make out the distinctive superstructure of the D class cruiser somewhere in the middle. On the horizon ahead was the outer screen of the fleet destroyers. The close escort leader, *Lapwing*, was ahead of the columns of merchant vessels and the other close escort ships, like us were guarding the flanks. There were almost as many warships as there were merchant ships.

Our flagship, *Campania*, was a rather small aircraft carrier, a merchant ship hull with a flight deck on top. She looked like a real fleet carrier until you saw her single engined fighter planes ranged on deck. Her small size made them look like four engined bombers. To make up for a short flight deck she had to steam full speed into a reasonable headwind so the planes could take off. Nevertheless, she and her sister ship, *Trumpeter*, were the most powerful units of the convoy. They were also the most vulnerable. They would be the prime target for enemy aircraft and U-boats. They had no armour, just the thin steel of a merchant ship and they were loaded with bombs and aviation spirit. The Vice Admiral who flew his flag on *Campania* was commanding the show from the least safe place in the convoy. To the rest of us, this was a most consoling thought.

After supper, I relieved Tony Baynon at the wheel. It was 8 o'clock, the wind was light but the swell was still running. Steering was not difficult but it was going to be a long four hours. Today, I had steered from midnight to 4.00 am, worked during the forenoon and steered again all the afternoon. I was fairly tired. The off-duty look-outs lit cigarettes which glowed in the shadowy wheelhouse. I stared at the giro compass repeater and tried not to look at the clock whose hands never moved. At midnight I could go below and sleep for nearly seven hours. In the meantime, I had to contend with tiredness and boredom. The only hope was poetry. If you learned enough poetry you could manage without books. Poetry was in your head like secret gramophone records that no-one else could hear. By this time, I had a fairly extensive knowledge of poetry, suitable for all occasions – fear, loneliness or escape. In the introduction to an anthology, W. H. Auden had written, 'Of the many definitions of poetry, the simplest is still the best; "memorable speech".'

I found his definition entirely satisfactory. You could read good novels or histories but they were not much use to you if you were steering a ship with your eyes unremittingly on the compass. You could not remember them. You could, on the other hand, remember poems – the exact words. I decided to begin with escapist poetry. A poem then selected itself. It was 'The Daisy' by Tennyson written in Edinburgh remembering a holiday in Italy. I had bought the poetic works of Tennyson in Kirkwall in the Orkney Islands in January 1944 and I had decided that this light unpretentious poem was the best thing in the book. There were twenty seven four-line stanzas and I thought I could manage them all. The exercise would probably take up the first hour of the watch.

> O love, what hours were thine and mine
> In lands of palm and southern pine
> In lands of palm, or orange-blossom
> Of olive, aloe, and maize and vine.

> What Roman strength Turbia show'd
> In ruin by the mountain road;
> How like a gem, beneath, the city
> Of little Monaco, basking, glow'd.

'Steer 060 degrees, 150 revolutions.'
I turned the wheel to port and the bosun's mate rang the engine room telegraph. I could feel the speed increasing. I reported, 'Course 060 degrees, 150 revolutions.'

> How richly down the rocky dell
> The torrent vineyard streaming fell
> To meet the sun and sunny water
> That only heaved with a summer swell.

> What slender campanili grew
> By bays, the peacock's neck in hue;
> Where, here and there, on sandy beaches
> A milky-bell'd amaryllis blew.

'Steer 055 degrees, 160 revolutions.'
I repeated the order and brought the ship slightly more round to port. The convoy was taking up a new after-dark course and we were increasing revolutions to keep station on the merchant ships.

> At Florence too what golden hours,
> In whose long galleries, were ours;

CHAPTER FIVE

What drives about the fresh Cascine
Or walks in Boboli's ducal bowers.

   In bright vignettes, and each complete,
Of tower or duomo, sunny-sweet
Or palace, how the city glitter'd
Through cypress avenues, at our feet.

   Who was the girl in the poem? She didn't really seem to
exist. The poem was not a love poem, it was about places. She
was just an idea. I might as well create her myself since Tennyson
had neglected her. She began to look like a fair haired Wren I had
talked to in a bar in Sauchiehall Street when we were last in harbour. It was not difficult to imagine myself with her in Florence
instead of in this hard edged steel ship in the North. I would be
rather shy with her but as a former architectural student I could at
least talk knowledgeably about the buildings. Her hair was light
gold in the Italian sun and her eyes were bluer than I had remembered them in Scotland. She said, 'We have looked at paintings
and seen an awful lot of architecture. Let's go back to the hotel?'
   She could see I looked a bit disconcerted by this suggestion. So far, it had been like a brother and sister on holiday. I
seemed to have been at sea a long time; I wasn't any good at girls.
   I suddenly felt a blind need for her.
'Starboard 10.'
'10 of starboard wheel on, sir.'
'Meet her.'
'Course 065 degrees, sir.'
'Steady on 065.'
In the last two verses, it was no longer an escapist poem;

   And I forgot the clouded Forth,
The gloom that saddens heaven and earth
The bitter east, the misty summer
And grey metropolis in the North.

Perchance, to lull the throbs of pain,
Perchance, to charm a vacant brain
Perchance, to dream you still beside me
My fancy fled to the south again.

Tennyson, like me, lived with a sense of loss. He at least had memories; I had only lost a dream of something I had never had.

When Taffy Jones relieved me at midnight, I had had enough steering. He looked tired, too. He had had only two hours sleep and now would be steering for the four hours of the middle watch. After I had reported to the bridge, he took the wheel and gave me a pale smile but didn't say anything. I went below to the dimly lit messdeck. One of the men coming off watch had got a jug of cocoa from the galley and filled my mug. With almost seven hours sleep to look forward to, it would have been a pity to turn in immediately and not enjoy this prospect. The ten or fifteen minutes that it took to drink the cocoa were the best in the three day watch cycle. I took off my sea boots and swung into my hammock fully dressed and wearing my uninflated life belt. I was asleep before I had even wrapped myself in my blanket.

I was awakened at 7 o'clock by the bosun's mate calling the hands. Only it wasn't the usual bosun's mate and it wasn't the usual call. One of the leading seamen of the Blue Watch was rousing us up and making an awful noise. Trilling his pipe, he shouted;

Heave ho, heave ho, heave ho,
Lash up and stow
Come on my lucky lads, you've had your time
The mornings fine, no sign of rain
We're off the sunny coast of Spain
Come on my lucky lads, show a leg
The sun's burning your eyeballs out
Hands off cocks

On socks
Rig of the day, sailor suits
Buckets and spades.'

As I ruefully abandoned the idea of another ten minutes with my head down, it occurred to me that this frightful din came well within W. H. Auden's definition of poetry.

On the upper deck, it didn't look a bit like the sunny coast of Spain. It was now quite cold and the fresh breeze made your ears hurt and your nose sting when you breathed. The sea was black and flecked with white under the cold sky and some spray was coming on board. There were flurries of snow and ice patches were forming in odd corners around the Oerlikons and depth-charge throwers. We were now on the same latitude as the North of Iceland but a long way east. I was glad to be in the wheelhouse where it was fairly warm. The men at the guns and the look-outs came down from the bridge into the wheelhouse with cold pinched faces. These sort of conditions were unfamiliar to many of the crew. We were entering foreign seas.

The two eighteen year old ordinary seamen in the Red Watch were quite excited about it all in an unhappy sort of way. Leading Seaman MacLaughlan said, 'We'll be crossing the Arctic Circle fairly soon so keep a sharp look out.'

Scott asked, 'When will we see icebergs?'

MacLaughlan said, 'We can do without bloody icebergs,' and resumed his reading of the Reader's Digest.

It was not very warm in the seamen's mess in the afternoon. The cold seemed to have descended on us like a great hand. I sat reading near an electric fire and tried not to shiver. Everyone was asleep huddled in blankets except three seamen in No. 5 mess who were drinking coffee and talking quietly about what they would do after the war. There was no thermal insulation in the ship and the condensation was beginning to freeze on the inside of the steel plates of the hull.

I didn't seem able to read. I wished MacLaughlan or

Gordon Powell were awake. I felt alone and unlucky in a fateful sea.

The Navigating Officer had pinned up a chart on the bulkhead outside the sick-berth. It showed the projected route of the convoy to Russia. He had drawn on it two arcs with their centres at Banack and Bardufoss airfields in North Norway. Against this, he had written 'area of probable aircraft attack'. We were now entering this zone. Why hadn't the Navigating Officer written 'possible' instead of 'probable'? He seemed to have acquired the skipper's knack of making everything look fairly bleak.

I was not all that scared of an air attack. You could see the planes coming and we had two carriers. It was the U-boats that frightened me.

Still the Navigator's chart was a reminder of hazard. I wished I were somewhere else. I wanted to be outside the neatly drawn circles. I sat feeling cold and depressed.

I was relieved when leading seaman Ron Teece came and sat down at the table opposite me. He had been one of the men awake drinking coffee in 5 Mess. Hammocks enfolding sleeping men bumped gently above us as the ship rolled.

'You look fed up, Henry,' he said grinning cheerfully. 'What's up?'

'Those circles on the chart.' I said, and then, because I was talking to Ron Teece and nobody else, I added, 'I think they rather frighten me.'

I could talk like this to Ron Teece because he and I shared action stations in the plot cabinet and hence worked together in times of maximum tension. It was a bond between us. He stopped smiling.

'You aren't the only one,' he said seriously.

Ron Teece was the life and soul of 5 Mess. All the big laughs that came from the starboard side seemed to emanate from him. Everything was a joke. Afloat and ashore, he was one of the boys. I knew, however, that there was a lot more to him than that. His home was in Nottingham and he had worked in a tobacco factory before he joined up. His hobbies had been his old car and rowing on the River Trent. He was about my age but had had more sea experience. Behind his charm and sense of fun, was an intelligent and sensitive mind. I knew, that like me, he was in fact often afraid. We were both glad that our action stations were high on the fore superstructure.

Ron was looking at me attentively. Although he talked a lot he was also a good listener. He made me want to talk to him.

I said, 'The bloody officers in this ship seem to go out of their way to put the fear of God in us. We all know about Russian convoys. Are they adding a bit more fear to keep us on our toes? It's a funny way to manage the show; I thought officers were supposed to encourage the troops.'

Ron considered what I had said. I must have sounded quite angry because he said, soothingly, 'You're only really talking about the Navigating Officer, Henry.'

We both knew him well. The young man who was next in seniority to the First Lieutenant ran the action plot. The three of us spent hours huddled together round the plotting table listening to the ticking motor that automatically recorded the ship's position and the pinging of the adjacent asdic set. The Navigating Officer was alarmingly detached. When the asdic indicated that we might have detected a U-boat, he would draw calm lines on the plotting table. It was if he were proving theorems in geometry rather than hunting the enemy.

Ron lit a cigarette and tossed the match into the gash can.

'The others aren't like him,' he said. 'I heard sub lieutenant LaTouche telling some of the chaps who were looking at the chart that he thought the Germans had sent their best aircraft to southern fronts. He said they were only fielding their second eleven. He cheered me up. He made it seem like a game that we could win.'

I had to concede that the Gunnery Officer was usually optimistic but I wasn't yet ready to be comforted. I said in a more even voice, 'I'm afraid of people who aren't afraid and the

Navigator is one of those. They don't recognise fear in other people. Luckily there aren't many like that. The trouble is we've got
another one on board – the bloody Skipper. I hate it when he talks
to us.'

Ron grinned inhaling smoke, 'The Skipper's okay. He
makes rotten speeches but he keeps us out of trouble. I don't
think he wants to win any medals. I think he wants to get out of
the Navy and go home like the rest of us.'

In truth, I shared this view about the Skipper. It had just
been the circles on the chart that had got me. I moved along the
bench so that I could warm my hands on the electric fire. Ron
could see that I was out of my black mood.

'There's bloody Jimmy too,' Ron said and he started laughing. Jimmy the One was the name we gave the First Lieutenant.
He was responsible for the efficiency of the crew.

'He's okay. The only thing is, he frightens me more than
the Germans do!'

He stubbed out his cigarette and stood up, 'I've got the first
dog watch' he said.

He had cheered me up and I was grateful to him. I didn't
even mind his last teasing remark as he left Six Mess. 'See you
at action stations any time now.'

I found I could go on reading again.

By the time I relieved Tony Baynon for the morning watch
at 4 o'clock on the following day, we were across the Arctic
Circle. Darkness concealed the cold waves and the remorseless
routine of the ship seemed to anaesthetise both fear and wonder.
The wheelhouse was lit by the dim red glow of the giro compass
repeater. The magnetic compass slopped from side to side in its
bowl of light. The men on the upper deck muffled in their cold
weather gear were hard to identify. They came stamping through
the wheelhouse, glaring disparagingly at the compass. Then I
could recognise the boys' faces under their hoods fringed with
fur. The off duty look-outs sat on the wheelhouse deck by the
radiators visible only by the glint of their cigarettes.

CHAPTER FIVE

Tony said, 'You'll have a quiet time, Henry. Jimmy's got the watch.'

I liked it when the First Lieutenant was on watch. The other officers were alright but I felt safer with him up there on the bridge.

I reported to the bridge and heard the First Lieutenant's acknowledgement. 'Very good.'

I could hear other voices muttering through voice pipes, 'Radar, plot, radar plot . . . plot here, plot here . . .'

'Is that you, Jock? . . . bridge, WT office, can I have that last signal?'

Red Watch was now in business for the morning.

I felt depressed. There didn't seem to be anything to look forward to. I supposed the war would end one day and I could go back to being an architect but at 4.15 in the arctic it seemed an unbelievable idea. The future was steering the ship for ever.

Watching the giro compass, I felt alone and tired. I thought of the inevitable action with the enemy in the next few days and wondered what it would be like. I hated the morning watch, nobody was talking in the wheelhouse. Perhaps men were thinking thoughts like mine. Dawn was hours away.

The Skipper came through the wheelhouse on his way to the bridge. I wondered why he was going there; nothing seemed to be happening and he never needed to supervise the First Lieutenant. Keeping station on the convoy would be easy on a calm night like this.

Through the voice pipe I could hear snatches of conversation between him and the First Lieutenant. Reassuringly, it seemed to be just chat. I heard the First Lieutenant acknowledging MacLaughlan's first hourly report to the bridge. I was steering 010 degrees. The morning watch was proceeding with deadly monotony.

It was a relief when the First Lieutenant came down to the wheelhouse. Perhaps he was going to have a look round the ship whilst the Skipper had the watch or perhaps he just wanted a smoke. He pulled off his gloves and put them in the pockets of his duffel coat, unwound his scarf and lit a cigarette. He didn't seem to be in a hurry.

Lieutenant Scrivenor was in his mid twenties and as tall as I – six foot two. He seemed to be able to combine a restless energy with a relaxed confidence in himself. He had an animal magnetism that I thought would be attractive to women. More important to us was his sense of humour. This was in marked contrast to the rather gloomy Skipper and the nervousness of the junior officers. He was one of the few men in our ship who seemed to enjoy life.

He stood silently looking at the compass. Steering was no problem. In this calm sea I was keeping the ship's head within two degrees either side of the course. MacLaughlan was sitting at the table trying to look alert. In the faint light I couldn't see his expression but I know his gaze would be fixed watchfully on the officer. The First Lieutenant said, 'It's nice to have a calm night, Henry.'

He drew on his cigarette. 'Bloody dark though, you can't see anything on the bridge, just a few stars.'

This reminded me of something and since he seemed to be in a conversational mood, I said, 'Do you mind if I ask you a question, sir?'

'Fire away,' he said.

'What's the star you refer to as Wiggy?'

'How do you know about that?' he asked.

I said mildly, 'I hear quite a lot down the voice pipe, sir, and I've heard you and the Navigating Officer talking about it.'

'Bloody eavesdropping,' he said, 'but I suppose it helps to keep you awake.'

I glanced at him and in the light from the compass I could see that he was smiling. I knew he would tell me about the star. He was interested in stars. On one occasion when I had been lookout on the bridge on a clear night, he had noticed me looking at Jupiter. In the 7 x 50 lookout binoculars the four satellites of the big planet showed up clearly – Jupiter was in my lookout sector so I was doing my job all right. He had wandered over and looked at the planet through his own glasses.

'Pretty, isn't it?' he had said.

Now in the wheelhouse he said, answering my question, 'We take star sights pretty regularly and Wiggy is the one we often use – it's the star at the tail of the Plough.'

'I thought that one was called Alkaid.'

He looked quite impressed for a brief moment. Then he said, 'I suppose you've been creeping about the chartroom looking at the star globe, Henry.' But I knew he didn't mind. He was glad to have someone to talk to about stars. The Skipper and the Navigating Officer knew all about stars too. They looked at them through their sextants and fixed the ship's position with them but that was all. The First Lieutenant wondered about them.

'Alkaid is only one name for that star, it's got another name – Benetnasch.'

Instantly I made the connection. Our Chief Stoker was called Wiggy Bennet.

He went on, 'It reminds us of the Chief Stoker.'

He may have said this jokingly but I knew what was going on in his mind. Those stars out there were beautiful but also slightly scary. The North Atlantic sky in winter on a clear night was an unbelievable sight. If you thought about it for a while, you began to feel fairly small. Jimmy had put the kind hearted and genial Chief Stoker up in the sky to domesticate the whole thing.

The First Lieutenant stubbed out his cigarette in the gash tin and went down the wheelhouse ladder. The conversation had been an intermission, a relief from boredom, and the clock's hands showed that it was fifteen minutes nearer dawn and the end of the watch.

MacLaughlan said, 'Are you a friend of fucking Jimmy – all that crap about stars? He behaves like a shit.'

MacLaughlan was standing up and I could just make out an expression of curiosity on his face. I thought of the First

Lieutenant's rough but grinning enthusiasm and his splendidly abusive language.

I said, 'He's okay. He's only doing his job. First Lieutenants are supposed to be shits. If it wasn't for him we would all be sitting in the mess drinking tea half the day.' I was surprised to see the leading seaman nod in agreement.

'Yes, he's pretty fair with us,' he said, 'and for a Reserve Officer he knows his stuff. He gets his hands dirty too.'

MacLaughlan sat down at the table but before relapsing into silence said, 'I still think he's a shit, though.'

The First Lieutenant had one other good quality that appealed to very young men who made up most of the crew. He had a reputation for recklessness.

I had been an unwitting agent for creating this reputation. The event had occurred when the ship had been based in Tobermory harbour in September 1944 for working up training after commissioning. The Flag Officer, Commodore Stephenson, through whose hands all new Western Approaches ships passed ran a fairly tough outfit. Day-long anti-submarine exercises off the west coast of Mull were followed by simulated emergencies in harbour – the ship is on fire, the anchor is dragging, the Skipper is dead. The Commodore's training staff speeded up the solution to these problems by tossing thunder flashes. It was a hard two weeks but the Commodore was much harder on the Skipper and the officers than the crew. The crew began to resent this and tried quite hard to help them. In a new ship where people hardly knew each other, there was gradually born a sense of solidarity and a loyalty to the officers. I didn't appreciate it then but this was precisely what the Commodore intended.

It was rumoured that when a corvette was at moorings at night with officers and men enjoying a brief and exhausted sleep the Commodore with his gang of gunners mates wearing gaiters would creep out in a whaler with muffled oars and unshackle the ship's mooring chain. Next day her skipper would be put on a charge for failing to guard his ship. On our first night in

CHAPTER FIVE

Tobermory I came on duty for the first watch – 8 o'clock to midnight.

As sentry, I was wearing a regulation watch coat and web-
bing equipment. The Smith & Wesson revolver on its white
lanyard was more of a badge of office than a weapon. I had in fact
armed myself with a small book of poetry in my pocket to guard
against the long lonely hours of darkness. I had just taken over
when the First Lieutenant appeared on the main deck in the fading light.

'Here you are, Quartermaster,' he said. 'Take these.'

He handed me five .38 cartridges. I must have looked rather
surprised. I said politely, 'Thank you, sir,' and put them gingerly
into my pocket.

'Not there,' he said, 'in the bloody gun.'

I was puzzled but took the revolver out of its holster and
slowly loaded it.

'Now,' he said, 'if any boat approaches the ship I want you
to fire at it.'

I couldn't see how there could be any Germans in
Tobermory so I said, 'Supposing it's the training people from
ashore, sir?'

'That's precisely who it will be,' he said, 'and they'll be
trying to unshackle the cable. It's your job to stop them.'

'Shouldn't I give them a hail first, sir? I might shoot the
Commodore.'

The First Lieutenant looked exasperated. I didn't know
what orders the Skipper had given him but it must have been on
the lines of, ' . . . and by the way, No. 1, make sure those dozy
quartermasters are on their toes.'

He said patiently, 'I want you to kill him. As far as you're
concerned he's the enemy and by the way take off the safety
catch, you'll have to shoot fast.'

He could see I was getting the message. He grinned and
said, 'Pass those orders on to your relief at midnight.'

He left me staring uneasily into the growing darkness. The

73

revolver was back in its holster but my hand was on the butt. I wasn't going to read much poetry on this watch.

I imagined the First Lieutenant sitting in the ward room listening for a fusillade of revolver shots on the upper deck and even the cries of the wounded.

In the event the Commodore must have had a night off because nothing happened but the matter was not without consequence. Next morning as we were getting off our moorings to go on our first anti-submarine exercise I noticed that the seamen on the fo'c'sle were looking at the First Lieutenant in a new way. Their normal expressions of complete indifference had changed to something approaching respect. As we left harbour I heard one of them say to another, 'Our bloody Jimmy told the quartermasters to shoot the sodding Commodore if they could. He dished out rifles, live ammunition, hand grenades – the lot.'

The phrase 'our bloody Jimmy' struck me. It indicated that in the minds of the ship's company, that although he was still the hated First Lieutenant he had been accepted as a member of the same firm.

Daylight and the end of the morning watch showed the ship rolling and pitching easily in the long Atlantic seas going north and east. The sea was black and speckled with white horses. The clouds had raw ragged edges and there were occasional unexpected patches of blue sky. We were not far from Jan Mayen Island.

On my way below to the messdeck, I had another look at the chart pinned to the bulkhead. Apart from Jan Mayen Island, it showed that we were hundreds of miles from anywhere. The enemy coast was far away to starboard and the polar ice a long way off on the port bow.

At supper time, Jim Pickthall asked, 'What's this about not being able to go ashore in Russia?'

He was a very young seaman and spoke with a Lancashire accent, made fashionable by Gracie Fields and George Formby.

MacLaughlan said, 'You can go ashore in Russia but there's got to be a leading seaman in charge.'

Jim thought about this for a moment and then said, mildly, 'Perhaps some leading seamen don't know their way about Russia.'

He carefully secured his woollen drawers around his waist and looked at me a bit doubtfully with his narrow face because he saw that I was laughing. There was a pile of clothes heaped on the mess table and over it I could see MacLaughlan continuing his game of patience and the White Watchman eating supper. The wireless which was on all the time tuned to the BBC Forces Programme suddenly called attention to itself by playing "There's no place like home". This made everyone look miserable.

In the dog watches, the seamen off duty wrote letters. They wrote to wives, girlfriends, mothers and friends. They wrote pages and pages. The letters were addressed and piled up in the ship's post office. We shall bring them back with us from Russia and they will be posted only when we get back to the Clyde. If leave is granted, some of the writers might easily arrive home before their letters but letters were a link with the outside world. They were all censored by our officers so you could not say anything about the ship or where you were or what was happening. In these circumstances, it was quite difficult to write good letters.

I didn't have a wife or a girlfriend to write to so I wrote to previous student colleagues, my mother in Exeter, my uncle in Bideford and occasionally to my younger brother who was in a Hunt class destroyer in the Mediterranean. I didn't like writing to my mother. Until recently, my regular correspondence with her had been the most important. A few weeks ago, however, I had received a letter from my father advising me that my mother was upset by my letters home. Could I ease up? I am sure he was quite right to tell me this; both sons were on active service in the Royal Navy but my father's letter was like a kick in the teeth. It wasn't all that marvellous being an able seaman in a corvette and it hurt me to think that my parents didn't want to know about it. Now my letters home were carefully contrived essays. Writing them was just a chore.

Nobody ever read anybody else's letters even if they were left lying about the mess tables so I never knew what sailors wrote. Some of the letters, however, to girlfriends must have been wild and wonderful because occasionally, I acted as consultant.

'Can I have some more adjectives, Henry?'

I was even expected to do quick drawings of the authors to accompany the texts. A seaman who was writing said, 'What shall I write to her about, Henry?'

'Well, just tell her how much you love her.'

'I'm not sure that I really do.'

He could see I was listening and went on, 'You see, sometimes she seems to want me, at other times she doesn't but she just needs me around.'

I thought I could help here. I said, 'There was a bloke in your position who wrote about it three hundred years ago. What he wrote was this,

Or love me less or love me more
but play not with my liberty
Either take all or all restore
bind me to you or else set free.

The sailor said, 'God, what happened?'

I said, 'I can't remember any more but it was written by a pongo who got killed in the end by Cromwell's soldiers.'

'Bloody hell, tarts don't change much do they. Can you say it again, only slowly.'

I could hear the bow wave rushing past the thin plates of the hull, the Forces Programme music and the vibration of the screw as I dictated for his girl the four lines from Sydney Godolphin's poem. It seemed a funny thing to be doing in the arctic.

Chapter Six

Callisto arrived at Bodo at nine o'clock in the evening. The city was a disappointment. I suppose I had expected something beautiful like Alesund and even more magical for being in the arctic. Instead it revealed itself as an ordinary medium sized seaport with modern buildings under a grey sky. It could have been anywhere. The intrusive sound of aircraft engines reminded me that it was a forward NATO base. After the wonders of the Nordland coast Bodo seemed prosaic.

My disappointment was only momentary. Bodo was a safe harbour and we had arrived ahead of schedule only 36 hours from Rorvik. *Callisto* was doing fine. We had sailed 200 miles and were more than two degrees of latitude northward. We were thankful to tie up to pontoons by the long mole that sheltered the harbour. There was none of the tension of entering Rorvik: the harbour was wide and deep and there were yachts at moorings.

It had been a good sail. The breeze that had greeted our entry into the arctic had held through most of the day. It had been variable from the north and north east. We had sailed at six knots some of the time mostly hard on the wind and occasionally as we altered course around islands the wind came from astern. This meant easier sailing but the wind blew into the saloon through the open hatch with a raw coldness. The crew below wrapped themselves in their sleeping bags.

On deck it was hard work as it always is in a sailing boat going to windward. One member of the watch was steering all the time concentrating on the luff of the genoa and altering course in response to the shifting direction of the wind. You can't use the autohelm in these conditions. The other member of the watch would be keeping lookout for marks and going down the ladder at intervals to examine the chart. Sometimes it would be necessary to tack. The helmsman would steer the boat through the wind and the other would grind the big sheet winches to bring the genoa to its correct setting on the other side. Even in a light wind the big genoa on *Callisto* has a pull of about 12 horse power – getting it in even with the full power of the sheet winch is a two handed job. Tacking made you sweat. Tacking wasn't popular with the crew below washing up, cleaning or relaxing. The saloon had been heeling 15 degrees to starboard for perhaps half an hour then quite quickly it would heel to port. Cups, books, buckets, pencils would slide to the other side sometimes falling off the edge of tables and worktops. The cutlery and saucepans in the cupboards in the galley area would rattle alarmingly. It would be five minutes before things settled on the new tack and at any moment would come a shout from the cockpit,

'Sorry, we're tacking again.'

We all loved it, of course. Even I with my obsession with covering miles was prepared to forgo the rather faster method of motoring straight into the wind. Yes, I wanted to get to Russia but even that had to take second place to the excitement of beating to windward in a thirty four foot yacht in smooth water.

The enjoyment of fast sailing did not distract the watch on deck from the need for continuous navigation. The track of the ship had to be shown at all times in pencilled lines on the chart and her position checked continuously by cross bearings from lighthouses and beacons. The Decca Navigator co-ordinates needed to be recorded on the hour. We were sailing a well marked seaway but the sea is never safe. To remind us of this we came upon the wreck of a fishing boat. She was lying on her side on a reef, the waves quietly lapping her torn sides. We stared at her in silence. For all the lighthouses and all her radar and electronic navigation systems she had got it wrong. She was an eerie reminder that eternal vigilance was the price you paid for sailing the wild coast of Nordland.

'We're very lucky with the weather,' Kate said. We were sitting in the saloon drinking tea; Ashley was with the others in the cockpit. 'We've only had a few spots of rain since Bergen and we've had no gales.'

Recently my conversations with Kate had been confined to routine questions and comments such as, 'Can I have the log reading, please?' or 'You ought to be wearing your safety harness.' Now she seemed to want to engage me in conversation. She drank her tea carefully as the yacht heeled to the gentle wind. The sunbeams swayed across the polished wood and cushions of the saloon.

'Yes,' I said, 'it couldn't be more settled; we've only had to shorten sail once. Perhaps it's always like this here at this time of the year.'

She was silent for a moment drinking her tea. 'You're very lucky with your two watch leaders,' Kate said and nodded towards the cockpit hatch where Tom and Ashley were discussing the correct position for the jib fairleads. 'They really do know what they're doing. I'm now feeling quite confident.' She smiled.

She had lowered her voice. Talking about other members of the crew, even saying nice things, was to be done with discretion, especially when the motor wasn't going.

'Yes, they're doing extremely well,' I said and thought about their dedication to accurate pilotage and the safe management of the ship.

'You've done well, too,' I said. 'You're acting like an experienced yacht crew.' She looked pleased. I collected the mugs to wash them up. I was glad Kate was talking with me but listening to her had made me feel somewhat diminished. She had talked too much about luck. There is a lot of luck in sailing but a skipper tries to arrange things so that as far as possible the luck goes his way. We were indeed lucky with the calm settled weather but Roy and I had done our homework on meteorology.

The dates we had chosen to sail would give us a good chance at least of encountering the continental and arctic high pressure systems with their light winds and clear skies. Even the fast schedule we were keeping to was determined by our decision that *Callisto*, wherever she got to, had to be south of the arctic by mid August. We were prepared to meet adverse conditions but we had as far as possible minimised their likelihood.

And, yes, I was lucky with my watch leaders too and yet they weren't entirely accidental either. I had sailed with Tom and Ashley on previous occasions, teaching them all I knew and giving them more and more responsibility. I had encouraged them to attend evening classes on navigation. I had surely made some sort of contribution to their present excellence. I had managed a large architectural practice on the basis of delegation and I didn't see why I should run a yacht any differently, but I appreciated that my laid back manner could be deceptive. Even so I rather resented the fact that *Callisto*'s modest success so far had been attributed by Kate to blind chance and the skill of other people. As I dried up the tea mugs I said to her mildly, 'It wasn't all luck, you know, Kate.'

But she had gone back to reading her book; her long dark hair concealed her face and hid her from me.

Bodo was larger than I had expected. With a population of 37,000 it was bigger than both the ports of North West Scotland – Oban and Stornaway – put together. It was the centre of communications for north Norway with a busy airport, a fine harbour and even a railway connecting it to Trondheim. It was all new. The old Bodo had been destroyed by German bombs in May 1940, during Britain's ill fated attempt to help Norway resist invasion. Its buildings were undistinguished but the town centre with it's trees and good shops had a nice feel about it. Hemmed in by mountains and focussed on its great asset – the harbour – it was an assertion of Norway's determination to make a success of the far north.

We stayed in harbour the next day: we could spare the time and the weather was cloudy without wind. There was water on the pontoons and showers at the SAS Hotel. We didn't really have time to see the two main tourist attractions. I should have liked to have seen Svartisen – Europe's second biggest glacier but to visit it would have meant a motorboat trip and I wanted a day off from the sea. The other natural marvel near Bodo is Saltstraumen – a ferocious whirlpool caused by the tide funnelling rapidly between islands. It was a hazard to ships. I was quite happy to miss out on Saltstraumen and instead spent time in an extremely well stocked bookshop.

My lack of enterprise in sightseeing is matched by my avid reading of travel information. Anne had collected the Bodo Guide from the tourist information office. I liked its style; it seemed both scrupulously honest and poetic at the same time. The English translation on page 3 said,

"Bodo is the first town north of the Arctic Circle where you can see the midnight sun like a red ball just above sea level before it starts rising again. From June 2nd until July 10th you can see the midnight sun in Bodo, provided a not too cloudy sky."

I think only the Norwegians would have included the last six words.

The Norwegians are confident enough to write their own English which sometimes gives it a special quality. At the end of the brochure an advertisement for bus hire caught my eye.

"For you who want to reach a destiny not supported by

public communication we put up a touring program adapted to your spesific needs regarding hotels, guiding, etc."

It made me feel that if I boarded such a bus I would arrive at some great truth.

Ashley didn't go sightseeing either. He went fishing on the quay and caught three cod. I hoped Kate disapproved. She is a vegetarian and high principled about animals but she didn't say anything; Ashley disappeared to a nearby Norwegian motor yacht further along the pontoons and watched television – Egypt versus the Netherlands in the World Cup. There was something reassuringly normal about Ashley.

After supper I got out the charts and looked at the way ahead to Harstad. We would be for a time out of the shelter of the inner leads and sailing in Westfjord. The Lofoten islands would be on our port side sheltering us from the Atlantic but they would be forty miles away. A westerly gale would blow up a big sea. In this event I resolved to head west crossing the fjord to sail in smooth water in the lee of the islands. No problem. A south west wind would be a different matter; the great fjord would be totally exposed to the ocean. On the chart it looked like the Bristol Channel. I was a bit apprehensive. After some thought I decided that in the event of strong winds from the southwest I would just run on northwards in the narrowing fjord. Unlike the dreaded Bristol Channel there appeared to be plenty of islands and anchorages which would give shelter. I am not a quick thinker and like to have my contingency plans made beforehand. On this occasion however, I didn't think I would need them. Ashley's television friends in the motor yacht had predicted that the light weather would continue.

We sailed next day, 13 June, slipping quietly away from the pontoons under sail. As grey Bodo dropped astern the sun came out: we were back in the eternal summer of the Norwegian seas.

I wrote in my diary,

"The white summits of the Lofoten Islands are on the port side on the western horizon. The sun is streaming into the saloon as we tack into a northwest breeze. The sun is warm but the wind is cold and we need oilskin jackets over our jerseys. It couldn't be nicer weather.

It had been the best days sailing so far. Before sailing I changed down to No. 2 genoa but the clouds cleared and we reset No. 1 soon after we got under way. As we passed the Karlsover Islands we saw White Tailed Eagles flying and at their nest in a tree.

Tom and Anne are on watch and Kate is testing Ashley on the names of the parts of a yacht. It is very relaxed with the acceptance of a long slow sail to Harstad or somewhere."

The wind dropped at 7.00 pm. *Callisto* slowed down to bare steerage way. The low sun was dazzling us reflected in a glassy sea. We had sailed thirty miles from Bodo.

'What do you want to do?' I asked. 'If we want to keep going we'll have to use the motor.'

Tom groaned. 'Not the motor,' he said. 'Let's anchor for the night like we do in Scotland.'

Anne looked interested. 'Could we?' she said. 'We've only stopped in ports so far. It would be nice to get away from the Coastal Express route.'

I wanted to keep going but it was their holiday and we had time in hand; Harstad and Tromso were not far away. Tom went down to the chart table. He reappeared in the cockpit a moment later.

'Let's go to Helesund,' he said, 'it's a little bay that looks perfectly sheltered and the chart shows it's an anchorage. It's only two miles away.'

He pointed to the wooded coast to the east. 'There it is.'

So we anchored in a quiet landlocked pool. The low shores were tree clad. There were a few houses among the trees, a couple of fishing boats and a small quay. The rest was ours. In the clear water we could see our anchor and chain cable eight metres below us on white sand and fish swimming. In the heat of the sun it looked like pictures I had seen advertising yacht charters in the

Caribbean.

We sat in the cockpit in the still heat drinking before dinner. We looked at the snowy ranges of mountains and listened to a silence intensified by the occasional piping of oyster catchers. Tom said, sipping his gin slowly, 'This has been the best day so far. We sailed all the time and we saw the eagles.'

After dinner the sun dropped behind the trees and the shadows spread across the harbour but the mountains were a blaze of sunshine. We slept well that night in the bright daylight of the arctic.

Next morning the crew nearly mutinied and it was my fault. We had arranged to sail early but I had gone on deck whilst the others were still having breakfast. It was a beautiful morning and the light north wind had come back. I wanted to get going. Why bother the others, I thought I'll get underway by myself. I had often done it before. I hoisted the mainsail and then went onto the foredeck and heaved in the cable. With 40 metres of chain and a 35lb anchor this was hard work but in the freshness of the morning I loved the labour. The people below would have heard the cable coming in but would have assumed that I was just shortening in in preparation for sailing. I walked aft and took the tiller. The forward momentum of hauling the boat up to her anchor gave me steerage way and I bore away on to starboard tack for the harbour entrance and as the wind filled sail let the main sheet run out through my hand.

When I was unfurling the genoa Ashley and Kate appeared in the cockpit. They had the forenoon watch but it wasn't yet eight o'clock. Ashley was eating a bacon sandwich and looked silently at the trees on the harbour entrance passing by. I handed the tiller to Kate and went below for a cup of tea. I had enjoyed sailing *Callisto* for once by myself but I hadn't liked Ashley's grim look. I had probably upset him. I lingered over my tea feeling rather worried. Half an hour later when I went back up into the cockpit the air was stiff with disapproval. Kate was still steering and not looking at me. Ashley was sitting on the windward seat beside her. He stood up when I emerged from the hatch.

'Kate and I want to make a formal protest,' he said. 'You aren't running the ship properly. You make rules about starting times and which watch is responsible and then ignore them yourself. Kate and I were preparing to get going at 8 o'clock. as you said last night.' His young sunburnt face was neutral but I could detect underlying hostility in his voice. 'If you wanted to do macho things by yourself without our help you ought to have told us.' He stood there with his scarlet sailing smock bright in the morning sun and he was quite right. There is no place for maverick behaviour in a sailing boat on a long voyage: information has to flow freely. I wondered why I had done it and the thought came into my mind that it was partly because of my conversation with Kate two days before which had seemed to imply that I was being carried by my two watch leaders. The one-man operation of leaving harbour may have re-established my confidence as a sailor – I could manage without them – but it had landed me into a first class problem as a skipper. There was a silence between us. Perhaps Ashley had expected me to justify my action or even assert my authority. Instead I said quietly, 'Formal protest accepted. Enter it in the ship's log.'

I didn't really see what the ship's log had to do with it but it sounded correct. It wasn't much but it was enough. I felt the tension easing in the cockpit: anger faded. Kate looked at us both. We had all become very fond of each other sailing together through the long seas of Norway.

We sailed until tea time with a light northerly breeze that just enabled us to lay our course north east along Westfjord. The shining mountains of the Lofoten Islands got closer and closer on our port side as the sea narrowed. Tom, who had been encouraged by the White Tailed Eagles, spent time in the cockpit with binoculars looking for more birds. He didn't have much success.

'There seem to be hardly any sea birds,' he said. 'All the travel brochures make wild life a tourist attraction. All the time we've been in Norway we've seen a few eider ducks, some oyster catchers, the odd herring gull and one lonely gannet.' He sighed, 'That one had probably lost his way from Flamborough Head.' He went on dolefully, 'No seals and only two small dolphins near Bergen.' He let the binoculars dangle from the strap round his neck. I suspected that Tom liked watching birds because it gave him an excuse to go off on his own without other people but he knew a lot about them.

'It's probably over fishing,' I said, 'nothing for them to eat.'

'Well, Ashley can catch fish,' he replied reasonably.

Kate said cruelly, 'I expect the Norwegians shoot birds for fun.'

There was a shocked silence for a moment as we tried to imagine the kindly Norwegians hunting puffins with double barrelled shot guns.

'They hunt whales, don't they?' Kate said.

'They're not like us.'

I think we had all expected the thousands of islands and skerries to be teeming with wild life like the Hebrides. Instead we had seen less birds in all Norway than we should have seen in an afternoon's sail off the North Yorkshire coast. I thought of our industrialised over populated land. I said, 'It makes you feel that Britain is one huge wild life sanctuary.'

Our disappointment with this aspect of Norway was a real plus for our own country.

We arrived at Harstad next day at four in the morning. We had had to motor through the narrow sounds that separate Hinnoy, the big island of the Lofotens, from the mainland. We had passed the entrance to Ofotsfjord which led to Narvik and there were a lot of merchant ships. We had, at one point, been overtaken by a frigate of the Royal Norwegian Navy. I had dipped our ensign politely. This had been acknowledged by a friendly wave from the officer of the watch on her bridge. I hadn't managed to get much sleep: I had been anxious about entering another unknown port. At that time in the morning nobody was about in the harbour. We secured alongside a visitors' pontoon near the middle of the town. I went straight to sleep but was awakened not long afterwards by the ceaseless wash of fishing boats and the ferries that connect Harstad with the mainland.

Harstad was smaller than Bodo but prettier. Sheltered by islands its climate seemed more benign. Although a long way north it was less off the map: we felt the relative proximity of the two big towns of Narvik and Tromso. The off shore oil prospecting was not obtrusive but there were fishing boats everywhere. The town was mostly new and it had the usual good shops. There were showers at the nearby swimming bath, water on the pontoon, diesel oil and propane gas. We would linger here before the last leg of the journey which would complete our passage to Tromso. Tourists come to Harstad to visit the wild beauty of the Lofoten islands and many bus tours were on offer. Tourists like the great open spaces but sailors wanted the local amenity of a town. It seemed a waste not to explore the islands but we had been looking at the jagged summits of the Lofotens for the last 24 hours. I was content with a sailor's view. Happiness was diesel fuel and fresh food.

At the edge of the town I came across a small war memorial. It was an obelisk on a plinth with a five pointed star on top. It stood on the shore of the sea with mountains in the background. There was a simple inscription on the plinth 'in memory of the Soviet Soldiers'. After forty five years of Cold War Norway had still not forgotten the soldiers of the Red Army who had defeated the Germans in north Norway and then gone home. It was a kind tribute to the young men of a foreign country who died on Norwegian soil.

Late that night when the others had turned in I quarrelled with Kate and Ashley. They had spent all day together in Harstad and it was quite late when they returned to the yacht. I can't remember what I said but it included hard words about disrupting the community of the yacht. Kate gave as good as she got but

Ashley looked as if he wished he was somewhere else. Afterwards as I tried to sleep all I could think of was that I had been thoroughly unfair to two good crew members.

Next morning Kate asked me to go ashore with her for coffee. She wasn't smiling. I followed her along the pontoon to the quay. The sky was overcast but it was quite warm. We walked along the quayside in constrained silence. My feet dragged on the paving stones. There was no spring in my step. The quay was cluttered with fish boxes and mooring lines; and the air was heavy with the sound of the diesel engines of fishing boats. I found a cafe that faced the harbour on one side and the bus station on the other. It was the first time Kate and I had been alone together for a long time.

Kate looked at me over the coffee cups with green searching eyes. 'Why did you call me a shit?' she said.

'I didn't mean it,' I said. 'I hadn't had much sleep and I'd drunk too much whisky. You've been a marvellous crew member.' I was going on to make further apologies but Kate interrupted me.

'Cut out the bullshit,' she said. 'Last night you were being honest for once. It was the first time you expressed any real feeling since Newcastle. I'd rather be called a shit than ignored. You've been cutting yourself off from me completely.'

I took a gulp of my coffee. My hand was shaking. There was a lot of noise from the quayside traffic and a bus started up.

Kate said, 'You warned me when you invited me to come on this trip that you would be preoccupied with the navigation and management of the yacht but I didn't expect to be totally disregarded. You haven't looked me once in the eye and even when I've asked you a straight question you've usually managed to direct your reply to Ashley.'

I wanted to say, 'On the contrary, you were ignoring me.' But it would have sounded like something from a second class movie. There seemed to be a great gulf of misunderstanding separating us across the coffee table. I sat in hurt silence.

CHAPTER SIX

After a while Kate said, 'What's really the matter?'

The anger had gone out of her eyes. My instincts were prompting me to reply evasively to her question and say something about the pressure on me to keep going endlessly through new seas. But we were in Harstad and I was talking to Kate and I decided to tell the truth.

'I'm jealous of you and Ashley,' I said. It was a terrible admission but I immediately felt better. No bullshit.

She looked at me wonderingly. 'You silly idiot,' she said, 'why do you think I came and why do you think we're sitting here now?'

I must have looked surprised.

'I need another coffee.' she said.

For some reason the waitress was wearing a cowboy hat. She looked at me curiously. We hadn't been talking loudly but other people in the cafe could detect the intensity of our conversation. I didn't care what people thought. Kate reached across the table and took my hand. It was very un-Norwegian behaviour.

Kate was smiling. 'You actually said something rather nice last night before you fell asleep. You said that even though I was a shit you thought I was the most beautiful woman in the arctic.' She let out a loud giggle. I could see the look of relief on the faces of the coffee drinkers around us. These English had got their act together. We drank four coffees each in that cafe and talked for nearly two hours.

When we left the overcast was clearing and Harstad was lit by a flashing sun.

It was a rough and exciting sail to Tromso. Before leaving Harstad we filled up with diesel fuel and changed the engine oil. By two thirty we had cleared the harbour and were tacking well reefed into a fresh north east wind. The sea in the fjords was quite calm but *Callisto* was heeling more than 20° in the gusts. Tranoyfjord, Solbergfjord, Gesundet, Straumsfjord were the names on the charts with the Island of Senja on our port side. In

89

my mind they were just a blur of high wooded shores and blue channels. We drove *Callisto* to windward with as much sail as she could carry for thirty hours through continuous daylight. The wind hummed in the wire rigging, the genoa cracked and roared as we tacked and the loud ratchets of our sheet winches echoed back from the trees. Spray rattled on the deck. It was quieter below in the yacht's double hull but it was hard to get comfortable. At one point Ashley, sound asleep, was thrown off the starboard saloon berth. Somehow Anne managed to cook: we seemed to have plenty to eat, but with the heeling of the boat it was like cooking on the roof of a house. The snowline got lower and lower. Before Harstad the snow had been on the mountains – here it was a couple of hundred feet above the shore. It hung wetly in the trees. I had never sailed through snow before. We were going to make Tromso alright. I was not thinking about Murmansk. At Tromso we would have time to rest and consider the future then. To have sailed to Tromso in the far north was already quite an achievement. There was a sense of exhilaration in the crew of *Callisto*. They were sailing her like an ocean racer.

We saw a school of dolphins. It was a good mark for the Norwegians. Tom stared at them carefully through binoculars. He said, 'If the sea hog jumps look to your pumps' but they weren't jumping, and the barometer was steady. It was set fair for Tromso.

We used the motor to assist the sails during the last hour or so. There was a strong tide running through the channels and it was against us. There were whirlpools – the dreaded straumen. They seemed to grip our keel but they didn't worry us. *Callisto* had been blooded in the racing tides of the British coast. There hadn't been any tidal streams worth bothering with in Norway until now.

Tromso announced its presence long before we saw it. There were brightly painted country cottages on the green promontories with Norwegian flags stiff in the breeze. They seemed to be telling us that we were approaching a great city.

There were bridges, fishing boats and ferries and Sunday after-noon sailing boats. They built up a sense of expectation.

Since Harstad I had stopped feeling tense. On the last miles to Tromso I spent half an hour in the saloon with Anne. I didn't think I had paid her enough attention. She was drinking coffee looking rather tired.

'Thanks for feeding us so well,' I said. 'You've been a good sailor too.'

She said dolefully, 'I was never good enough for Tom. He didn't teach me things the way Ashley taught Kate.'

'You can steer and handle the sails,' I said. 'Nothing went wrong in your watch.'

'Tom's a perfectionist,' she said. 'He didn't want to let you down. He was afraid I would make mistakes but I'm glad you saw how hard I was trying.'

She didn't say anything for a while. There was a lot of noise coming down the hatch as *Callisto* tacked. Then she smiled.

'I think I've begun to like sailing. Can I come with you next year?'

I thought it isn't hard to tell people that you appreciate what they are doing and yet it makes the world of difference. It seemed to be a necessity in a small yacht, perhaps it was equally needed in other human enterprises. There didn't seem to be enough of it going on in Britain.

She changed the subject.

'I'm looking forward to seeing Tromso again. I think you'll like it.'

We came to Tromso in the late afternoon. The wind had dropped, we furled the sails and motored slowly into the harbour. The city seemed to be set in an amphitheatre of hills and islands. Buildings, trees and ships were mirrored in the calm water. White mountains dazzled in the sunshine. Snow and forests: it was like some alpine town with the sea in it. I was enchanted. Tromso is the capital of the north: after the lonely Norwegian coast it seemed like the centre of the world.

We moored alongside a visitors' pontoon and tidied up on deck. Oilskins and jerseys were stowed away. Someone opened the forehatch. *Callisto* had never been in such heat. Bewildered by the sunshine, only half believing that we were here, we stood an irresolute group on the pontoon photographing each other like tourists. *Callisto*, immaculately white, and in perfect condition was the background to the photographs.

The delights of Tromso would be there for us tomorrow. In the meantime there were drinks before dinner in the cockpit. We drank to *Callisto*'s achievement and her success in the future. We could hardly believe that it had only been thirteen days since we left Bergen. As I drank my gin I felt relief to be here but also a tiredness. It seemed to have been close quarters pilotage through all the reefs and islands of Norway, with a few of my own thrown in. It had been eight hundred miles and at the moment I was feeling every one of them.

Chapter Seven

'Let's be trippers,' I said, 'no need to bother with the ship tomorrow.' We had plenty of time. We had arrived at Tromso early. When planning the trip I had arranged to change crews at Tromso with a new crew arriving on 24th June.

In the event we had arrived in harbour on 17th June. In planning my passage it had been necessary to allow for a possible three or four days delay to shelter from strong winds. There had been no gales consequently we had been able to keep going. Looking at the tired faces of my crew I realised that I could have taken it a little more slowly. In compensation they did not have to leave yet and they could rest and enjoy beautiful Tromso before catching the plane south.

Tromso is an island city connected to the mainland by the longest bridge in Norway. From the yacht harbour it looked big with trees spreading the buildings out along the low hills. The city centre was a ten minute walk along the quay and through the ship repair yard. It greeted us with a criss cross of busy streets lined with 19th century timber buildings and new hotels beautifully cared for and painted in bright colours. Unlike Bodo and Harstad it had been undamaged by war. With 50,000 inhabitants it had all the amenities of a metropolis – shops, restaurants, night clubs, museums, art galleries, a cathedral and a university. The whole of arctic Norway looked towards Tromso. After the empty seas and the raw look of the other towns I appreciated its vibrance and feeling of security. Cars and buses filled the streets, people sat in the shade under the trees in the squares or walked along the shady sides of the streets. It was a town of shirt sleeves, T-shirts and thin summer dresses with a background of high snowy mountains. The city encompassed its great harbour. Its streets ended at quays and the white superstructures and rigging of ships. The permanence and stability of its unpretentious timber architecture and waterfront warehouses was a backcloth for the endlessly changing quayside scene with cruise liners, fishing boats, coastguard vessels and merchant ships, entering or leaving. Tromso was European, sophisticated and up to date, but it was still far into the arctic, a frontier town. You were reminded of this not just by the snowy horizon but by the fact that people had time for each other. In not many other towns in the world did the cars stop for you if you wanted to cross the road. In Britain cars did it at pedestrian crossings – here they did it anywhere whenever you stood on the kerb and looked as if you wanted to cross. It made you feel fairly important as a long line of buses and cars waited for you.

I don't remember much of that first day in Tromso. I wandered through the streets glad to be freed from the anxieties of the yacht and the sea. I was too tired to take much in. It was sufficient to be among the sights, smells and sounds of a city with time on my hands. My only constructive action was to buy the remaining charts I needed. What a marvellous country, I thought dreamily, where all bookshops carry a full set of charts. I got lost in the unfamiliar bustle of the streets: it was as if I had left my sense of direction out among the islands and rocks of the coast. It was tea time when I found my way back to the yacht. Walking through the shipyard a loud radio was playing and men were knocking off work. Everything stopped at 4 o'clock in Tromso. The patches of grass between the big sheds were ablaze with the colour of wild flowers.

The others had been more energetic. Drinking tea Kate said she had taken the cablecar to the summit of Storsteinen, 420 metres above sea level. 'What was it like?' I asked.

'Well, it was nice to be by myself,' she said honestly with a smile. 'There was lots of snow and the sun was very hot. I made a snow ball and looked at the view. The cablecar was full of fit looking Norwegians with back packs wearing shorts and setting off to God knows where.'

I remarked on how balanced and sensible the Norwegians were. Anne, who had been to the museum at Folkeparken and was now even more well briefed on Norwegian history, said, 'I'm not sure about that; they've got one very nasty habit. They set fire to their towns.'

It sounded worse than shooting sea birds.

'The Germans destroyed Bodo,' I said.

'The Germans saved them the trouble there,' she answered, 'but at some time in their history they burnt down all their towns.'

She smiled indulgently. She loved Norway. 'I'm glad they've got a mad streak,' she said.

Ashley said, 'The book about Tromso says they've got the most northerly brewery in the world,' he sighed, 'not much use to us at this rate of exchange.'

I was off duty as far as sailing was concerned but I was still obsessed with weather forecasts. I had learnt that Norwegians never intruded but were extremely helpful if you asked them. After tea I approached the skipper of a motor yacht moored near us on the visitors' pontoon.

'Could you give me some advice about coastal radio stations?' I asked. He got up from the deckchair he was sitting on in the cockpit of the motor boat and lent on the guardrail. He looked at me enquiringly. 'I don't seem to be able to get local weather forecasts from them,' I said.

'Ah,' he said sadly, 'you usually can but I'm afraid they're on strike just now.' He made it sound like a fairly normal occurrence.

'What ought I to do?' I asked.

He looked at me sympathetically. 'Let me think,' he said. He started thinking aloud. 'You could buy a newspaper,' he said, 'they publish forecasts there.' He hesitated. 'No good, unless you speak Norwegian you wouldn't be able to understand them.' He was silent for a moment looking at the cloudless blue sky. Perhaps he was wondering why English sailors needed weather forecasts the way other people needed drugs. I waited hopefully. Suddenly he produced a relieved smile. I knew exactly what he was going to say.

'Don't worry,' he said, 'the weather is going to stay settled like this for quite a while. It said so on television.'

I thanked him then said, 'I've got another question. I don't understand the direction of the tidal streams. I can work out the times of high and low water at Tromso from the Nautical Almanac but which way does the tide run?'

If he thought I ought to know the answer to that simple question myself he didn't show it. Very few British yachts visited Tromso and he would have expected them, at least to some degree, to depend on local knowledge.

'Easy,' he said, 'when the tide is low you go north, when it's high you go south.' It didn't sound very scientific but it was all I needed to know. I was grateful to him. He relapsed into his deck chair.

Tom went home early on the 19th June. Before he left I thanked him for his great help in getting *Callisto* north. I saw him off to the airport bus. At breakfast in the saloon after he had gone I said, 'Do you think he enjoyed himself? He never talks about his feelings.'

Kate said cynically, 'Few men do.'

I found the quaysides fascinating. I looked in wonder at a huge up to date German cruise liner. It seemed to be totally enveloped in a streamlined superstructure with windows through which the passengers could view the passing scenery. Were they ever allowed on deck, I wondered? Was there any deck? Perhaps they were permanently encapsulated in the sealed air conditioned interior. It was like a space ship.

The *Statsrad Lehmkuhl* was a complete contrast. She was a three masted barque rigged training ship. Her high masts and yards towered over the quayside buildings. She was one of the sights of Norway. I hadn't seen her come in but now parties of visitors were being shown around her to marvel at the complexity of her rigging and the mechanisms of sailing an old time square rigger.

The First Officer was standing near the gangway directing guests. He was wearing a smart uniform with gold braid on his sleeves. At a moment when he did not appear to be busy I said, 'Where are you bound for?'

He looked up at me from the deck below – his face shadowed by the visor of his cap. 'Murmansk,' he said.

I said, 'We're going there, too, in our yacht.'

'I'm afraid you won't be able to enter the port,' he said, 'you've got to get permission.' He resumed his duties with the visitors. I could hardly believe my ears. I thought of the seven months it had taken us to obtain permits. Did he seriously believe that I was sailing to the Soviet Union on some sort of amateurish English impulse? Okay, we were a tenth the size of his bloody great windjammer but the Russians had invited me in: the guest of the Murmansk City Soviet and the war veterans of the USSR. I thought meanly: I don't suppose they ever use those sails – they've probably got twin diesels.

I had another difficult conversation with Kate over coffee. We went to a restaurant called Le Mirage. It sounded French but it was very Norwegian with leather armchairs and expensive coffee. We had been talking to each other since Harstad but there

97

was still a feeling of reserve. For all the miles from Bergen we seemed to know less of each other. She looked at me over her coffee. I thought her suntanned face was very beautiful and she seemed to radiate the vitality that had first attracted me to her.

'I talked to Ashley about you last night,' she said. 'You had gone to bed but it was sunny on deck. He asked me why I liked you.' She paused. I didn't interrupt her: she had a story to tell.

'I said I didn't know and then he said something rather interesting.' She smiled. 'He said he thought I liked you because of my anarchist, feminist convictions and you were a man, part of the awful establishment, with a CBE and an expensive yacht. You gave me something to hate. I needed you.'

I said in rather a small voice, 'Is that true?'

'No, it isn't,' she said gleefully, 'but I thought it was a pretty penetrating comment. I hadn't expected it from Ashley.'

I went to the counter and got two more coffees. They were only half the price this time round.

'What did you say to him?' I asked.

'I told him my friends thought I went out with you because of your money.'

There was a long silence. The coffee was strong and hot. I wanted to ask her what she really felt about me but I knew she didn't know the answer to that. University, *Callisto*, Norway and I were stages in a process of re-evaluating herself. After a false start she was looking freshly at the world not yet sure of her feelings. I was content to leave it like that. I had been slightly cheered by the thought that Ashley, even if he had been wrong in his analysis of her motives, had at least seen that there had been a little more to it than Henry simply ignoring Kate. I felt a kind of cautious tenderness towards her. The third coffees were free.

We went out of the restaurant into the blaze of the sun. 'Let's look at the Norwegian navy,' I said. A flotilla of patrol boats had entered harbour yesterday evening and were moored in tiers alongside one of the quays. They looked reptilian and incongruous in peaceful Tromso. I hadn't really looked at warships for

45 years. They still appeared fairly familiar with a gun on the foredeck and a lot of aerials.

Kate said disparagingly, 'Toys for the boys.'

They were symbols of violence in sunny Norway. I felt depressed. Then I caught sight of the sentry guarding the gangway. His sub-machine gun was on a sling round his shoulder but, inspite of this, he was about the most unmilitary figure I had ever seen. His helmet was tilted on one side of his head. His hands were in his pockets and a cigarette hung loosely out of the corner of his mouth. His young face expressed boredom and resentment. What he seemed to be saying was 'Okay, Norway's got to have a navy but we don't have to like it.' He immediately cheered me up. In Norway with its fleet of merchant ships that sailed in the oceans of the world I didn't think the Navy was the senior service. As in Sweden and Denmark everyone in Norway had to serve for a time in the armed forces. If such peaceful countries preferred armies and navies of reluctant civilians rather than career professionals that was alright by me. The young sailor had blurred the dark grey outlines of the war ships.

A statue commemorating the whale hunters of Tromso seemed to project a more brutal image than the Norwegian Navy. High on a pedestal a bronze figure stood in the bow of a whale boat, harpoon in hand. We joined a group of Norwegians dutifully admiring it. Kate looked at it distastefully. The eager aggression of the hunter was in marked contrast to the relaxed brightness of the leafy square. She shook her head angrily.

'They still do it,' she said.

I had once been cox'n of a Royal Navy whaler. We didn't use it for hunting whales but it looked like the bronze replica. Only twenty seven feet long and pulled by five oarsmen it had seemed a frail enough craft carrying mail between ships in the open sea – never mind engaging whales.

I felt incautiously that I had to defend the statue. 'It's only a hand held harpoon: they had to get close,' I said, 'they were pretty brave and the whale often won.'

'You're just as bad as they are,' she said in a clipped voice and turned away.

I felt overcome by the heat and wanted to get back to *Callisto* and be by myself. It was difficult to live up to Kate's high principles. I had done enough sight seeing.

'You go on,' Kate said, 'I want to see the Polar Museum.' I left her to it. The Information Guide for Tromso had said -

'Founded in 1976 and located in an old customs warehouse from the 1830s which is scheduled as a monument. The exhibitions show activities in connection with hunting and research in polar regions, especially in the arctic.'

I had a feeling that this was not the sort of museum I wanted to see, least of all with Kate.

I walked slowly back along the jetty to the small world of *Callisto*. It was still very hot but there was a faint breeze ruffling the harbour water and I took off my shirt. The Norwegians in the two adjacent yachts at the visitors pontoon were delighting in the hot sun and dozed on cushions. I was glad to be by myself. I looked at the check list I had prepared of things that needed to be done before sailing – propane, rigging, backstay tension, motor filters, batteries. We had only been in Tromso two days and there was plenty of time to think about the next stage of the voyage. In the meantime there was this God given summers day in the arctic and my crew not back till supper time. I arranged the cushions on the cockpit seats and followed the example of the somnolent crews in the nearby yachts. I tried to read my Russian grammar but I was interrupted by the interesting activities of the harbour.

I watched a big white ship come in and moor half a mile away at the town quays near the sailing vessel. I admired the way she tied up alongside without fuss – professional sailors. There was something familiar about her and I reached for the binoculars. She had a Union Flag at the jackstaff and a White Ensign at the stern. A Norwegian courtesy flag fluttered from her foreyard. British I thought, the first British ship I had seen since Newcastle.

She was probably a Royal Navy survey vessel far from home. Although it was nice to see a British flag she was just part of the changing harbour scene contrasted with the changeless stillness of the white mountains beyond.

Half an hour later a man and a girl wandered onto the pontoon and silently studied *Callisto* in detail. Not Norwegians I thought. After a while they approached me.

'Where are you from? Where are you bound?' – The opening of conversation between yachtsmen the world over. They had just arrived at Tromso in a German yacht I vaguely remembered her obscured by rain alongside the Fish Quay at Bergen.

'This is where we come every year,' he said. He was a big man wearing a baseball cap with a large peak.

'Is the weather always like this?' I asked.

'Yes,' he said, 'better than further south. No gales. But you have to be careful: it is not a coast to be trifled with. I brought you this.' It was a list of Norwegian weather forecast frequencies and translations into English of Norwegian meteorological terms. He was a foreigner too, and had guessed that I did not share the Norwegian's confidence in their weather or their television. He did not smile much yet he was kind and helpful. I had not met many Germans in my life. The last ones I clearly remembered were pale faced men dazzled by the bright day light in 1945 on the decks of surrendered U boats.

'I wonder why more English yachts don't come here,' I said, thinking of the unsettled cold summers of our own islands.

He gave me a rare grin and the girl laughed, 'For God's sake don't tell the English about this part of the world.'

When they had gone I resumed my reading but was distracted by the Norwegian yacht moored on our starboard side. She was called *Brisinga*, British built and registered in Oslo. Her skipper seemed to be alone on board carrying out various small tasks stripped to the waist. Although we had been a few feet from each other for two days we had successfully managed to avoid any form of communication. Now he started tipping buckets of sea water over himself. The water gurgled out through his cock-pit drain holes. Even in Norway I didn't see how I could ignore this rather unusual activity.

'Hot, isn't it?' I said. He grinned and wiped his face in a towel.

'Twenty five degrees at midday,' he said, 'and going up.'

He seemed revived by the cold water.

'I'm waiting for my crew,' he said, 'I keep getting messages from them but they never seem to get here.'

He didn't look very impatient: he seemed happy alone in his pretty yacht.

'None of them know how to sail,' he said scathingly. 'We'll just cruise locally around the islands and I'll do all the work. Never mind, where could there be a nicer place to sail? My wife will be here and she is a good cook.'

His sunburnt body was drying in the sun. I envied him his relaxed cruise exploring the outer skerries with his holiday friends. I wished I was doing the same.

'You've chosen the right time of the year,' he said when I told him I was heading for Russia. 'It's still a bit early in the season for us. You'll see more yachts next week.' He seemed to have all the time in the world. I lit my pipe. We talked companionably: two skippers temporarily unencumbered by crews.

'People don't seem interested in sailing-yachts here,' I said. 'In England people come and chat with us. Norwegians keep miles away.' I explained my theory about the respect for privacy.

'I'm afraid it's not just that,' he said, 'they think you are a rich pig. Motor boats are alright – they are just a way of getting about like a car.' He looked up at our tall masts. 'We're rich men doing it for fun. It is a class thing so they keep clear.'

I said, rather surprised, 'I've encountered that feeling sailing in Greek waters but I wouldn't have expected it in Norway.'

He laughed, 'I know England quite well. In your country people sail anything anywhere. Sailing has no particular social status. Every river, gravel pit, estuary is full of small sailing boats. I think in England anyone who really wants to can afford to sail. It is not so here.'

It may have been my reading of the Icelandic Sagas because somehow I had never really thought of Norway as a foreign country. Our two lands were now being moved far apart. Yet what he was saying to me had the ring of truth. The last sails I had seen in more than ones and twos had been a vast fleet of dinghys racing off Tynemouth as the Bergen ferry left Newcastle. He could see my discomforture and let out a loud chuckle. 'I wonder what the Russians will think of you and your yacht when you get to Murmansk?'

'Now I must go ashore,' he said, 'and find out where my bloody crew is.' He put on a shirt and strode energetically off along the jetty.

The shining spars and white decks of beautiful *Callisto* seemed somehow tarnished. A rich man's toy! And yet she had come all those miles from Whitby. She was jointly owned and the cruise expenses were shared with the crew. She was British designed, British built and British owned: part of our way of life. To hell with foreigners and their class attitudes I thought, especially in countries where you couldn't afford a round of beers.

When Anne, Ashley and Kate returned to the yacht one by one for supper I felt rested and once again reconciled to Norway. Along the coast we had not met a Norwegian who had not been helpful and friendly. In banks, shops, harbours and markets we had met nothing but courtesy and kindness. Whatever they thought about yachts with tall masts to them the British were friends.

It was still hot – there was no night and cool evening in arctic Tromso in June. We sat in the cockpit before eating and compared notes. As I had expected Kate's visit to the Polar Museum had been a disaster.

'It showed you how to kill seals and walruses – it was all about death. I hated it.

'Amundsen and the conquest of the South Pole wasn't so

bad, that was quite interesting.'

I wasn't going to tell her that Amundsen had shot his sleigh dogs as his loads got lighter and fed them to the remainder. Perhaps the museum had omitted that bit for the benefit of the British tourists.

Anne said, 'I called in on the travel office. I think I've found a way to go home that gives us time to explore Bergen.' Everyone still looked tired. There was too much heat, too much daylight and too much to see.

Anne and Kate left on the evening of the 21st June, four days after we had arrived. Ashley and I helped them carry their luggage to the hotel where the bus left for the airport on the mainland. They would fly to Bergen and catch the Newcastle ferry.

Earlier in the day I had said my goodbyes to Kate over coffee in the Mirage. We had not said much. I sensed that she was glad to be going home – back to normality, away from me and the tensions of the ship. I felt that I had failed to pass some kind of test but she said, 'Bring me something from Russia. Write to me if you can.' Perhaps I would see her when I got back to Nottingham. I didn't know.

I had a few words with Anne before she left. She said, 'Thanks for a super trip; the holiday of a lifetime.' She paused and then said gently, 'I didn't want to add to your burdens – you seem to have got enough problems on your plate – but it would have been nice to have gone ashore with you for a coffee occasionally.' She smiled at me. 'You're a good sailor but not so good with people. I wish you had enjoyed it as much as I did.'

They waved to us happily as the bus left, to the world of aeroplanes, hotels and ferries. Ashley and I walked back to the empty yacht lying at the visitors pontoon.

The new crew of four would arrive on the 24th June. In the meantime Ashley and I worked on the yacht. With just two of us on board it was possible to clean her thoroughly and prepare her for the last leg of the journey. Whilst Ashley scrubbed the deck I folded and put away the charts from Bergen to Tromso and laid out the charts to Murmansk·in sequence on the saloon dining table.

We had already sailed more than half the distance but the passage ahead looked formidable. Hammerfest, North Cape, the Arctic Ocean, the Barents Sea and beyond them the Russians – the unknown people who had sent the telexes and the letters of invitation. I didn't doubt I could do it – all had gone well and we were on schedule – but I had to admit I was frightened. I suppose none of us would sail at all if we didn't like living on frontiers but this was a bad one.

I tried to tell myself it was only a frontier for me. It was a frequented sea route. The Coastal Express ships ran to the Russian border at Kirkenes. Russian factory fishing ships and bulk carriers sailed from Murmansk. When the ice melted the timber ships came from Archangel and the Kara Sea. The chart showing the entry into Murmansk which lay at the bottom of my pile even showed separation zones for ships entering or leaving the Kola Inlet. It made it look like Dover or Felixstowe. However, the thought of occasional sightings of great indifferent ships gave me little comfort. The charts showed me the unimaginable ragged headlands of Europe's most northerly coast. They faced a sea which had no shore to the north, just the ice of the frozen Arctic Ocean. We should be traversing the edge of the world. *Callisto* was a 34 foot sailing vessel with a three cylinder auxiliary engine and an amateur crew: she seemed small and fragile to dare such a sea.

After a while I began to realise that I was not just suffering from the reasonable fears of a careful yachtsman examining a difficult passage ahead. I began to feel uneasy. Bright sunshine still lit the familiar saloon but there was a coldness in the air. Something alien had entered the yacht. It was as if I were facing ghosts from the past.

'Don't come here,' they said, 'remember what happened last time, and the time before that.' They were the ghosts of dead men and dead ships from a long forgotten war. The Barents Sea is full of ghosts.

Through all the years of peace the Russian convoys had been fearful but faint memories at the back of my mind. They had not troubled me. The action had been in the unimaginable arctic, nothing to do with the seas I sailed on or the land I lived in. The ghosts had been far away. Here in Tromso they seemed very close.

I experienced a moment of panic: my hands were shaking. I gripped the edge of the table. 'Leave me alone,' I said aloud, 'it's because of you that I've come here, I've not forgotten.' I felt cold. There was sweat on my forehead. There seemed to be nothing I could do. I sat for several minutes staring with unfocussed eyes at the chart. Then slowly the chill began to go out of the saloon. Perhaps the ghosts had heard me. My hands stopped shaking. I could hear Ashley sluicing water down the side decks. *Callisto* was part of today's world. We would encounter the northern seas as they were now not in memory. I was still rather afraid of what lay ahead but the moment of irrationality in the saloon had cleared my mind. I had confronted the ghosts: I could deal with the problems shown on the charts.

The next two days were strangely peaceful. In a now uncrowded yacht Ashley and I worked on rigging, motor and sails. We did not know what facilities there would be in the north. In the meantime at Tromso we could make sure all was in order and obtain any spares we needed. I worked from bow to stern with pliers and spanner tightening all shackles, cotter pins and replacing any worn or doubtful item. It was a task I enjoyed with the hot sun burning on my back and enough time to do it thoroughly. There was, in fact, little that needed doing but examining each fitting, wire, or rope began to allay my fears. Ashley checked engine lubricating oil, counted out spare dry batteries and light bulbs, checked safety harnesses and recalibrated the Decca Navigator. In the process we cleaned and burnished each part of the ship. From time to time one of us would go ashore and walk through the hot streets to buy detergent, copper wire, lubricant or distilled water. We were going round North Cape to Russia. By the end of two days we were confident that we had the perfect vehicle with which to do it. We might have problems with gales or crew, or bad luck but failure wouldn't be *Callisto*'s fault. I believe ships respond to loving care like people. *Callisto* shone white and radiant in the sun at the visitors pontoon: she looked as if she were loved. Ashley didn't talk much but perhaps he felt as I did that the quiet routine tasks of caring for the yacht had, in turn, taken care of our own anxieties.

By the evening of 24th June there was nothing more to do. Ashley and I sat in the sunny cockpit smoking our pipes and drinking very expensive gin. The new crew would arrive some-time later in the evening on the plane from Bergen or Oslo. There would be all talk then, stories to tell, decisions to make, people to worry about, watch routines to set up. I had resolved to sail tomorrow. In the meantime there was just the two of us in the cockpit, not saying much, celebrating the quiet days in Tromso and our confidence in *Callisto*.

We didn't sail until after tea next day. The crew, Alice Nunn, Ana Mason, Lesley Potts and Sandy Simpson had had a long journey delayed by engine failure on the Bergen ferry. They did not arrive until midnight marvelling at the snow and flying straight into the eternal daylight of the arctic. I thought a quiet day in harbour was indicated. They slept, sat in the sun or wandered indecisively col-lecting impressions of Tromso. They had done heroically to get here on the day they had promised weeks ago, joining a small yacht in an unknown country. They deserved a quiet day.

We sailed at 6 o'clock in the evening, tacking into a light wind. A Coastal Express ship was arriving at the quays, the ham-mering diesel engines of fishing boats echoed from the tall warehouses. Tromso harbour was all movement and interest. We stowed mooring lines and fenders and unfurled the No. 1 genoa as we quietly cleared the harbour entrance.

We turned north heading for an uncertain future.

Chapter Eight

We left the inner leads next morning. The sea was calm but out of the shelter of the islands we could feel the long swell of the Atlantic and see the white fringe of surf breaking on the mainland coast. Everything in the lockers rattled as *Callisto* rolled, the noise mingling with the incessant clatter of the motor. The sky was packed with lead coloured stratus clouds.

During the night we had crossed the 70th parallel and Norway had hid her smiling face. The sun had gone, the trees had gone. Here was the north as I expected it. This was the climatic zone of the tundra – bare rock, moors and scrub flayed by the ocean and the arctic winters. Leafy Tromso was a world away in the hot south. When the rain came just before noon the coast faded; only Loppa was in sight on the port side – the southern-most island of Finmark. When I handed over the watch to Ashley I was glad to leave it all and go below.

After lunch I sat at the saloon table and wondered about my new crew. I wrote in my diary, 'I had the first watch yesterday night with Lesley and also the forenoon today. Lesley is an apt

learner and went through most of the process of coastal navigation. She is asleep now in the pilot berth.

We are in three watches so everyone is getting enough
sleep.

I'm feeling a bit tired, however. I awoke at 0330 for the
watch change to make sure Ana and Alice could manage OK.
They did very well and I turned in again at 0500.

I am lulled by the noise of the engine. I keep forgetting
about Murmansk. It is hard to remember that we are heading for
another country. Russia is still a fairy story.'

I had decided to have Lesley in my watch because she was
the least experienced member of the crew. She was a young
woman of 34 whom I had only met socially and I was rather surprised when she had said, 'Can I sail to Russia with you?'

'Have you done any sailing?' I had asked.

'No,' she said, 'but I'm pretty handy.'
She looked fit and active so I had signed her on. She had a law
degree and was a director of a company in Scotland building
small hydro electric plants. She had certainly been handy and in
less than twelve hours could steer on the wind or by compass.
She was already a useful sailor.

I had not really needed to check on Ana in the night. She
had sailed with me many times and was a qualified yacht skipper.
She could sail the boat as well as I and I was glad to have her with
Ashley and me as the third watch leader. She has a slight figure
and a diffident manner that always makes me feel unnecessarily
protective of her. It was this impulse that had got me out of my
warm sleeping bag during the night. I hoped she would get on
alright with my niece Alice who was a very different personality.

I must have dozed as I sat writing at the saloon table and
was awakened by a change in the sound of the motor. It had been
throttled back and was now at tickover in neutral. I put on my oilskins and went on deck. Ashley and Sandy were alert figures in
the cockpit undeterred by the rain. There was nothing to be seen
but a one mile radius of grey sea around the yacht. The big island

of Soroy was twelve miles ahead of us but as yet invisible. There was a ruffle of wind on the sea.

Ashley was steering. 'I think we can sail,' he said. I unfurled the genoa and winched in the sheet. We began to pick up speed.

Ashley said, 'Sandy, turn off the motor.'

'How do you do it?' Sandy asked.

'Go into the saloon, lift up the top step of the ladder and pull up the decompression lever, then turn off the power switch and switch to number 2 battery.'

Sandy hesitantly complied. The sound of the motor died giving place to the hum of the wind in the rigging and the gentle crunch of the bow wave.

'Not that switch,' Ashley called down into the saloon. 'That's the starter button. Power is on the right.'

When Sandy came up into the cockpit Ashley said, 'Now you know how to stop the motor,' and grinned. In the falling rain he was teaching Sandy the tasks of a crew member.

'Navigation next,' he said.

'I don't want to learn how to do that,' Sandy said. 'I'll do the basic stuff but I'm not really a keen sailor.'

She had made this perfectly clear from the start. Her main contribution to the voyage had been getting the visas out of the Soviet Consulate in London. She was a fairly high powered secretary in a big company and she had once worked for me. The idea of sailing a yacht to Murmansk had captured her imagination. I do not think I alone would ever have cleared a path through the undergrowth of bureaucracy. The Russians in the Consulate had been different from the people we wrote to in Murmansk who did their best to smooth our path. I remember one occasion when we had almost given up hope hearing her say on the telephone to someone in the embassy. 'You didn't stop him entering Murmansk in the war when he was a sailor in the Royal Navy. He just walked ashore.' In the end her administrative skills and patience had been rewarded. Entering Murmansk would not be the end of a sea voyage for her but the climax of the seven month persistence that had made it possible.

Ashley had been looking forward to her joining the ship at Tromso. She was older than he and he was influenced by her sparkling personality and tough realism. I looked at her standing in the rain with her high cheek bones and blonde hair. I thought that perhaps he was a little in love with her, too.

I went below to the chart table. In the absence of anything to see we were sailing on dead reckoning. The distance run since our last fix at Loppa showed me that we were approaching Soroysund. We could alter course to the east for a while.

'Steer 060,' I shouted up at Ashley and recorded the course alteration in the log book. As we turned to starboard the wind came free. Sandy and I eased the main and genoa sheets. For once we had a fair wind. The dial of the Walker log mounted on the stern showed that we were sailing at a respectable five knots. I wished the rain would stop but on the other hand I was quite glad not to see the intimidating coast of Finmark.

I was about to go below to get out of the rain when I noticed that Ashley had not got the lanyard of his safety harness secured to the yacht.

'Clip on your harness, Ashley,' I said.

He smiled. 'Sorry, ' he said and took the lanyard out of his oilskin pocket and snapped the spring shackle to the strong point in the cockpit. I realised I wasn't clipped on either and did the same. Safety harnesses were a nuisance. The lanyards got tangled when sails were being handled and you had to keep clipping and unclipping if you wanted to move about the deck. For this reason I did not insist on their use in the cockpit except in the dark, poor visibility or when alone. Now, in the rain they were clearly needed. I suppose every yachtsman has nightmares about hearing the dreaded cry 'Man overboard'. It would turn an enjoyable sail into a sudden life threatening emergency. We had practised the drill of recovering a casualty many times. The action had to be automatic because the loss of a crew member might replace cool thinking by panic. All action depended on not losing sight of the crew in the water and manoeuvring the yacht rapidly but calmly. In the cold sea of the arctic you would have to get it right the first time. It was better not to let it happen.

I noticed that Sandy's harness was properly made fast. One of the advantages of women crew was they they looked after themselves. Men took risks: in my experience women hardly ever did. They ate properly, dressed warmly and hence were less likely to suffer from sea sickness. They told you if they couldn't manage something and they kept clipped on. I was very happy to be sailing to Russia with a crew of which four of the six were women.

Below in the saloon I took off my wet oilskins and relaxed. Soroysund was wide and free of outlying dangers and the Decca Navigator was working well confirming Ashley's dead reckoning. It was quiet without the motor. The other three members of the crew were still asleep. I thought of following their example but it occurred to me that we could well be in Hammerfest before midnight and I could sleep then.

For this part of the voyage I had a pilot book. I got it out of my locker. It was Othere's account of the discovery of the White Sea and it had been written over 1000 years ago. It had been incorporated into the Anglo Saxon Chronicle by Alfred the Great and I had read it first in Old English. The copy I laid on the saloon table had a parallel text. When I had previously read it it had simply been an interesting story and an exercise in translating Old English which I had rapidly discovered was not a foreign language at all. Now sailing the wild coast that Othere discovered I found the story strangely comforting.

'Othere told his lord, King Alfred, that he lived the furthest north of all Norwegians. He said that he lived in the north of Norway on the coast of the Atlantic. He also said that the land extends very far north beyond that point, but it is all uninhabited, except for a few places here and there where the Finnas have their camps, hunting in winter, and in summer fishing in the sea.

He told how he once wished to find out how far the land extended due north, or whether anyone lived to the north of the unpopulated area. He went due north along the coast, keeping the uninhabited land to starboard and the open sea to port continuously for three days. He was then as far north as the whale hunters go at their furthest. He then continued due north as far as he could reach in the second three days. There the land turned due east . . .'

Othere's voyage had not been prompted by desire for fame or riches but simply curiosity. I liked to think of him being received well at Winchester, the guest of the king, inspite of being a Norseman. He would have told his story in Old Norse and King Alfred's scholars would have understood and recorded it in Old English. It was a piece of Norwegian history in our own language.

He had sailed from just south of Tromso so he had taken a little longer to round North Cape than we intended. Although his ship would have been three times as long as *Callisto* with a tough professional crew he would have had to feel his way carefully through the sounds and islands that had been carefully surveyed for us. Wisely he sailed only in daylight.

I found it easy to identify with Othere. His slow, cautious coastal cruise depending on the wind seemed much more real than the fast and certain schedules of the Coastal Express. If Othere could bloody well do it, so could I.

Othere discovered the White Sea long before Archangel was built or before Russia was even a name.

'Then from there they sailed due south along the coast as far as he could sail in five days. A great river ran up into the land there. They turned into the river, not daring to sail beyond it without permission, since the land on the far side of the river was fully settled.'

You could set that against the stories of the raiding murderous Vikings. I felt in a strange way that I who was also sailing north for fun and curiosity was quite close to Othere. I must have been feeling rather lonely.

At three thirty Alice woke up and started preparing to relieve Ashley and Sandy. She and Ana had the short first dog watch – four until six. She burrowed under cushions and in lockers to find her foul weather gear. She had not yet got into the routine of stowing everything away where she could put her hand on it immediately.

'Have you seen my safety harness?' she asked me.

'It's under your pillow.'

I heard her muttering, 'I ought to take a sea-sick tablet. Where did I put them?' A moment later I heard her say to herself, 'I don't think I need one: it's getting calmer.'

She had an unsettling habit of thinking aloud. On a previous cruise I had had to tell her not to express her internal dialogue in words because she was driving the rest of the crew mad. I had said, 'You sound like a committee meeting.'

There had been a relieved laugh from the others and she had joined in. She was very good tempered. Now she always tried not to do it and on this occasion with only a lapse for sea-sick tablets managed to assemble the rest of her gear – oilskins, scarf, sea boots and woolly cap in silence.

Ana and Alice vanished up the ladder at four o'clock. A moment later Ashley came down to the chart table in dripping oilskins to make up the hourly position on the chart. Ana joined him.

'We're here,' he said pointing to a small triangle that indicated the estimated position. 'The Decca puts us here.' A square showed the Decca fix; it overlapped the triangle. Decca and dead reckoning were confirming each other.

'You ought to see land soon; Soroy to port, Stjernoy or Seiland to starboard.'

'OK. I've got her,' Ana said and went up to the cockpit where Alice had relieved Sandy at the tiller.

I stood half way up the ladder with only my head in the rain. There was no need for me in the cockpit; the new crew were

114

settled in to the routine of running the ship. I could see Ana methodically looking at the angle of the sails and the position of the fairleads.

Alice addressed Ana. She said, 'Let's put her on autohelm, I want to do the navigating on this watch.' She was very keen to develop her skills as a sailor. She had been to evening classes. Ana thought for a moment.

'I'd rather do it myself,' she said in a gentle voice. 'I haven't got the feel of it yet like Henry and Ashley. You can do it later.'

Alice looked disappointed; she liked taking charge of things. The two crew members now running *Callisto* were complete opposites. Ana was introspective and non assertive but she was a more reliable and careful sailor. Alice was strong, full of enthusiasm and noisy. She was my niece and had sailed with me many times. I was very fond of her. She had a boring job in British Telecom and all her energies were devoted to scuba diving and music. She had enlivened many yacht parties with her violin and her folk songs collected from Cornwall to the Shetland Islands. She never introduced me to any men friends or talked about them but she was not a loner like her elder brother, Tom, and was usually surrounded by people and action. Although I sometimes suppressed her high spirits and excitement she always came sailing with me.

Later in the evening when Lesley and I were on watch Ana came up to the cockpit and said she wanted a word with me.

'I'm sorry,' she said, 'I can't manage Alice.' She sighed. She probably thought it was her fault. Briefly I wondered if I should have put Sandy in Ana's watch. She would have done what Ana said unquestioningly. Ana was secretary and administrative officer in a London interior design office. I guessed she tended to sink into a secondary role whenever she could. Now she was watch leader of a yacht bound for Hammerfest in the high arctic. It was no secondary role.

I said, 'I'm impressed with the way you are managing

Alice. She knows her stuff but she needs to be sat on occasionally. You seem to be doing that very well. Nothing has gone wrong in your watches.'

Ana knows me very well. She gave me a look that indicated that she knew I was being the skipper – building up people's confidence. All the same it worked. She looked hard at me. 'I knew you would say that.' She smiled. 'OK, I'll keep the show on the road. Next watch I'll let Alice navigate but keep an eye on her.' She hesitated. 'I'll also tell her to stop muttering to herself.' We both laughed.

The relationships you have with each other in a small yacht on a long voyage are essentially functional, in our case directed at getting *Callisto* to Russia.

This gave a sense of common purpose. Nevertheless in the narrow world of a cruising yacht people could get very irritated by each other. It was the skipper's job to ensure that it became no more than this. Personal relationships were as complicated and potentially hazardous as the reefs and skerries drawn on our charts and deserved at least as much attention. I didn't think I was very good at this aspect of running a ship: I had not done very well sailing to Tromso with Kate and Anne.

We came to Hammerfest on the evening of 26th at 11 o'clock. The rain had stopped but the town was grey and austere under the low cloud. Mist hid the bare hills. We furled the wet sails and motored slowly into the harbour. All was quiet. We tied up alongside a floating pontoon near the town centre and stopped the motor.

School children know that Hammerfest is the most northerly town in the world. At latitude 70° 39′ it is as far north as the northernmost tip of Alaska. Fishing boats alongside the quays, warehouses, a fish processing plant, oil drums and new buildings indicated a tenuous prosperity but no charm. A city of 8000 inhabitants I guessed it would have all the amenities of every other Norwegian town but it seemed to have no roots in the past or connection with its deserted northerly landscape. Nature had something to do with its air of depression: its polar nights and its cold sea but people had not helped. It had been burnt down in 1900 and again destroyed in the Second World War by the Germans. It had been thoroughly ill treated.

In *Callisto*'s saloon someone had lit a candle to make it seem dark. We drank a glass of whisky looking at its flickering light. The crew who had joined at Tromso had had a hard first sail but they seemed happy enough. After all, not many people could say they had sailed a yacht into Hammerfest.

After a day in harbour we sailed on 28th June in a fresh breeze. After taking on board fuel and water we motored out changing down to the no. 2 genoa and reefing the main. Clear of the harbour the wind strengthened and *Callisto* heeled to it throwing up cascades of spray.

I had not done any sight seeing in Hammerfest the day before. I had stayed by the yacht uneasily feeling the wind rising. Some swell was entering the harbour and the fenders between the yacht and the pontoon groaned. We had to round North Cape now only sixty miles away. The passage would be mostly in the unsheltered Atlantic: the last thing I had wanted was a lot of wind.

I wondered whether we ought to have sailed. The wind was from the west – a fair wind for North Cape but blowing off the ocean making the mainland coast a lee shore. We were still in the shelter of Soroy but it was blowing force 6 and already I could see the waves increasing in size and breaking all around us. There was a raw violence in the wind. Occasionally there were sudden stronger gusts that blew the tops off the waves and made the yacht heel so that her lee deck ran with water. *Callisto* would be butting into the seas until she was north of Kvaloy when I could ease sheets and run with the wind on the port quarter for North Cape.

I looked at the crew. Lesley, the only one that had not sailed before was steering, watching the luff of the genoa. She was catching rather less spray than I was in the for'ard part of the cockpit and was concentrating on the totally absorbing task of sailing a boat to windward. Ashley and Alice were standing by in case I ordered another reef. Inspite of the sea water running off their oilskins they seemed to be quite calm. Ana and Sandy had gone below to brew tea – no easy task in the wildly gyrating saloon. I had a tough ship and a tough crew. We would be round North Cape in ten hours. It seemed that I was the only one suffering any anxiety. I didn't think the wind would increase to gale force 8, the barometer was perfectly steady but what would the Atlantic be like in a force 6-7 at this latitude? I could imagine the explosions of white surf as the waves broke on the bare cliffs and fountains of spray from half submerged rocks. Had the west wind been blowing long enough to generate a big sea when we sailed out of the shelter of Soroy? Perhaps not yet I thought, but there were hours to go. The coast was unknown to me and I had no really reliable picture of the weather. What would my partner, Roy, have done? He had already put *Callisto* through her paces in a gale force wind in the North Sea but the wind had been blowing off the land. He didn't take chances with the wind in the other direction. I hated to waste a fair breeze but we were sailing a 35 foot yacht into the arctic ocean. No past experience or anybody else could help me. I had to decide whether to go on on the basis of my own judgement. Sometimes when I have to make a difficult decision, and have weighed all the pros and cons, I say to myself – yes, but how do you feel? I did this now and the result was blindingly clear. I was afraid. I didn't want to sail *Callisto* round North Cape in a strong onshore wind.

'We're going back,' I said. 'Bear away slowly, ease sheets. Lesley, steer towards the harbour entrance.'

As the wind came astern *Callisto* came upright and the spray stopped flying.

Nobody said anything but after a few minutes Sandy was passing up mugs of tea and everyone was chatting and smiling. Perhaps they had all had secret fears, but had not said anything. If there was going to be any chickening out it was going to be done by the skipper.

As we sailed back into Hammerfest and secured once again alongside the pontoon I felt like a beaten dog. I let the crew make all fast and went below slumping on the saloon cushions still wearing my oilskins. Ana came down first and saw my tense expression. She touched my hand.

'You did the right thing to come back, Henry,' she said softly. 'And you did the right thing to go out and have a look at it too. We're all terribly glad to be sailing with a skipper who doesn't take risks.'

I said, 'I would have sailed in those conditions normally. North Cape has made me into a sort of coward.' She smiled at me. There was understanding and warmth in her smile. 'Thanks very much though, for saying what you did,' I said. 'I feel OK now.'

When you have left a harbour once and then because of the weather find yourself back in it is an anti-climax and it loses all charm of novelty. I just wanted to get out of Hammerfest but it seemed sensible to leave sailing until next morning when the wind might be less. I went for a walk along the quays and around the point where I could see Soroysund. The wind was still strong but there were less white caps to the waves. The cloud was breaking up and there were small patches of blue sky.

Walking back along the quays I found a group of about thirty Lapplanders. This distracted me from worrying about the wind. I looked at them curiously. They were Asiatic with narrow eyes. They wore padded jackets and appeared to be waiting for a bus or a ferry. I know the Lapplanders were treated well by the Norwegian government but I hadn't expected to see them carry so many cameras. Back in the yacht I told Ana about them. 'I must see these,' Ana said and stepped ashore. Lapplanders and reindeer were the sights of Finmark. Ten minutes later she returned grinning.

'They aren't Lapplanders at all,' she said. 'I'm sorry to disappoint you, Henry, but they're a party of Japanese tourists.'

The others went ashore in the evening and explored the town. They had a round of half litre beers at the Hammerfest Hotel and Ashley had told them about the voyage from Bergen to Tromso. They met a coastguard called Ulf.

When Alice came back on board she told me indignantly, 'Ulf said we shouldn't worry about whales, there were lots of them, they were not getting extinct, and they were good meat.'

She looked shocked: I don't think she had met anyone like Ulf before. After a minute she said fairmindedly, 'He wasn't all bad. Earlier in the day he had arrested a Russian fishing boat for using too fine a filament in its nets.'

Next day, 29 June, things took a better turn. The swell in the harbour had gone down during the night and *Callisto* lay still at her moorings. Hammerfest and its high hills were lit by bright sunshine and the sky was a faultless blue. The depression in the Greenland Sea that had probably generated the stiff breeze from the west had moved away. It looked as if we were back in the settled weather of the arctic high pressure. I sat down at the chart table and did some tidal calculations. It seemed rather strange looking up the time of low water at Dover, England, and calculating the time difference nearly 2000 miles to Hammerfest. It would work alright, low water would be about 1030. The skipper of the motor cruiser in Tromso had said go north at low water. If I sailed at 1030 I would have a six hour fair tide out of Soroysund. I would need that: the wind appeared to have gone back to the north east. It would be blowing off the land giving a calm sea but we would have to tack against it. I would need the help of the tide.

Alice handed me a cup of tea and a peanut butter sandwich. My spirits rose. I liked working out the tides. They were one of the few absolutely predictable things in life.

Everybody was having breakfast in the sunlit saloon. 'We're sailing at 10,' I said allowing half an hour for them not being ready with last minute postcards and fresh milk.

We tacked north through Soroysund in a light wind, we had

motored out of Hammerfest in good order at 10.30 a.m. In the bright sunshine it looked more friendly than when we had arrived. The figure on the pier in smart uniform saluting us was the coastguard, Ulf. As the town diminished astern I felt grateful for its safe harbour and hospitality. Even if its inhabitants left you alone somehow you felt like a welcome guest. They charged us nothing for the use of their harbour.

The wind strengthened as we sailed out of the lee of Kvaloy. We were sailing at six knots. I managed to call up Hammerfest radio on the VHF. They now seemed to have settled their strike and predicted a NE wind force 4. It was now force 3. The sea was blue with some white horses but no spray came on board: it was a perfect day for sailing. The land was lower here with big cliffs rather than mountains. There were only small patches of snow. Occasionally there were low lying shores of bright green grass with a scatter of houses. Soon only the Atlantic was on our port side. The land became distant as we diverged from it on starboard tack.

In the afternoon it was quite warm in the sunshine inspite of the breeze. Lesley and I were on watch. Alice was relaxing in the cockpit. She had peeled off her jerseys revealing her Greenpeace T-shirt but there was an edge of coldness in the breeze.

'It's a bit like a soft cats paw,' Alice said. 'You know that underneath the fur is a paw full of sharp claws.'

I was steering. The wind was intermittently altering direction as much as 10 degrees; you had to make use of the windshifts if you wanted to drive the boat to windward. I could steer by the wind automatically.

Lesley was working the winches when we tacked. It was like sailing on a fine day on the British coast only there weren't any other ships. We were heeling to the wind with our wake stretching astern sparkling white in the sun.

'When shall we get to North Cape?' Alice asked.

'A while yet,' I said. 'We're making six knots through the

121

water but we're having to tack: only three knots over the ground. We may do a bit better than that though, say ten hours.'

'That'll be in our watch,' Alice said. She sounded excited. 'I can't believe this. What are we doing here?' she said.

When I handed over the watch to Ashley at 1600 hours we were tacking into the channel that separates the small island of Rolvsoy from the mainland. Once through there the coast ran north and we could sail parallel with it for many hours without tacking.

I went below but I couldn't relax. I looked at the barometer and hunched over the chart. I fiddled with the radio wondering if I could hear Hammerfest or Vardo. Everything was going well and we were running off the miles to North Cape but like Alice I couldn't believe we were here. Beyond North Cape was another world full of new challenges and discoveries. I couldn't think about that. Life had narrowed down to getting *Callisto* through the forty miles that separated us from a grim headland that had haunted me for months.

At half past five I could feel the wind increasing. The yacht was heeling more and loose gear in the saloon began to slide. The noise of the bow wave increased. Two china plates slid out of the sink to smash on the cabin sole.

Ashley shouted down from the cockpit. 'I'm going to put in a reef. She's getting hard to steer.'

'OK,' I replied. 'Do you want any help?'

'No, Sandy's going to do it. Good practice.'

For a couple of minutes I could hear the sails rattling as Ashley brought the yacht closer to the wind and then the sound of winches. Back on course *Callisto* sailed more comfortably. This was the predicted force 4 NE wind.

I took over the watch again at 8 o'clock. We were close hauled on starboard tack running north out to sea. There were more breaking waves but the weather looked settled and the low sun shone in our eyes.

After half an hour Lesley went below to have supper. Sandy handed me up up a small gin and apple juice. I drank it slowly as I steered making it last. There wasn't enough of it to allay my anxieties but a drink before dinner was a familiar ritual to set against the strangeness of this sea. Sandy passed up a bowl of beef stew.

'D'you want to eat it up there?' she asked.

'I don't feel hungry, I don't want it.'

Sandy said, 'You aren't looking after yourself.' There seemed to be a tight knot in my stomach. Beef stew would be indigestible lumps. Food would begin again after North Cape.

We didn't tack until nearly midnight. By then we were almost ten miles from the nearest land. The cliffs were low and unimpressive on the southern horizon. The new tack would take us into the shore again and more in the direction we wanted to go. I thought I could see North Cape twenty miles away on the port bow. With a wind like this in any other direction than NE we should be there in three or four hours. As it was it would be a long slog to windward all night. I didn't mind. I hoped that the wind would stay as it was blowing off the land and giving us a calm sea. We had plenty of time.

Lesley asked, 'Did you see North Cape in the war?'

'No,' I said, 'there were German air fields at Banak and Bardufus. We kept as far away as we could, close to the ice. This is a new experience for me.'

There was silence for a minute. Then I said, 'We've crossed the 71st parallel during this watch.' Lesley nodded. It was her first sail. It ought to have been a two hour trip from Whitby to Runswick Bay with lunch at the pub. 'You've done jolly well,' I said.

Ashley and Sandy relieved us at midnight. I showed Ashley the position on the chart. 'North Cape is due east. The wind is still shifting about so keep on the favourable tack and keep well out from the land. We'll lose the wind if we get too far inshore. Pass that on to Ana at four o'clock.'

Ashley shouted up to the cockpit. 'Are you OK for a few minutes, Sandy?' I heard a muffled 'yes' from Sandy at the tiller.

Ashley took his pipe from his pocket and lit it. He seemed to use a lot of matches. It was a major operation which reminded me that he was a chemical engineer.

He said, 'I like the way you don't use the engine unless you have to. It is quite an experience to sail to North Cape against the wind.' He looked young and confident. He was going to enjoy his watch.

Before he went back to the cockpit I said, 'If I don't wake up, take a bit of trouble handing over to Ana at four: she's going to sail past the bloody thing.' I had a feeling that Ana was the only member of the crew who felt fear the way I did.

I went below to the crowded heeling world of the saloon lit by the rays of the low sun. Lesley had already turned in. Alice and Ana were asleep. I settled into my sleeping bag still wearing my safety harness. I tried to sleep. I was very tired: I was skipper as well as watch keeper. I only seemed to doze fitfully. I wasn't on watch until eight in the morning.

I heard Sandy making hot soup in the galley. Ashley tacked at 3 o'clock. The direction of the sun through the saloon lights indicated we were once again heading out to sea. At 4 o'clock, just before the watch changed, Sandy shook out the reef. The wind was getting lighter. I heard Ashley quietly talking to Ana at the chart table. I felt confidence in my watch leaders. They would get me up if there were any problems. In the meantime the ship's routine was running like clockwork. I slept quite well for the next three hours.

At half past seven I gulped down a cup of tea and went up into the cockpit. Alice and Ana were bulky figures in jerseys, scarves and oilskins. They looked cold. The sun was shining through a thin layer of clouds in the north east but the sky was dark over the land to the south with wisps of mist on the hills. *Callisto* was running just north of east over an uneasy grey sea. The wind was light now. It had backed more to the north and blowing off the ice. The cat that Alice had referred to was showing its claws.

124

'There it is on the beam,' Ana said. She was steering and she didn't take her eyes off the luff of the genoa. North Cape was a great inert black cliff seven miles away, at 1000 feet, the highest point in a high coast. This was the most northerly point in Europe, the end of the world. There was a low building on its summit. This was a restaurant and interpretation centre. The travel brochure said, 'Here you can sit in the bar and enjoy a glass of champagne ... warm and snug behind an enormous panoramic window!' I wondered if there were any tourists there now looking at a far distant white sail: the only object in the empty Arctic Ocean. I wished the bloody building hadn't been there: it seemed to defile the great emptiness of the north.

Shortly after Lesley and I took over the watch at 8 o'clock I got out a new chart and layed off a course for the next headland, Nordkin. Nordkin was forty miles to the east. The great fjords of Porsanger and Lakse which ran in to the south made it seem like a small ocean crossing.

'Steer 090,' I said. Lesley altered course to starboard.

'We can free sheets,' I said and eased the genoa sheet around the winch. I let the mains'l out. For the first time since leaving Hammerfest we were not hard on the wind and were steering a compass course. *Callisto* picked up speed joyfully. The log showed seven knots. With the wind free we were heeling much less. I looked at the compass delighting in three figures – 090. For the first time since leaving Bergen there was no north in our heading. We were round the corner. From now on it would be east and south for Murmansk.

I wondered if we ought to have had some sort of celebration like yacht crews did when they rounded Cape Horn and turned north to run into the tropics. Perhaps I should have made a speech! There would have been a rather small audience: Ashley and Sandy were still asleep and Ana and Alice just off watch had turned in too.

As I set the autohelm Lesley said, 'We've done it, Henry. What does it feel like?' Her hair was tangled in the wind and she was smiling. She looked at me kindly: she knew how much I had been fretting.

'It seems like an ordinary headland,' I said, not believing it.

Lesley stared at the great cliff.

'It looks rather scary to me,' she said 'and I don't think Ana liked it very much, either.'

After a few moments I said,' I think we deserve a cup of tea. I'll put the kettle on.'

Lesley and I drank tea as the others slept below. *Callisto* surged through the waves of the Barents Sea east towards Russia. It was a sufficient celebration.

Lesley had reminded me that I had rounded North Cape once before. It had been unseen below the horizon. On that occasion there had been nothing at all to celebrate.

Chapter Nine

On 17th March, the fifth day from the Clyde, HMS *Lancaster Castle* entered the Barents Sea. The sun came out. This was the last thing we wanted near the enemy coasts. The sky was pale blue with small woolly clouds that diminished in size towards the horizon in endless perspective. They showed you the curve of the earth. The low sun shone flatly and there were no shadows under the whaler slung on the davits. The sea was calm and blue, complete with shearwaters and fulmers flying along the surface. The ships of the convoy were small and steady like ships in bottles. I heard one of the seamen looking at the scene from the quarterdeck say, wonderingly, 'It looks like a bloody picture postcard.'

It was good flying weather. It was rumoured that one of the reconnaissance planes from the carriers had reported that there were about 35 Junkers 88 bombers and 50 fighters on the Norwegian airfields. The Buffer examined the chart pinned on the bulkhead and ran his fingers along the indented coastline of Norway. He was a chief petty officer with a lot of experience and sense. I was glad when I heard him say, 'If that's all they can put up, we've got damn all to worry about.'

On the quarterdeck, Gordon Powell was smoking his pipe and leaning on the bulwarks appraising the clear sky and the convoy hard in the sunshine. He said, thoughtfully, half to himself and half to me, 'Well, Jerry's missing a grand opportunity today,' and he shook his head slowly in disbelief.

'Do you think they'll come, Gordon?' I asked.

He looked at me and thought for a moment. 'I don't know,' he said. 'Perhaps the weather isn't like this over the airfields or maybe they haven't got enough planes left in Norway.'

He re-lit his pipe, shielding the match with his hands against the light breeze. 'They'll have a hard time if they do come,' he said. 'We've got Grummon fighters and a cruiser and the destroyers can put up a lot of anti-aircraft fire.'

He looked at the nearest merchant ship. You could see Oerlikon guns mounted on her superstructure as well as the four inch gun aft. 'That lot aren't exactly defenceless against aircraft either.'

He turned and grinned at me. 'There's plenty of time yet, though.'

No attack came out of the dangerously shining sky of that day. Gordon Powell's assessment of the tactical situation had probably been right but I had another rather depressing thought. Perhaps the Germans simply had other ideas. They were not short of U-boats.

In the mess before supper, John Brooksbank and Len Tilley were talking about Ingrid Bergman. Her picture was stuck to the bread locker alongside General Zhukov. She was wearing a green dress that set off her golden hair. John Brooksbank said, 'She's super, isn't she – the sort of girl you would like to meet.'

Len Tilley, older than John Brooksbank and married didn't say anything for a moment. He stared levelly at Ingrid Bergman and his face softened. Then he grinned and said, 'When we get back home and I get leave, I'll be sleeping with one like that, only bare.'

John Brooksbank looked at Len with a puzzled expression. He was probably thinking similar thoughts to mine. Len often talked about his wife in Market Harborough and when he did so, conveyed a picture of a fulfilling and genuinely loving relationship. He was always writing letters to her. How could he equate her with his simple lust for a film actress with no clothes on? Len seemed different.

It occurred to me that perhaps this is what happened to you on the road to Russia; feelings had become basic and simplified.

John Brooksbank believed in the ship. Other members of the crew probably believed in her too. If so they concealed their feelings. From the Skipper downwards the prevailing attitude was one of unalleviated cynicism. John Brooksbank, on the other hand, talked quite openly about the importance of our various missions and their contribution to winning the war. Still only twenty years old he had had a lot of sea experience. When he had heard we were assigned to the Russian convoy he had said to me, 'We've both done this before: we ought to set the younger chaps an example!'

His narrow boy's face looked keen. At this stage of the war his positive attitude was rather out of date. In spite of this he was well liked. Other members of the crew shook their heads and wonderingly said, 'Bloody John's all for it.' I was very fond of him.

Supper was, as usual, awful but worse for me because I had a row with John Brooksbank.

Simmonds shouted, 'Any sod interested in grub?' his hands truculently in the pockets of his overalls. 'Well, hop up to the galley and get it,' he said.

Somebody unrolled the oil-cloth all over the letter I had been writing and the man carrying the big fanny of tea pushed past.

'Gangway, or I'll make a bastard.'

The plates were spread over the table and Simmonds slapped the grub out of the big tins with a saucer. 'How many on watch?'

'Three in Blue Watch.'

He put three platefuls aside.

'Alright lads, dig out, fill your boots.'

John Brooksbank was cook for the day and had to square up the messdeck after the meal but we all washed up our own plates. My diary entry conveys the shameful banality of our exchange.

'"I'm just telling you to dish up your shit," John said.

"How can I when you have not got the water? Extraordinary person you are," I replied crossly.

"Well, I am just reminding you," John said.

"Why not remind Taff; he's not dished up yet?"

"Taff always does his bit – you don't."

"Why the hell don't you look after your own affairs and leave me to mine?" I said and later added, "Shut up, you make me sick."'

Perhaps common sense and friendship were other casualties on the road to Russia.

I was glad when the red watch was piped at eight and I could leave it all and go to the wheelhouse.

It was quiet steering. I had stopped worrying about air attacks and began to worry about mines. If a small ship hit a mine, there would not be very much left and what there was would sink quickly. I hadn't worried about mines so far on this trip; there weren't any in the open ocean but I knew that there were extensive minefields on the approaches to Murmansk. They were 'friendly' minefields. They had been laid to restrict the movement of U-boats and we knew the way through the swept channels. Mines were moored to the sea bottom by wires to sinkers. They floated invisibly just below the surface at a shallow enough depth to be hit by the underwater hull of any ocean-going ship. It wasn't these mines that worried me, however. It was the ones that got loose. Sometimes the wire cables that held them in position parted and the mines floated to the surface drifting in the currents – an equal menace to both friend and foe. The nearer you got to minefields, the more likely you would come across floating mines.

I had had a personal encounter with one of these last December when our escort group had been patrolling the gap in the minefield between Shetland and the Faeroe Isles. I was masthead look-out at the time and dusk was falling. Searching ahead with my binoculars, I saw a small black spot in the sea almost dead ahead. It vanished and re-appeared in the oily swell. I shouted down to the bridge, 'Object bearing green 010.'

I had no acknowledgement to my report and I didn't even know if the skipper could see it too but the ship made a quick alteration to port. In these waters a floating object was best avoided. The bridge below me seemed to fill up with officers staring through their glasses to starboard. I felt as if I had over-turned a beehive. Everyone could see the mine now as it passed safely on our starboard side. It was a sinister sphere barely awash, with horns sticking out of it. It was not my responsibility any more but I watched it with interest. How were they going to deal with it? The Skipper reversed course to get closer to the mine. I saw George Seeley open fire on it with the starboard single Oerlikon and the First Lieutenant fired at it with a 303 rifle. The quiet of the Atlantic evening was rent by the sound of gunfire; 20mm Tracer shells and bullets made the sea boil around it and I hoped for the sight of a violent explosion. Nothing happened. The small black sphere floated unresponsively and dangerously in the swell. Twilight was spreading from the east and the Senior Officer's corvette came nosing towards us. She was rising and subsiding in the seas. There were rust patches on her hull above the foam of her bow wave. She rather meanly took over the business and we resumed our patrol station. Her Oerlikons fired and I heard the deep bark of her four inch gun. There was no explosion. They may have sunk it or abandoned it for some other alert look-out on a ship to spot another day.

I awarded myself a recommendation for reporting the thing long before anyone else could see it and I was encouraged by the fact that the Skipper had probably altered course on the basis of my report alone. It was typical, however, of this ship that none of the officers took the trouble to shout up at me, 'Well done, look-out.'

It would not have cost them much.

It was only when the watch ended and night had fallen that I remembered with dismay that the mine had not been detected by either radar or asdic. It had required eyesight and there was a lot of darkness at this time of the year in these latitudes.

MacLaughlan was a dark still shape sitting at the wheel-house table. I could see he was awake by the glow of his fag.

'Mac,' I said, 'can asdic detect floating mines at night?'

MacLaughlan laughed. 'Still thinking about that bloody mine you saw before Christmas? Shook you up didn't it, Henry?'

Then he said rather to my surprise, 'It was a good bit of work you did, though.' Then he addressed himself to my question. 'A good asdic crew might pick up a floating mine in really calm weather but not our dozy lot. Sharp look-outs by day and good luck by night are what we need.'

After a moment's reflection he added, 'Long odds, really. They are not trying to get us you know.'

He didn't say any more but he left me with a thought – it was not blind chance I had to worry about but efficient German sailors in U-boats going about their lethal business.

After that the wheelhouse relapsed into silence. The hours stretched ahead of me until midnight. There were some steering orders from the bridge but nothing else interrupted the throbbing silence and the steady rolling of the ship in the arctic night. I felt depressed and alone.

After the watch ended at midnight, I fetched a jug of cocoa

from the galley. I handed a cup to John Brooksbank who had also
come off watch. He said, 'Thanks, Henry, just what I need.'

He looked grateful. We drank in silence for a moment in the
half lit fug of the messdeck. Then he said, 'No aircraft today then;
perhaps they don't know we're here.'

I did not believe that for a minute and nor did he but it was
a signal that our quarrel at supper time was forgotten.

The following day was Sunday. On the previous Sunday, we had
heard that we were going to Russia and now we were three quarters of the way there. In the forenoon, the ship was quite steady
and the lee door of the wheelhouse was open. The sea was flat
and the sky was still light blue. The air was transparent and clear
as a prism. It was not even cold. MacLaughlan decided to test the
off duty Red Watch look-outs in aircraft recognition. There were
models and drawings in the wheelhouse. He questioned Jim
Pickthall reading down the list of planes. He asked, 'Can you
recognise a PBY2?'

'Yes,' said Jim, confidently. 'A Yank flying boat.'

'A Hurricane?'

'Yes.'

'A Kitty Hawk?'

More doubtfully, 'I think so.'

'A Shite Hawk?'

'No, I don't know that bastard.'

MacLaughlan was delighted. He had to tell everyone that
Jim didn't know about seagulls.

'Why don't you buck up, Jim?' he suggested.

Jim grinned apologetically and said gently in his
Lancashire voice, 'I know fuck all. An ordinary seaman isn't supposed to know anything.'

After dinner, Gordon Powell and Leading Torpedoman
Higginbottom started teasing MacLaughlan in the mess. Jim

Pickthall listened quietly. Gordon Powell said to MacLaughlan, 'You know, you remind me of one of those old time sailors.'

He pointed with his pipe, 'Stripped to the waist, tattooed, unshaven . . .'

Higginbottom said, 'All he needs is gold earrings.'

MacLaughlan, the regular seaman, by this time in the war represented a rather exotic minority. There may have been a time when the ratings who came from a civilian life to join the professionals in fighting the war were made fun of. Now the boot was on the other foot. For most of us, joining the Royal Navy was a response to an emergency; the idea that anyone would choose it as a way of life was beyond our comprehension.

Higginbottom said, 'In ten years time, Mac, you'll be sitting in a bloody messdeck like this, drinking coffee.'

But MacLaughlan could look after himself and retorted, 'And what will you be doing? You'll be outside the Andrew going to the same factory every day and wondering which bloody film to see in the evening.'

It was quite amiable and soon Higginbottom and MacLaughlan were discussing a Scouse they both knew who really did wear earrings.

In the quiet afternoon, Gordon Powell, went on writing his endless letter on foolscap to his girl. After a while, he stopped to fill his pipe, looked at MacLaughlan and said, 'You'll be a dirty matelot all your life, Mac. You won't even know what it's like to be civilised.'

MacLaughlan just grinned.

I put my sheepskin and gloves on and went on to the upper deck to take a look at this strange sea in the blaze of the sun. We were on latitude 73 degrees. The North Pole was just over 1,000 miles away. We were north of everything and everybody.

There was no land near except Bear Island to the south west, a small lost piece of ice and rock in the arctic. Beyond that was North Cape. I couldn't see the Polar ice-fields but they were quite close over the horizon on the port side. It all looked unbelievably blue and golden. The screw churned creamy white water astern and the foam of the bow wave spread out either side of the ship.

Last time I was in this part of the world, the weather had been as bad as I had ever experienced it. The Fleet destroyers had taken green seas on board and it had been quite dangerous. I had watched a man drown. He had been washed off the deck of the destroyer just ahead of us. I had been look-out on the bridge at the time and the accident had occurred in my sector. I reported it but I lost sight of the man in the great breaking crests of the waves. It was extremely sad but not an uncommon event and I wrote an account of it for a magazine. It had been published in *Tribune* in August 1944. The Literary Editor was George Orwell. He sent me two guineas. The story was accurate enough yet I now realised that I had missed the point of it all. What struck me now was the humanity of the skippers of the two big destroyers who let the convoy pass as they searched and searched in that wild sea for the one lost lamb. There had never been much chance of saving him but they only abandoned the search and resumed their convoy screen positions when all possibility of his being alive in such a sea was gone. The safe and timely arrival of the convoy was their only care and yet this overriding responsibility could be interpreted to permit a significant part of the convoy defence force to look for one man. It was extremely impressive.

Now this same sea was calm and sunny and when I climbed to the rear of the bridge, I could see most of the convoy.

The twenty four merchant ships were a compact but huge rectangle. The Fleet destroyers were ahead fanned out almost on the horizon. One of the carriers was steaming head to wind flying off a fighter patrol. I could see the big radar scanner on the mast of the corvette ahead of us endlessly revolving. A signal lamp winked from the cruiser. It was a scene of disciplined and purposeful activity. The convoy looked invincible. The dreaded Barents Sea was a calm blue lake on the edge of the ice-fields.

There were white seabirds skimming its surface. I looked with wonder at the blue sky. The transparency of the light and the bright sun shining on white ships. For a moment I seemed to forget the war and the ice-fields. Then I noticed the flags on the sterns of all the ships – red, white and blue – sharp bright squares of colour. The whole thing suddenly became a summer regatta in the Solent.

Monday, the 19th March, began badly for me. I never liked the morning watch, taking the wheel at four in the morning was not much fun but in addition, you could not sleep after the watch was over. On this occasion, I was slightly apprehensive of what was going to happen. You usually cheered up when you were approaching harbour. In this case, however, the nearer we got to land, the more dangerous it would be.

I felt extremely tired. My limbs were heavy and I had difficulty in focussing my eyes on the giro compass repeater. For moments the numbers became indistinct in a blur of red light. I didn't seem to be up to the job of steering and I worried about making a mistake. Except for my sea boots, I was wearing the same clothes that I had slept in and I felt uncomfortable and unwashed. I steered and fought against tiredness, trying to keep alert whilst my whole self was crying out for sleep. Somehow I managed to comply reasonably efficiently with the steering orders from the officer of the watch. His voice sounded tired too. We were all short of sleep.

I knew that with the ship's company divided into three watches, one could go on indefinitely, but after more than a week at sea, it didn't feel like it two hours before dawn. With only one third of the crew closed up and ready for action there were sixteen hours off watch everyday for everyone. But there were many activities that had to be fitted into this time in addition to sleeping. We had to work in the forenoon when we were off watch, we had to feed ourselves, keep clean, wash and mend our clothes and, above all, keep out of each other's way. I suppose I could have turned in last night before 10 o'clock and had more than five and three quarter hours in my hammock instead of reading but the messdeck lights weren't turned off until ten and there were the messdeck loudspeakers.

I must sleep every afternoon when I'm off watch I thought and catch up on the backlog. I was reluctant, however, to abandon the time for reading and writing. These activities kept me sane even if they contributed to my tiredness. I took my hands off the wheel and briskly rubbed my face. I knew I could manage. I wondered if the quartermaster steering the *Campania* and *Trumpeter* and the fleet destroyers and *Lapwing*, not far ahead in the darkness, were feeling like me. I thought of the great convoy running south east through the night towards Russia with tired but watchful men in the ships. It helped a lot. When dawn came, my need for sleep disappeared as it always did. I hadn't made any mistakes but I was sick to death with the wheel, the compass and the voice pipe – the slavery of steering.

At 8 o'clock when the morning watch ended, I went to the bathroom to shave and clean up. I was feeling rather depressed but found Able Seaman Kenneth Buckler, even more depressed and in a very bad temper too. He was shaving drearily, swearing under his breath.

'What's the matter, Ken?'

'Every bloody thing; it gets me down.'

He swept his hand around in a gesture which included the narrow crowded bathroom cloudy with steam, the tired faces, the dirty water slopping about our boots and the yellow light. Sailors were getting in each others way and cursing each other. He resumed shaving, carefully looking in the mirror and muttered, 'Bloody uncivilised conditions. Fancy making people live like this. God, how long is this going on for?'

I liked Ken Buckler in spite of his moods. I didn't see a great deal of him at sea because we were in different watches and he was in No. 5 Mess but often went ashore with him. He was good company when he was out of the ship he hated. He came from a comfortably well off family in Dudley and was on the way to becoming a qualified accountant. He was 22 and had recently got married. He was a good amateur musician and played a church organ. YMCA canteen pianos were easy for him and when we had last been ashore together he had played Dreamy Afternoon on the piano in the seaman's hostel at Gouroch. That was the time when he heard that HMS *Bluebell*, the corvette, had been lost off the Russian coast. He was an efficient seaman and also assisted sub-lieutenant Chown, the Signals Officer, with the ship's accounts and paperwork. Off watch in the mess he read company law and economics disconnecting himself from the ship, stroking his forehead with his sensitive fingers. Quite a lot of people liked him but some didn't. He never tried to understand or come to terms with the predominantly working class culture of the lower deck. He was a piece of high principled middle class England in the wrong time and in the wrong place.

After dinner, he got into a fight. I don't know what caused it. Possibly he was shooting off his mouth about the canned music from the messdeck loudspeakers or someone could have taken his complaints about life in general as a personal insult. A seaman we called Tanky hit him twice and then went for him with the nearest weapon, a tin opener. He had washed off the blood and changed into clean overalls which he wore like a lounge suit. There was a black patch over his right eye and his left eye stared greyly and hopelessly under his long eye lashes. He said, 'They file you, number you, dip you, treat you like swine herded together with other swine . . .'

Then he said, changing the metaphor, 'It's a yachting party for officers with the rest of us brought on for comic relief.'

I did my best to cheer him up without any success at all. Rather treacherously I began to feel a tiny bit of sympathy for Tanky!

In the last dog watch I told John Brooksbank about Ken Buckler. John had admitted once to me that he enjoyed talking about other people. He had said that it made him feel happy afterwards. We were sitting at a table in the crowded mess, glad to be on good terms again. John Brooksbank said, 'Ken never learns. He looks around him at the behaviour of the rest of the crew and finds it falls short of the standards of middle class Wolverhampton and rejects it. He doesn't seem to realise that it's not worse here – it's just different. He never tries to see the good side.'

I said, 'You mean fighting with tin openers is okay but not being late on watch?'

'Yes,' John said, 'but it's more than that. For instance, there's never any stealing. We never have to lock anything up.

'In my last ship,' he continued 'we had a seaman drafted to us who did lock up his things. He had keys for his locker, his ditty box and attache case. Chaps didn't like this and eventually the killick of the mess had a word with him and told him that it wasn't necessary to lock things in Forrester. He got told again the next day but he wouldn't listen. He went on locking thing up in front of everyone. God knows what ship he had been in before Forrester. One day when he came down from watch, all his possessions had gone – ditty box, case and a lot of things from his locker. All he had left was his sea-going gear. The whole lot had been chucked over the side. The odd thing was that whoever had done it had remembered standing orders and had punctured the ditty box and suitcase with a marline spike or something so that they had sunk and left no trace of the convoy.'

'What happened?' I asked.

'Nothing happened, of course. Nobody knew who had done it because it could have been done by any of us. We were pissed off with him.'

John went on, 'There's something to be said for a community in which stealing can't happen. There's even more going for one where even the suggestion that it might happen is not tolerated.'

Trying to be fair, I said, 'We can be thieving bastards if we want to be. What about the time after we had tied up alongside the cruiser – we found we had a new outfit of heaving lines and fenders?'

John said dismissively, 'That's different, they weren't personal possessions. It's only your mates you don't steal from and we never pinch gear from other corvettes either. They need the stuff like we do.'

Later in the evening, one other incident occurred that made me think about the social order in the ship. A seaman from No. 5 Mess came up to me and politely asked if he could borrow the dirty book.

'They're all dirty,' I said, slightly aggrieved at the downgrading of my small library.

'I mean the blue one about the world in the future where everyone has any tart they want.'

'You mean *Brave New World*.'

'That's it,' he said.

I rather grudgingly got the book out of my locker and gave it to him. It was well thumb-marked having been read by three people already on this trip. I was not all that impressed with Adlous Huxley's satire about the totally hedonistic and materialistic future but everybody else seemed to be enjoying it. H. G. Wells had called it 'the bible of the impotent genteel' and I thought I agreed with him. If Huxley was making fun of a world where people lived with all material needs satisfied but lacking any spiritual values, the satire was completely missed by the readers in Number 5 and 6 Mess. If you were men who had grown up in the back-streets of the big cities in the 1920s and 1930s, a future that offered security, comfort and entertainment was, indeed, not a satire but a utopia. Now, sharing their hard world, I was inclined to agree with them. To hell with spiritual value; I wanted to be clean, warm, well fed and, above all, safe, and that was all.

As the seaman went off gratefully with the book, I thought about those other Utopians – the men who had set out to change their own social order – the Russians. The revolution of 1917 made by Lenin had turned the world upside down and now these same Russians in their brave fight against Nazi Germany were turning the world upside down again. I was fascinated by them.

We would soon see the coast of Russia, but what else should we see? I tried to concentrate on reading to still my hands but no book I had could distract me and I remembered that the last Russian convoy had been attacked in these waters. I hadn't thought about the coast much on this trip so far; getting through each day without violence had been enough. Our merchant ships were taking tens of thousands of tons of war materials to the Russians. To get to Murmansk we had to pass through the channel between the minefields of the Kola Inlet. If German sailors wanted to help their soldier friends defending their country against the Red Army, they would know where to find us.

Behind my restless unease before action lay two contradictory thoughts. I must not show my fear and it is going to be interesting.

No. 6 Mess looked quite ordinary. Supper had been cleared away. Two men were playing cribbage – some were reading and writing letters, one was sewing. It was all reassuring and apart from the frozen condensation of the ship's side and the scattered arctic clothing gave no indication that we were approaching the northern coast of Russia. Other men must have shared my worry but if so didn't talk about it.

Faintly, I heard far distant under water explosions hammering against the ship's side. Men looked up for a moment listening. Someone asleep on the lockers turned over and opened his eyes, then everything went on as before. The depth charges stopped after a few minutes. It had probably been an attack on a doubtful asdic echo by a tense corvette.

Chapter Ten

Each hour I read *Callisto*'s log and plotted the distance run on the chart. As North Cape faded astern the line showing the easterly course with its little triangles at 6 mile intervals was the only evidence of our progress. Nordkin was still ahead – but unseen. Under a pale overcast sky the Barents Sea was grey and neutral – its sole feature the wake that we ourselves made stretching astern of us. It was very lonely.

With the autohelm steering there was little for Lesley and I to do. The wind was steady from the north east and the sails needed no attention. We kept watch for other ships and for the low shadow on the horizon that would indicate the promontory of Nordkin. The rest of the crew would wake up soon and there would be coffee handed up to the cockpit and perhaps the sizzling of bacon.

The watch keeping and the domestic routines of the yacht went on wherever she was. They were in marked contrast to the alien nature of this strange sea and the bleak coast of North Norway just over the horizon. Above the steady crashing noise of the bow wave I could now hear voices in the saloon where other members of the crew were waking up. *Callisto* was a speck in the Arctic Ocean but she was still our home. To go below was to enter a familiar world of soft cushions, books, the chink of cutlery and chat. It looked and sounded exactly the way it did in the English Channel. I had anticipated that in sailing to Russia I would sometimes be afraid. What I had not expected was the way the yacht herself would help me to live with fear. Norway, Russia and the Barents Sea were foreign and remote but *Callisto* wasn't.

Sandy appeared at the hatchway, 'There are bacon butties for you down here.'

'I'll go first,' I said to Lesley. I was hungry now we had passed North Cape. 'Give me a shout if you see anything.' I went down gratefully into the saloon.

When both of us had eaten there was still more than two hours on watch before handing over at noon. With no sight of land and no problems with the weather it was rather tedious. After a while Lesley said, 'Tell me what it was like on the Russian convoys.'

Lesley must have been as bored as me: nobody usually wanted to hear stories about the war.

I described the life of an able seaman in a small warship. This wasn't too difficult. After all, she was steering, standing watches and turning out at all hours. She nodded understandingly. I didn't emphasise the war part of it. After forty five years of peace it seemed unbelievable even to me that men had traded violence and sudden death in these waters. How much more so for her. She and all the other members of the crew had not been born at that time. As I looked at the smooth curves of *Callisto*'s sails white against the pale grey sky it seemed hard to imagine we were traversing a tragic ocean.

She looked at me with puzzled eyes. 'Why weren't you an officer?' she asked.

'I tried to be,' I said, 'but I failed. They chucked me out on the last day of the training course at HMS *King Alfred* and sent me back to sea in the lower deck.'

It hadn't been quite as brutal as that. They gave me the option of doing the course again and when I had declined this allowed me to join a small ship which was what I wanted.

'What went wrong?' she asked.

'My fault,' I said. 'I didn't try hard enough. I was recommended for a commission by the skipper of my first ship. I was just twenty at the time and quite bright, but things had come easily to me. I had already passed my intermediate exam as an architect. The navy wasn't just looking for brains but leadership qualities. They were quite good at assessing people and I didn't hit their standards.'

Lesley was looking at me curiously. She didn't know me very well. I feared that she was thinking that the Navy's judgement might still apply.

I went on, 'I felt an awful failure afterwards but it was probably the best thing that ever happened to me. I don't think I ever failed anything again for lack of trying. Later I got promoted to leading seaman. It wasn't much but it cheered me up a bit.'

Lesley seemed slightly reassured. Her question had exposed the weak point in my track record. I had changed since then and I hoped Lesley appreciated this. Perhaps I needn't have worried. *Callisto*'s sharp bow now slicing into the small waves of the Barents Sea was sufficient evidence that I had tried hard enough this time.

I felt I had talked too much about success and failure. I said, 'I was in the Navy for three years and I wouldn't have missed a minute of it. That's hindsight, of course. Looking back on it now it was good for me to serve on the lower deck. I was with men who hadn't got my privileged background and had different priorities and values. I learnt a lot from them.' I paused. Lesley was still looking interested: there was an hour to go before the end of the watch. 'I don't want to sentimentalise,' I said. 'We were a rough lot but I learnt that it was alright to have feelings. A man called George Whiting allowed me to cry, another called

144

MacLaughlan accepted that I was afraid, Higginbottom taught me to grieve and Ron Teece and I looked at death together at action stations. They've stayed with me.'

Lesley nodded. I wondered if she understood. She had an even more privileged background than mine.

Ashley and Sandy relieved us at noon and I went below to plot the hourly position on the chart and make up the log book. When I recorded the latitude and longitude shown on the Decca I got a shock. The decimals of the longitude seemed to be changing very rapidly yet our speed had not varied. It took me about a minute to realise why this was so. We were running east on a constant latitude and only the longitude was changing. What I had forgotten was that the meridians came together at the North Pole. Here on latitude 71 degrees 14 minutes North they were much closer together than they were in England. I was fascinated by the rapidly changing figures on the Decca display. I experienced for the first time something I had learnt about at school but never encountered in practice. Russia wasn't so far away. It was much closer than it had looked on the map.

Relaxing in the saloon after lunch I got another shock, this time a rather nasty one. I found it difficult to breathe. I'm getting an attack of asthma I thought. I could feel the air rasping in my throat. I hoped no-one else could hear it. I was dismayed: a bad attack could incapacitate you – stop you even climbing the ladder to the cockpit. I was still only suffering discomfort but I knew anxiety always made it worse. I had to think carefully. I remembered that I had brought with me a supply of steroid tablets that my doctor prescribed for me. I was reluctant to take this drug but it would relieve my breathing and the only side effects were slightly shaking hands. I found the bottle in my locker and swallowed six small tablets. I sat with my elbows on the saloon table and my head in my hands waiting for the drug to work. I wondered what had brought on the asthma. I had had asthma all my life and its cause, at least sometimes, seemed to be psychosomatic.

I had not been able to play games at school but I had managed active service in the Royal Navy. It was as if the adrenalin caused by fear and excitement had kept the illness at bay. So far on this trip I had been perfectly alright sailing north. Perhaps the asthma was a reaction to the successful rounding of North Cape – the release of tension. Then I had a more alarming thought. We were very rapidly approaching a part of the ocean that was full of fateful memories. It was possible that my difficulty with breathing resulted from the denial of fear. The Decca had shown how quickly we were reaching this sea. I needed to slow things down a bit, I thought, give myself time to adjust.

I had intended to keep going through the night to Vardo, the most easterly point of Norway. Murmansk would then have only been a day's sail. There was a good breeze and *Callisto* was sailing fast and comfortably. The crew would have been quite happy to continue. It had been a hard passage for me, however, since leaving Hammerfest yesterday morning. It had left me short of sleep but in addition it had included the emotionally charged experience of rounding North Cape. Now I had an attack of asthma too. What was it Sandy had said last night? 'You ought to look after yourself.' But it was my mind not my body that needed care and attention. I decided to find a harbour for the night. I wanted out of it.

At the chart table I ran my eye along the indented coast. Twelve miles beyond Nordkin which was now close on our starboard bow was the small port of Gamvik. The chart gave no details but the travel brochures indicated that it was a ferry point for the Coastal Express. We would go there.

I went up into the cockpit and told Ashley what I had decided. He didn't notice my difficulty with breathing.

'Pity to waste this wind,' he said.

'We've got plenty of time,' I replied. 'Everyone's done jolly well since Hammerfest. I think we would all benefit by a night tied up in harbour.'

He didn't demur. 'We'll alter course when we've rounded Nordkin.'

146

CHAPTER TEN

We had sailed a long way. Going into Gamvik was quite a reasonable thing to do. I hadn't told anyone that I had originally intended to sail to Vardo. Ashley did not know that I was once again chickening out.

Gamvik is on the edge of things; a few houses and some fishing boats in the small harbour facing the Arctic Ocean. We sailed in at six o'clock in the evening rounding up head to wind inside the piers to lower the sails. Starting the motor seemed to shatter an absolute silence. There was nobody to consult so we secured to an apparently disused fishing boat moored alongside a quay. I had never sailed to such a remote settlement as this. It was encompassed by low hills of rock and thin grass stretching away greyly to the horizon. A burnt out warehouse dominated the dilapidated pier. Turning off the motor brought back the silence and Gamvik lay neglected and deserted under the overcast sky. It seemed as if the magnificent achievement of spreading prosperity the whole length of Norway had finally run out before reaching this place. It was rather sad. Nevertheless it was a safe harbour. The thirty hour sail from Hammerfest had not been difficult but I felt mentally and physically drained. I went down to the saloon like a hunted fox returning to its lair.

There were too many people below taking off oilskins and making tea. I felt jostled. Usually the yacht doesn't feel crowded. At sea there are always two members of the crew on watch on the upper deck and people go ashore in harbour. I sat down at the chart table to keep out of the way and make the final entry in the log book. We had only needed to use the motor for fifteen minutes all the way from Hammerfest. Against my previous entry '1740 approaching Gamvik' somebody had written 'Ghost town'.

Lesley handed round tea. The crew relaxed sitting around the saloon table drinking and talking. I drank mine a little apart at the chart table. I heard a voice say, 'What are we doing in this end of the world arctic dump?' and everyone laughed. I felt a sense of resentment and anger. I concealed this but I didn't join in the laughter. What did they expect? A holiday cruise with every harbour carefully pre-selected for its charm and amenities? A ship run by superhuman professionals immune to fear and failure? They could have stayed at home, I thought. I felt isolated from my crew hating their unconcern for me. I drank my tea in silence. After a while the anger and self-pity slowly subsided. As the conversation turned to other matters I calmed down and started thinking. It had only been a light hearted remark and it hadn't been directed at me. It was I who had interpreted it that way. I had come into Gamvik because of my own weakness and concealed it because of pride. I should have been more candid. I could have said, 'I'm bloody tired, this sea is full of ghosts for me and I've got slight asthma. Do you mind if we have a night in harbour?' Nobody would have objected or thought the less of me for it. I would have shared my feelings and could have shared in the laughter. Another lesson I thought sadly, on the way to Russia. Leadership means taking people into your confidence and letting them see you as a real person not as an iron man. I said to myself, Henry, it's time you stopped bullshitting. It was the word Kate had used about me.

Ashley, Alice, Sandy and Lesley went ashore for a look round before supper. I had said I wanted to stay on board and clear up the saloon when they were out of the way. I wouldn't be able to do very much because of my breathing. Ana had hesitated and then said, 'I'll stay on board and give Henry a hand.'

They climbed over the high bulwarks of the fishing boat, walked along the pier and vanished into the barren landscape.

I started to wash up the tea mugs. 'Leave that,' Ana said. 'I'll do that and then sweep up. You sit down and have a rest.' She gave me a sharp glance. 'You look a bit bushed, and I'm not surprised.'

She pumped salt water into the sink. I wanted to tell her about asthma and fear and the Russian convoys. Somehow it didn't seem necessary. She was watchful and sensitive. Instead I

148

asked her, 'Ana, what did you think of North Cape?'

'I didn't want to look at it,' she said. 'It was brutal and alien.'

It wasn't just me.

We sailed next morning. It was seventy miles to Vardo in a south easterly direction. The wind had backed towards the north and was now on our port quarter. It was the 1st July and the sky was rapidly clearing with the sun shining between little white cumulus clouds. The sea was pale blue, flecked with white horses. Razorbills and puffins flew with rapid wing beats along its surface. After a night's sleep I felt very much better. In just over an hour we were off the Omgang lighthouse and heading across Tanafjorden. We were sailing at seven knots. My spirits rose with the joy of it. As Gamvik dwindled astern I felt a little guilty about my harsh thoughts. It had given us all we had wanted – shelter, rest and water. Sandy had even found a shop selling bread and milk which opened specially for her. The lady who owned it had told her,' My children watched you sail in. They were very excited. They have never seen a sailing yacht,' and she added, 'and such a small yacht, too, all the way from England!'

The north coast of Finmark is not the pretty Norway of the holiday photographs. It is black and low with only small patches of snow on the summits of the hills. A sailor perhaps sees it with another eye. There were no off lying reefs or islands and no nerve-wracking pilotage through narrow sounds. It allowed easy coastal sailing. As the sun strengthened I relaxed, warm and contented in the cockpit. The yacht was sliding down the short waves that were now coming from astern. I could hear the rumble of her bow wave and see her wake stretching astern in the sunshine. *Callisto* was running off the miles to Russia. There was an eagerness about the way she sailed as if she scented success.

When the wind died just before midnight it didn't matter. We were only fifteen miles from Vardo and we could hear Russian language as well as Norwegian on the VHF radio. The sea became smooth and glassy and the sun shone on us like a huge searchlight from the north. The shadow of our sails stretched away towards the coast. The sky was clear and there was no haze on the northern horizon. You could see the midnight sun above the sea ready to start rising again. Everyone came on deck to look at it. They took photographs of each other in its level light. It was all quite different from yesterday: I felt like a successful tour operator with happy clients. My asthma had gone.

When Lesley and I took over the watch at midnight we had just started motoring. The dreaded Barents Sea was a quiet blue lake.

'I wish we weren't making so much noise,' Lesley said. It was the first time we had needed the engine at sea for a long time. We had become accustomed to the wind and sea noises of sailing. I eased back the throttle lever.

'We're in no hurry,' I said. The sound of the engine became a muted purr. The dial of the trailing log showed that we were travelling at a bit less than five knots. 'We'll still be at Vardo before the end of our watch,' I said.

We grinned at each other. Neither of us were tired: why shorten our passage along this coast? I think the black and the blue and the radiance of the sun had gone to our heads.

At 2.00 a.m. Vardo, still six miles away, emerged on its island from behind a low headland. It was a kaleidoscope of primary colours in the blaze of the sun. It shone with a jewel like clarity in its setting of stony cliffs. The beautiful face that Vardo showed us that night was the last thing that I had expected at the remote North East of Norway. It was quite different from Hammerfest and Gamvik.

Vardo didn't disappoint us. We motored slowly into its great harbour flanked by warehouses painted in bright colours. It was full of silent fishing boats alongside the high quay walls. There were no people at all. It was three in the morning. The town was asleep in the sunshine. I had never experienced entering harbour like this.

I reduced the engine revs to tickover: I wanted to be as quiet as possible and also prolong the magic of our arrival.

'Can you wake Ashley and Sandy?' I asked Lesley.

They came up into the cockpit heavy with sleep, then stared around them marvelling at the brightness and silence of the port. With their help we tied up beside an empty quay with long mooring lines to allow for the rise and fall of the tide. I turned off the motor and *Callisto* lapsed into the stillness of sleeping Vardo.

Vardo is a frontier town. To the West, five hundred miles away is Novaya Zemlya and the Kara Sea. To the south, and quite close, is Russia. In the north is Spitzbergen and the polar ice. It has been a settlement for a very long time. On its island site with its natural harbour it is the meeting point between east and west. Its ownership had been disputed by Russians and Norwegians. A treaty of 1326 established more settled conditions. Only the native Lapps lost out: they found themselves paying taxes to both Russia and Norway. Since then Vardo has benefitted by trade in dried fish with the Russians who needed it for their numerous religious fasts. It was given town status in 1789 and became one of Norway's biggest fishing ports. Today it has an air of prosperity and nearly 5,000 people live there on the island and the adjacent mainland. All the buildings are new. The old town was totally destroyed by the retreating German armies in 1944.

We spent one whole day and two half days in Vardo and were sorry to leave. The unusual visit of a yacht even overcame the native reticence of the Norwegians. Some of them came to talk to us and invited us to use the facilities of the Fishermen's Club. The showers, laundry and good coffee were exactly what we needed.

I was reluctant to leave the yacht. I did my share of cleaning up below and on the upper deck. Then I got out the cockpit cushions and relaxed in the sun. The quayside buildings were reflected in the water of the harbour disturbed only by the entry or departure of fishing boats. Members of the crew returned at intervals from their various missions to buy post cards and fresh food. They told me what the town was like. I was content with that. I didn't want any excitement. I was between North Cape and Russia and I wanted nothing. The sunshine and the ships made me think of far off Tromso. I thought of the long voyage north from Bergen. The tree clad islands and the high snowy mountains seemed part of another country. The crew who had sailed *Callisto* with Ashley and me through the narrow sounds were now in England. Anne would be at her drawing board; Tom would be worrying about new commissions to inspect timber shipments; Kate would be working on her thesis. It was difficult to imagine them having their separate lives away from the yacht. I wondered what they had told their friends about their summer holiday.

Anne and Tom I would see again – they were part of the family – but what about Kate? In the long sail from Tromso I had had other things to think about, now in the peace of Vardo I felt a need for her. I saw her as I first remembered her in the bar high over Nottingham. She had been wearing a full red skirt and a black blouse and her long glass ear rings were the colour of her pale eyes. At the time I had been mainly conscious of our conversation exploring shared ideas and feelings but I had now been at sea a long time and my thoughts were dominated by the way she had looked. I reflected on the disordered relationships I had had with women since my first passage to Russia in the war. I had always seemed to have escaped from love into action. In the bright arctic sun Kate was suddenly more important to me than either architecture or Russia.

My thoughts were interrupted by the thump of someone jumping down from the quayside ladder onto the deck.

Alice, Tom's sister, came on board and reported that there was no Vinmonopolet in Vardo. She said reflectively, 'If you want to give up drinking a Norwegian cruise is a good way of starting.'

Recently happy hours had been enlivened only with orange juice and tonic. A moment later I heard her say to herself, 'I'm not sure I really want to.'

Lesley had been talking to a young fisherman called Fritz. She must have been charming and persuasive. He said, 'There's a vinmonopolet in Vadso in the south. I ought to be working on my boat but if I can borrow Carl's car I'll drive you there.' He seemed glad of the distraction. Vadso was forty miles away on Varangerfjorden. In the car journey across the flat tundra Alice, Lesley and Sandy listened to Fritz describing the Norwegian political scene and telling jokes about the Swedes. They only saw two reindeer but they got whisky, gin and wine. Alice told me afterwards that the tundra was a botanist's paradise – little white and cream flowers carpeted the ground. There were white and pink knot grasses, bog cotton, ladies smock, mosses, lichens and little knee-high willow trees. It only looked lifeless from the distance.

Fritz came to supper in the evening. He said, 'I come from Hitra near Trondheim where my parents live. I don't really belong here and I miss the trees terribly.'

He said that if you walked to the south of Vardo island you could just see the Russian coast. I decided not to do this: I wanted my first sight of Russia to be from the deck of *Callisto*.

At 4 o'clock next day when the crew happened to be all on board drinking tea in the saloon, I decided to brief them about Russia.

'The Russians may completely ignore us,' I said, 'but we have a personal invitation from the chairman of the Murmansk Soviet and also from the Veterans Committee. They may make something of our visit.'

I had their full attention. This was the first visit of a British yacht. After forty five years of Cold War none of us knew what to expect.

'I know they haven't forgotten about the Russian convoys in the war,' I went on, 'but we only played a small part in their victory over Nazi Germany. The Russians would have won the war anyway without us or, for that matter, the Americans.'

153

My audience looked slightly unbelieving, but I continued, 'It cost them a lot though, they lost twenty million people and from all accounts every family in Russia is still affected by this. I know the war seems like history to you but I guess it won't seem so to the Russians. When you meet them try and remember that. If it is any help to you,' I said grinning, 'it isn't history to me either.' I paused. It was getting a bit like a pep talk by Lord Louis Mountbatten. 'When I was in Murmansk last time there were scores of American and British ships in the harbour and the city was full of allied sailors. The day after tomorrow we could be the only British ship in Murmansk.' I stopped myself in time from referring to the British flag on our stern.

Sandy said, 'I'm glad you said all that, Henry, but we'll just be ourselves and say we've come to see them.' The others nodded. Little *Callisto*'s long voyage would speak for itself.

I wrote a lot of letters. I knew the mail service from Murmansk to Britain was slow. Better to post them in Norway. England and Nottingham seemed remote and insubstantial. My home was now a far wandering yacht. My letter to Kate was informative but neutral. I told her I missed her. It felt as if I were sending it into thin air.

We left Vardo under full sail. I suppose I was showing off a bit but the wind was just right allowing us to set the mains'l at the quayside. We cast off and unfurled the big genoa. As Ashley steered I watched the quays, warehouses and fishing boats sliding silently astern. The heading in the log book said, '4th July. Vardo towards Murmansk.'

Ashley was wearing his red sailing smock, there was an intent look in his eyes. The light wind ruffled his hair. Clear of the harbour entrance he said, 'I'm coming hard on the wind.' Sandy winched-in the genoa sheet. A moment later he shouted, 'Ready about,' then 'lee oh'.

He steered *Callisto* through the eye of the wind. Sandy threw the sheet off the port side winch and I wound in the sheet on the starboard side. We were close hauled on the port tack with the coast of Russia appearing ahead on the blue horizon. Ashley and I looked at each other. We had made many interesting passages but this was going to be the most interesting of all.

We had left Vardo later in the day than I had intended. After breakfast we had quite quickly topped up the fuel tank and filled up with water but the trouble had been communication with Murmansk. I had received a telex from the Murmansk Shipping Company before I left Nottingham. It said, 'Pilot will board in position 69 degr. 12 min. N. 33 degr. 31 min. 6 sec. E near Tyuva Bay.' It had also said that the shore radio was high frequency not VHF and therefore we should have to telephone them to give twelve hours notice of our time of arrival at the position.

Sandy and I had set off with high hopes and my translation into Russian of our time of arrival in my notebook to make the call. At the post office we found there was no direct dialling. A kind lady in the Town Hall next door offered us the use of her telex. We wrote out our message giving estimated time of arrival – 1700 hours 5th July. We had to wait a long time for confirmation that it had been received. I was sweating with anxiety thinking that there was going to be some last minute hitch.

Sandy said, 'Stop worrying. They know what they're doing in Murmansk.'

The lady at the Town Hall gave us coffee.

At 2.00 p.m. the confirmation came through. Murmansk was just over the horizon but the wire had gone via Oslo and Leningrad – nearly 4000 miles. I gritted my teeth, 'How much did that cost?' I asked.

The lady gave me a soft smile. 'Nothing at all,' she said, 'the town is glad to help you.'

It was a heart warming farewell from Norway.

Vardo and Norway faded astern in the pale north. We shifted the ship's chronometer and our own watches two hours forward to conform to Moscow time. Ana lowered the Norwegian courtesy flag and hoisted the red flag of the Soviet

Union in its place at the yardarm. We were crossing a sea frontier into another country.

Sandy took my hand. 'It looks as if we're really going to get there,' she said gently, 'a dream coming true for you.' We were both thinking of the Soviet Consulate in London and the endless phone calls to Murmansk. Her bright eyes expressed gladness for me. Now all we had to do was sail the boat.

All that evening we sailed south close hauled with the wind on the port bow. I was unable to eat the beef stew Ana made. I wished my nerves didn't affect my appetite. Lesley and I went on watch at 8 o'clock. At eleven fifteen I tacked. On port tack we should pass two miles to seaward of the Nemetskiy light, thirteen miles away. We would then be able to sail parallel to the coast of the Rybachiy peninsula.

I handed over the watch to Ashley and Sandy at midnight. The Russian coast was closer now. It was like Finmark – black, empty and treeless – a waste land. The sun was hidden by thin clouds but the wind was still light and steady. *Callisto* was running at six knots and heeling under full sail. There was absolutely nothing to worry about.

I lay down on the port side saloon berth and dozed off. I was awakened by the VHF radio. We kept tuned to channel 16 which is the calling and emergency channel. There seemed to be a lot of Russian being talked. It sounded quite loud. I felt uneasy and went up the ladder into the cockpit.

'Over there,' Ashley said, pointing at the northern horizon. 'They look like warships.' We watched them as they got nearer. The vague grey shapes became the hard silhouettes of three big destroyers. They had high superstructures and through binoculars I could see arrays of aerials and revolving radar scanners. Their bow waves flashed white in the greyness of the sea. They seemed to be altering course frequently.

'They look as if they are carrying out an exercise,' Ashley said.

They were very beautiful ships but I wished they weren't

there; I hated their air of menace. Perhaps the Cold War hasn't ended here in the arctic, I thought. Perhaps our visas and ship's papers would mean nothing to the Red Navy. They could still be guarding their coast against intruders. What did we look like from the bridge of a destroyer – a small yacht, her sails white against the dark shore? I felt, wretchedly, that we could be turned back at the last minute. Unaccountably my hands were shaking. The ships jiggled in the binoculars. They were suddenly not Russian but Royal Navy fleet destroyers: *Scourge, Scorpion, Savage,* ships from another time which had fought the convoys through. Soon the others would appear *Sioux, Opportune, Orwell, Zambesi,* then the carriers, then the merchant ships. After that there would be the loud depth charges and the quietness of fear. I let the useless binoculars hang on the lanyard round my neck and gripped the edge of the main hatchway. I tried to think. Don't panic. This is 1990 and you're skipper of a sailing yacht on a summer cruise. I looked at Ashley and Sandy watching the three ships. They had not noticed my shaking hands. *Callisto* held her course for Murmansk.

I began to calm down; no other ships appeared. I could now hear the faint rumble of distant turbines but there were no other sounds from the destroyers.

The warships fanned out in different directions. 'They aren't interested in us,' I said with a steady voice. 'You're right, Ashley, it's a routine exercise.'

I stayed in the cockpit for half an hour. The destroyers didn't seem to be coming closer.

'I'm going below,' I said, handing over the binoculars. 'Keep an eye on them.'

In the saloon I could still hear them calling each other on channel 16. I lay down on my berth but sleeping was out of the question. I was still anxious inspite of my reassuring words to Ashley

Suddenly the VHF was speaking English.

'Yacht *Callisto*, this is Soviet Warship, over.' I couldn't

157

catch the name of the ship.

Ashley slid down the ladder from the cockpit and picked up the handset. I lay where I was and watched him: he knew the radio procedures. He pressed the transmit lever, 'This is yacht *Callisto*, over.'

'Yacht *Callisto*, switch to channel 12, over.'

Ashley twisted the tuning dial.

The radio operator's voice said, 'Yacht *Callisto*. Where are you from, where are you bound?'

'From Vardo, Norway, to Murmansk, USSR.'

There was silence for a moment. Ashley caught my eye.

He said, 'They know our name. Surely they can't read it from four miles away.'

A new voice came on the VHF.

'Yacht *Callisto*. This is the captain speaking. Welcome to Soviet waters. Good sailing. I hope you enjoy your stay in Murmansk.'

It felt like a strong arm around my shoulder. Ashley said into the handset, 'This is yacht *Callisto*. Thank you for your welcome and good wishes.'

He hung up the handset and switched back to channel 16. We both laughed with relief. They must have been expecting us. The tension ran out of the ship. I wondered what sort of country this was where the captain of a great warship could personally welcome a small visiting yacht at 3 o'clock in the morning.

Ashley went up into the cockpit to tell Sandy what had happened.

I sat wakeful in the saloon for a while. I was grateful for the greeting of the warship captain and I was now sure that we would reach Murmansk. The destroyers, however, I had to admit had unnerved me. I knew that Murmansk was the base for the Soviet Northern Fleet but for some reason it had not occurred to me that we should meet their ships at sea.

As I lay down to sleep on the port berth the thought entered my mind that the white sailing yacht they encountered heading for their home port was a symbol of a more hopeful future.

At 3 o'clock in the afternoon Novolok lighthouse was close on our starboard side. Lesley said, 'Do you recognise this place, Henry?' The lighthouse was white against the grassy shore. It marked the entrance to the Kola Inlet.

I looked at it hard. 'No, I don't,' I said.

All the morning we had sailed south along the bleak cliffs of the Rybachiy Peninsula. As we crossed the Motovskiy fjord the coast ahead had become green. It was bare of trees but beautiful in the sunshine. The wind had gradually faded and veered to the south. We had been motoring since 11.00 a.m. The throb of the engine echoed back from the low hills. We were out of the ocean. Ashley and Sandy had the afternoon watch but everyone was on deck. Ashley steered close to the western shore where the chart showed the inshore traffic zone. We were entering one of the world's great ports. We passed a big merchant ship heading out to sea.

Suddenly I noticed that the high headland six miles on our port beam was detaching itself from the mainland. I recognised it instantly: it was Kildin Island. The whaleback of its great hills were still the same as I remembered. It had been snow covered then, looming white out of the driving snow showers but the shape was unmistakable. The geography of the whole coast fell into place. I thought of the destroyers we had seen twelve hours before. It was quite warm in the sunny cockpit but I suddenly felt chilled. I turned to Lesley who had now lit a cigarette and was sitting relaxed, enjoying the scenery.

'I can remember all this now,' I said. 'The sun wasn't shining then and I was rather scared.' She smiled at me encouragingly. My voice probably sounded slightly shaky.

Chapter Eleven

It was dark and the visibility was poor but the coast of Russia was showing on the radar. I had relieved Tony Baynon at the wheel at midnight. He had given me a wan smile. 'The Skipper's on the bridge,' he said.

A calm tension spread out from the bridge through the voice pipes and telephones to all parts of the ship. All departments were closed up and alert. There were a lot of steering orders and alterations of speed. The convoy was deploying from ocean disposition to line ahead for the Kola Inlet.

I could hear the loudspeaker on the bridge. The ships of the close escort were using the radio telephone. The senior officer in HMS *Lapwing* was giving orders. They sounded urgent but unexcited. Compliance with them was translated to me as new courses to steer by the quiet voice of the Skipper. Steering was hard work. I tried to concentrate to avoid thinking but my response to the orders was almost automatic and my mind was free to speculate. What was out there in the dark? What would daylight show? It was cold but my hands on the wheel were sweaty. I began to pray,

CHAPTER ELEVEN

'Lighten our darkness we beseech thee, O Lord, and by thy great mercy defend us from the perils and dangers of this night.'

I had learnt that prayer as a boy but I wasn't a Christian now: seeking comfort in prayers was cheating. I had to live with an emptiness inside.

I was very tired when Taffy Jones took the wheel at 4 o'clock. I went below to get some sleep but I wasn't going to use my hammock. I lay down on the bare messdeck as near to the steel ladder as I could get. It was quite comfortable sleeping like this if you lay face down wearing all your clothing including sheepskin and oilskins. I used my mitts as a pillow to rest my cheek on and spread my elbows out to avoid rolling with the ship's movement. It was not as good as a hammock but it was safer. It took about forty seconds to get out of a hammock and put on your sea boots. These forty seconds could make all the difference. Sleeping where I was I was also nearer the single hatch, the only way out onto the upper deck.

Sleep eluded me for a while. I remembered a poem by Louis McNeice. The last four lines seemed to help.

'. . . Sleep and, asleep, forget
    The watchers on the wall
    Awake all night who know
    The pity of it all.'

It seemed to summon up a picture of the Skipper and Taffy Jones and all the others in Blue Watch wakeful and on guard in the arctic night.

I was awakened by the distant rumbling of underwater explosions. The shock waves striking the ship's hull sounded as if depth charges were being dropped at irregular but frequent intervals. It wasn't like an attack: it seemed more like an un-aimed barrage. The ship clanged. I got to my feet and glanced around

161

the mess-deck. It looked as it always did at sea. Oilskins on their hooks swung with the rolling caused by the swell. Hammocks bumped gently together. The mess tables were covered with their usual litter of unwashed cups, magazines, bread crumbs and cigarette ends. Electric light bulbs gave shadowless light. Some men had been awakened by the impact of the explosions, others were still asleep. The ship didn't seem to be going particularly fast or heeling to excessive course alterations. Action stations hadn't been sounded. I tried to believe that the depth charges were purely a precautionary warning to any lurking U-boats.

I took off my oilskin, re-fastening the uninflated life belt around my waist. Collecting my washing gear, I went to the bathroom on the deck above. There were several seamen and stokers already there. They were fully dressed and were shaving carefully. I joined them, lathering my face as the ship shuddered at each explosion. This routine activity seemed to provide some antidote to my growing uneasiness.

I returned to No. 6 Mess for breakfast but I didn't want to eat anything. The depth charges sounded louder at waterline level. Everyone was awake now but no-one mentioned the interminable hammering on the ship's side. Conversation was not very lively at 7.30 in the morning at the best of times. Now it was confined to remarks like 'pass the jam' and 'that's my bloody tea you're drinking'.

I gulped down a cup of tea and decided I had to see what was going on. I put on my oilskin and gloves and made for the upper deck.

On the quarterdeck, torpedomen were setting the fuses on the depth charges. A rating wearing a telephone headset was calling numbers to the leading torpedoman. This was a fairly ordinary sight although it hadn't happened on this particular trip. Much more unusual was the view on the starboard side – the coast of Russia. I stood in the lee of the main deck out of the way of the torpedoman and stared at it. Against the grey sky the shore was pure white with hard bones of rock showing through the

162

snow. At times snow squalls obscured it. I was glad to see land again after all this time. The cold wind seemed to smell of pine trees. On the port side the ships of the convoy veiled by mist were faint smudges, one behind the other. Occasionally they vanished completely.

The ship increased speed and with the helm over, began to turn. The coast and the convoy rotated around us. Now our own depth charges rumbled down the rails and fell over the stern as the torpedomen heaved and sweated. I didn't think we were attacking anything detected by the asdic or we should have fired a full pattern using the throwers as well as the traps aft. The two charges were at shallow fuse settings but because of our speed, were well clear of us when they exploded. The huge expanse of the sea close astern seemed to flash. A second later a tall column of water climbed in the sky and hung over us like a great tree. Then came a sound that hit me through the steel deck I was standing on. The ship gave a kind of jarring sob and my jaw shook in my head. The tree of water astern collapsed into a massive turbulence.

We had dropped many depth charges but somehow I never got used to their loud violence. Uneasily I watched the torpedomen re-loading the traps aft. Gradually, I was joined by the other seamen mustering for the forenoon's work. Nobody was talking. They stood tense and irresolute. I was glad when at 8 o'clock the Buffer arrived on deck.

'Right, get fell in, lads,' he said, seeming to ignore the distant coast and the noise of the depth charges.

He detailed us off for the familiar tasks of cleaning and maintenance. Action stations might be sounded at any time: in the meantime we were working normal routine. Men went off to collect wire scrubbers, buckets, soap and tins of grease. There was an uncertainty and slowness in the way they moved. When the Buffer reached John Brooksbank and me at the end of the line, he seemed to have run out of ideas. The cold strictly limited the amount of work that could be done on the upper deck. He hesitated for a moment and then a thought struck him.

'Give the whaler and dinghy a good sweep out,' he said, 'but don't use water – it'll freeze. Check the plugs are in both boats whilst you're at it. Take the lashings off the Carley rafts; we might be needing the bloody things.'

Another depth charge exploding close astern seemed to give point to his words.

We mounted the ladder to the main deck and took off the raft lashings. When we had got into the boats, we found, as we expected, that they were in perfect trim. We checked that the plugs were in and that the critical disengaging gear had not frozen up. Then we left them. We sheltered from the searing wind in the lee of the fore-superstructure by the funnel. The noise of the boiler room fans masked the sound of the depth charges. We stared in silence at the small white wave crests and the ships appearing and vanishing in the snow showers. The coast of Russia was a frozen desert.

'There may not be any U-boats here,' I said to John Brooksbank. 'This could just be a barrage.'

John turned and looked at me sadly. It may have been the cold but there wasn't the usual light in his eyes. Snow flakes were settling on his cap.

'They're here all right,' he said. 'This is where they attacked the last convoy.'

After a few minutes I said, 'I wish we were closed up to action stations.'

John said dully, 'I don't. I hate action stations. It's bloody awful down there in the T.S. with fuel tanks all around and the hatches closed above you.'

I wished I had kept my mouth shut. The alarm buzzers would send me up onto the bridge but John would descend to the lowest part of the ship to the transmitting station. He wouldn't know what was happening – just hear the sound of explosions magnified by the sea. If the ship got hit, his chances of surviving would be extremely small. He would be lucky if he died instantly in the explosion. I tried to comfort him.

164

'We've been lucky so far on this trip. Perhaps there won't be an attack,' I said. 'We could be in harbour by teatime.'

Nothing more was said. Harbour and teatime were fifty lethal miles away. I felt the ship heeling as she again altered course. The roar of the fans increased. John moved away from the shelter of the superstructure to the guardrail where he could see ahead. He beckoned and shouted through the wind, 'Take a look at this lot, Henry.'

We were now steering on an opposite course to the long column of the merchant ships. These ships with their great bow waves were an unforgettable sight. Low in the water, crowded with deck cargoes, they steadfastly headed for Murmansk. Occasionally concealed by mist, the line seemed to go on forever. We were quite close to them and as we passed each ship, I had an overwhelming impression of their size. Their high bridges, boat decks and cargo handling derricks towered over us. Our corvette was small and tentative. They represented a formidable contribution to the winning of the war; they carried enough munitions to supply ten Red Army divisions. These great ships from the Clyde had an air of success about them. Now they were almost in safety. John Brooksbank and I stood at the guardrail in the cold wind watching the merchant ships passing. For a few minutes, we forgot the inconspicuous destroyers and corvettes and the sound of their depth charges. Briefly, I entertained a futile hope that there would be no attack on the convoy.

It was just after nine o'clock when our luck ran out. We crossed over the first line of U-boats. I didn't see the torpedo explosion. What I saw suddenly emerging from the swirling snow ahead was a merchant ship swung across the line of advance. She had stopped. She lay still and level as the other ships manoeuvred to avoid her. There was no smoke or fire. She lay dead in the water. She was going down. In spite of my long months at sea, I wasn't ready for this. There was a hollowness in my stomach. The grip of my hands on the guardrail tightened. Is this what sinking ships looked like? Is this how men die? The clouds shifted and sagged over the coast and white waves flashed like fangs on her steel hull. A seabird flew along the wave crests. The Barents Sea was cold and indifferent. Other escort ships were nearer to her than we were and a destroyer was approaching her. Then a snow squall hid her and I didn't see her again. She would sink quite quickly. Heavily laden with tanks, guns and lorries, she would have little spare buoyancy. I could imagine the rush of water through her smashed sides and bulkheads and her great holds filling. Would the crew be saved? She was a seven thousand ton United States ship, *Horace Bushnell*, and she filled me with sadness. Ironically, other lines from the poem with which I had comforted myself in the night seemed to match this moment too.

'. . . the pity of it all
    is all we compass if
    we watch disaster fall . . .'

A few minutes later, our ship altered course a hundred and eighty degrees to take up a screening position on the flank of the rear ships of the convoy. The sound of the boiler room intake fans diminished. We were now steaming in the same direction as the merchant ships. The convoy was proceeding to Murmansk. It was as if nothing had happened but my tight grip on the guardrail did not relax. I could see in my mind a vivid picture of *Lancaster Castle* seen through the Zeiss periscope of a hidden U-boat. I could see the cross wires centred on our waterline just below the mast and the calculating machines in the plotting table of the U-boat's control room allowing for deflection and range. This was a vision I often had when we were at sea but now there were U-boats down there and they had already selected one target. I looked around me. The Skipper was on the port bridge wing outlined against the sky, a still figure looking at the ships. Near him was the lookout searching ahead with binoculars for the sight of a periscope or a torpedo track. The torpedomen were aft on the quarterdeck firing single depth charges. The Oerlikon gunners were bulky shapes standing by their twin mountings. I felt the familiar rolling of the ship and throb of the propeller. Everything looked normal. Gradually, I loosened my hold of the guardrail. I became conscious of John Brooksbank standing beside me. He seemed to have been talking to me. I heard him say, '. . . and they'd be no bloody use anyway.'

He sounded angry.

'What wouldn't be any use?' I asked.

My voice sounded quite steady.

'Our aircraft,' he said, 'there aren't any. They probably haven't been able to take off and land on the carriers because of the visibility. They wouldn't be any help anyway. The U-boats aren't coming to the surface to be shot at.' He was silent for a moment then the anger went out of his voice and he said, with his usual fairness, 'It isn't really their fault.'

What was going on between the minefields was the maritime equivalent of house to house fighting. Aircraft were too sophisticated for this kind of affray. The brutal un-aimed violence of the depth charges dropping over the sterns of the escort ships and exploding in great geysers of sea and smoke represented a crude and simple method of defence.

At about ten o'clock I began to feel cold. I wanted to get out of the wind. The shock of seeing the torpedoed American freighter was still with me but nothing more seemed to be happening. I began to consider the trade-off of the discomfort of the upper deck against my fear of going below. Comfort won. I need only stay in the messdeck for a short while to warm up and surely the Skipper would sound off action stations if there was going to be any more shooting. John's face was pinched with cold and his eyes were anxious but he followed me as I walked aft towards the quarterdeck. The scene on the quarterdeck was purposeful and calm. The task of dropping single depth charges was not too onerous. The torpedomen were working as a well drilled team. It was an assembly line with the gut-shaking explosions as the end product. I envied them.

In the messdeck, seamen were waiting. The air was blue with cigarette smoke and smell of sweat. Action stations would be sounded any minute. In the meantime, there was nothing to do. Everyone was wearing lifebelts with the attached red lights. In spite of the frozen condensation on the steel plates, it was warm. It was full of noise – the crashing of the sea, the drone of the dynamos in the low power room and the depth charge explosions. Nobody was talking. Gordon Powell wet the tea. I poured myself a mug and warmed my hands on it. Gordon Powell sat down at the mess table with his attache case before him tidying his papers. Nicholson, the rum bos'un, was cleaning the rum jug. Simmons was counting bully beef tins. Jim Pickthall and young Scottie were sitting at the forward mess table. They were huddled together as if to comfort each other. MacLaughlan was tying a bowline around his waist. This would help if he had to be fished out of the sea. John Brooksbank lit a cigarette and offered his packet to me. He had forgotten I didn't smoke cigarettes. I took one and he lit it for me.

The mess was still our reassuring home but it had been transferred physically to alien arctic waters and shifted spiritually to a new dimension of anxiety. As I drew on my cigarette, I looked at the men around me. There always seemed to be two ways of regarding the crew of *Lancaster Castle*. One way was to see them as the world saw them and perhaps the way they really were – the tough crew of an ocean going corvette in one of the world's elite fighting services. The other way to see them was as they saw themselves, not when talking with girls ashore or writing to parents, but when they were alone with their thoughts as they were now. They were mostly ordinary young men quite frightened and trying not to show it. They were hoping to be spared the worst horrors of war and, above all, hoping not to die. Nobody wanted to get a crack at the enemy. Perhaps the fighter pilots on the carriers wanted to do this but no members of the crew of this ship wanted glory.

I didn't finish the cigarette. We heard the bosun's mate approaching. He came down the ladder trilling on his pipe and called, 'life belts are to be worn and are to be inflated.'

We had never had an order like this. I couldn't take it in at first. I looked at the bosun's mate in disbelief. He was a messenger from the skipper and his face was expressionless. The impact of the depth charges seemed to take on a new menace. I threw away my half smoked cigarette and felt a dryness in my mouth. Slowly a thought came to me for the first time – I might die. Up to this moment, I had in my heart believed that death only happened to other people. I could no longer sustain this illusion. Men fumblingly and automatically complied with the order. Their faces were blank. I sat at the bench with my elbows on the table.

At that moment I wanted more than anything to feel a sense of comradeship with the others. Strangely, they were cut off from me. They seemed to be just part of the fabric of the ship. I was fond of most of them. Simmons trying to keep some comfort in the mess, Gordon Powell with his correspondence course, even MacLaughlan with his rough efficiency. There were all the others too. I shared my life with them. Now they were unavailable. There came to me the slow realisation – you didn't share death. I felt alone in the crowded messdeck.

I was glad when a few minutes later the action station buzzers sounded loud and urgent through the loudspeakers. The mess was full of running men and the drumming of feet. I went up the ladders to the bridge, my face close to the heels of the man ahead.

Ron Teece was already in the plot cabinet when I entered. He smiled at me as I sat down in the corner by the telephone. He said, 'Brains of the ship, we're all right now.'

This was the first smile I had seen that day but his eyes weren't smiling. Then the Navigating Officer came in and sat down at the plotting table.

At action stations, I immediately felt better.

The ship was ready. All weapons were fully manned –

depth charges, Squid, Oerlikons and four inch gun. Asdic and radar would be operated by the most experienced and senior specialists. The Cox'n was at the wheel. We could hear through the voice pipe all stations reporting their readiness to the bridge and the guns closed up and cleared away. The ship was now at maximum effectiveness to deal out death and destruction. We often closed up to action stations. Today it was different. The sinking of the American freighter indicated that this time the enemy was there. A sense of tension and expectancy ran through the voice pipes and telephones but it was far more bearable than the passive waiting in the messdeck. I was still a rather scared individual but I was also third hand in the action plot – a unit in a fighting system. The ship was not afraid.

The Navigating Officer was fiddling with his parallel motion drawing instrument on the table with a pencil hopefully in his hand. He was waiting for information so he could draw triangles. The pinging of the asdic was loud and continuous, almost drowning the noise of the depth charges but there was no returning echo giving the solid sound of a submarine.

The minutes ticked by. Sometimes one of us would go out onto the bridge and stare into the wind. On the port side there were hills. The snow lay silky and white between the grey of the sky and the black of the water. There was a stranded ship on the shore. As far as you could see there were the ships of the convoy fading into the snow squalls, lost among the white promontories. There were no signs of the enemy. I went back into the plot saying, 'You can't see anything.'

We ran into the second line of U-boats at noon. I could hear the radio telephone on the bridge loudspeakers. I could not catch much of what was being said because of the noise of the asdic but I could hear the call signs.

'Cod fish, this is starch paste, starch paste, over.'

'Starch paste, this is Cod fish, over.'

The Senior Officer of the escort group in *Lapwing* ahead of the convoy was giving a lot of orders and we were altering course to comply. The realisation of what happened then came only gradually – separate pieces of a jig-saw that fitted together to make a picture of disaster. First the voice of the Senior Officer of the escort on the loudspeaker stopped in mid sentence. No more orders. Silence. Then the men on the bridge saw beyond the leading merchant ships black smoke in the sky above a snow storm. Then we heard a distant rumble of sound on the wind that was quite different from the noise of the depth charges. I did not understand what had happened. Then one of the officers shouted briefly into the plot.

'Pilot, *Lapwing*'s gone, tin-fished.'

There was an edge in his voice. The Navigator stopped fiddling with his instruments, his hands became still. Ron Teece looked at me with shocked eyes, his face suddenly pale. Then came once again the violent sound of our depth charges exploding astern which cut us off from each other.

I felt a sick surprise. My hands shook. I had been dismayed at the sinking of the *Horace Bushnell* but the fate of *Lapwing* was a horror in a different order of magnitude. Her crew were like us – 200 or so crowded in every compartment of the ship, closed up to guns, instruments and engines. I had experienced in my imagination what it would be like if we were torpedoed. I knew what was happening in *Lapwing*. First the mind numbing shock as the warhead of the torpedo exploded tearing everything apart. Steel and men would be shattered in smoke and blood. The ship would sink in a few minutes. The men on deck who had been remote from the explosion would have a chance of life. Some would die in the cold sea almost immediately. Others could swim to the liferafts and hold on to whatever debris floated off the sinking ship. The men below would have no chance at all. In the boiler room, engine room, magazines and transmitting station everyone would die. There would be the overwhelming in-rush of water and the smoke and the fire. Hatches would be jammed by the explosion and there would be no time. They would go down with the ship. The live and the dead would be imprisoned in a terminal darkness

– light, fire, life and hope quenched forever. Minutes after the destruction of the ship, the survivors on the surface of the sea would be rescued by other ships. What about the others on the floor of the shallow Barents Sea – short term survivors still alive in air pockets? My mind veered away from this last picture.

Ron looked at me with fear in his eyes. There was a sheen of sweat on his face. I could see his knuckles white as he gripped the edge of the plot table. Did I look like that? Death seemed quite close. I was glad I could not see what was happening in *Lapwing* behind the snow squalls.

Rapid alterations of course and speed suggested that the close escort ships were taking up new positions to close the gap in the defence. There was the voice of a new senior officer on the radio telephone. The asdic was searching through eighty degrees on the starboard side. The instruments clicked and hummed and the transmission sounded like iron hammers. The ratings in the asdic cabinets bent over their dials and intently listened for a returning echo.

The Navigating Officer was the first to speak. He said, 'I reckon we can cross *Lapwing* off.'

He got up from his seat and with his pencil reached over and put a line through the name of *Lapwing* on the call sign list. He made it seem that a ship which had been fully operational fifteen minutes ago had never existed at all. Ron's face showed surprise and distaste. The navigator resumed his seat. He pulled from his pocket a packet of cigarettes. He offered a fag to the leading seaman. It looked like a placatory gesture.

The minutes dragged. The convoy could be in safety in less than two hours but time seemed to go slowly. The U-boats were concentrated here and seemed invulnerable. My reaction to the loss of *Lapwing* had moved from near panic to a dull restless fear. Who will be next? I prayed.

I would have welcomed a sudden report of range and bearing of an echo from the asdic. This would have brought the action plot to life. Pencil lines would have directed the ship to an interception with an invisible enemy. We should be part of an attack system. It would have led to the dropping of a full pattern of depth charges on something; it might even be the U-boat that had torpedoed *Lapwing* but no such report came and we waited inactive and tense. My main impression was noise and the movement of the ship. The sound of the distant depth charges dropped by other corvettes was punctuated by the loud noise of our own charges exploding close astern of us shaking the ship. The ship heeled to steering orders, her rudder hard over bucking the slight swell. The radio telephone on the bridge loudspeaker jabbered unintelligibly and all the time I could hear the ceaseless pinging of the perfectly useless asdic.

Five officers and about fifty ratings were saved from *Lapwing* – only a quarter of her crew. She had been zig-zagging forty degrees either side of her mean course at a speed of seven and a half knots, screening ahead of the convoy. She had been torpedoed amidships on the starboard side four and a half miles north of Kildin Island. The death of a hundred and fifty men was small change in the brutal accountancy of war but it seemed to me at the time to be an appalling tragedy. It still does.

The coast was on three sides now. Soon the convoy would be entering the Kola Inlet. The U-boats would not be able to penetrate the Russian harbour defences. I was always glad to enter harbour after a long passage but this harbour represented life itself. The Navigating Officer went out onto the bridge to look around.

Ron Teece said, 'Just our luck to come all this way and then this mess.'

He thought for a moment and added, 'Thank God, there's land around us; somehow it makes it better.'

I said, 'Yes, it does,' but believed that it didn't make any difference at all but the thought had comforted him because he grinned and said,

'It's past dinner time and I want my rum.'

At two o'clock another merchant ship was torpedoed. The Navigator came back into the plot saying, 'I can see a cloud of smoke.'

Ron was looking doubtfully at his life belt.

He put in a few more puffs and I heard him muttering, 'Why did I ever join?'

The Navigating Officer nodded when I asked permission to go out onto the bridge.

Snow was falling lightly and there were little flurries of it unmelted in corners. The visibility was still poor but between snow storms I could see the torpedoed merchant ship. There was smoke coming out of her and she was going down by the stern. Fragments separated themselves from her. They were her life boats and a corvette was steaming towards them. It looked calm and ordered – a well rehearsed drama played before a back-cloth of the snowfields. It was hard to think about people, men dying and wounded. She was the 7,000 ton USS *Thomas Donaldson* and four of her crew were killed by the torpedo. Snow, smoke, noise and the killing cold of the sea – this was the face of war I saw that afternoon. I felt numbed but not because of the cold.

The *Donaldson* was our last loss.

Soon there was land in almost all directions. The merchant ships steaming in line ahead had now all entered the Kola Inlet. The water became calm and there were ice flows floating in it shaped like crazy paving. Two Russian patrol boats were threading through the flows like an expedition. The depth charging stopped and we followed the merchant ships, smelling the acrid fuel oil exhausts from their funnels. When land to the north hid the Barents Sea it was all over. We heard the First Lieutenant's voice on the loudspeakers, 'Secure action stations, Red Watch to cruising stations.'

I felt a heightened awareness. The copper voice pipes seemed to grow with a shimmering inner light. The drawing instruments were bright with brass and the dull glimmer of polished hardwood. I heard the wash of the bow wave. I felt a unity with the ship. Everything seemed to be existing strongly. I had a perception of the richness of life.

174

Ron Teece let the air out of his life belt and looked at me and grinned. The engine noise and the vibration of the ship diminished and the asdic pinging ceased. We tidied up the drawing instruments and left the plot cabinet. Then the fear ran out of me. We were entering the arctic port of Murmansk and in that moment it seemed to be the most beautiful place in the world. I saw the land, the ships and the water in a sharper focus than I had ever seen anything before. They were like life itself, fascinating and enduring. I was now on watch but as we were entering harbour, the Cox'n stayed at the wheel and I had time to look at Russia. In the wake of the merchant ships, destroyers and corvettes were slowly steaming south in the broad inlet. Snow covered hills stretched away on all sides broken by stands of birch trees in dark contrast. The wind was only ruffling the smooth water and ice lay in grey bands. Ahead of us I could see a signal station and a battleship alongside a jetty wearing a red flag on her jackstaff. Beyond her there was a line of huts on the summit of a hill. Roads cut through the snow and I could see lorries moving like black specks. Astern of us in the north, the sky was pale yellow and for a short time, our ships were lit by level sunshine. I suppose it was really a cold and barren land but I didn't see it like that on that afternoon. Russia to me looked magnificent.

We went alongside an oiler lying at anchor off Rosta, the destroyer harbour north of Murmansk. When we tied up the Skipper said down the wheelhouse voice pipe, 'Finished with main engines,' and the engine room telegraph clanged.

For the first time in ten days, silence spread through the ship and everything stopped rattling. Red Watch fell out and I went below. Somebody had opened the deadlights over the port holes and a wavering daylight lit the mess. The well known faces of the seamen in No. 6 Mess looked different, as if I had been to a foreign country and hadn't seen them for a very long time. Men were laughing and joking, pouring out tea, eating bully beef sandwiches and drinking rum. They were being very nice to each

175

other. They had been under some sort of stress for ten days and this had intensified in the last six hours but now it was over and everything was okay. Quite a lot of British and American sailors had died today but thinking about that would come later. In the meantime, relief and happiness united them and they could talk to each other about their experiences and impressions. I couldn't talk. I sat at the mess table and drank tea and thought, 'I'm alive, I'm alive' and hoped I would always remember that feeling.

I heard a seaman say, 'How did you feel?'

Another answered, perhaps for all of us, 'Like everyone else, all pee'd up.'

John Brooksbank said, 'It was pretty awful. I saw damn all and I wanted to go to the heads all the time.' His face looked drawn.

There was some talk about what had actually happened. We didn't know how many U-boats had been involved but for some reason we thought it was six and they sustained no losses. In fact there had been thirteen. Perhaps it was lucky for us that the Germans didn't know how bad the asdic conditions were or they might have been bolder and sunk more ships.

After supper, I joined a working party loading supplies from the oiler. These were to be off-loaded next day onto the crippled destroyer *Cassandra* alongside the jetty. *Cassandra* had had her bows blown off in a previous convoy action but many of her crew were still on board her. It was night now but the sky was full of stars. The deck lights were on as we man-handled the heavy boxes and crates. Over the smooth water I could see the flashing signals of ships and the milky gleam of a lorry's headlights on the hills. I was soon sweating in the cold dry air and enjoying the hard work. Before midnight I noticed a faint radiance in the sky like distant searchlights and gradually the whole sky lit up – shimmering curtains of fire. Men stopped working and looked up in wonder. We had often seen the Aurora but always pale and mysterious in the north. Here it covered the whole sky in gold, orange and red, flickering and flashing.

At about 1 o'clock all the stores were on board. We could turn in. I felt almost reluctant to leave that magical vision of the Aurora, the quiet water and the glimmering snow but I was tired. As we went below, sub lieutenant LaTouche served whisky to the working party. We drank it neat from wardroom glasses. It was the end of the 20th March 1945 and I had never needed a drink more.

In the dimly lit mess-deck, I slung my hammock next to leading seaman Higginbottom's. He was still awake. I could feel the warmth of the whisky combining with fatigue in my limbs. I was very drowsy. As I swung into my hammock I said, 'Hooky, thank God today's over.'

Higginbottom said, 'Worst bloody day I can remember.' His voice was muffled by his blanket. He pushed the blanket aside and looked at me over the edge of his hammock. 'We're the lucky ones, Henry.' There was sadness in his voice.

Most of the working party had not yet turned in and were chatting quietly and laughing. Before I slept, I heard Higginbottom say, 'Pipe down lads,' and then he added, 'you know, you bastards ought to think a few minutes about your mates in the sloop.'

There was a complete hush. The silence was absolute. It seemed to go on for a long time. It was the nearest we could get to a prayer for the men of HMS *Lapwing*.

Chapter Twelve

Five miles into the Kola Inlet scattered clumps of trees became a continuous forest close on *Callisto*'s starboard side. The trees were small but unexpected after the bare coasts of the Barents Sea. They covered the low hills and came down to the shore. To port ships of all kinds were homeward, or outward bound. Shadows of clouds moved slowly across the calm silvery water.

Had I really been here before? A sentence had, until now, always guided my life. Never go back. What had made me break my rule and bring me again to this fateful place?

I reflected for a moment. It was because of Russia that I had broken my rule. The vision of the grey ships in the Arctic might have faded but for forty years there had been the Cold War. The Soviet Union had always been in the news. It had been presented as the fearful super power capable of unleashing revolution and aggressive war, a potential enemy. I had to reconcile this with the knowledge that I had fought for the Russians and seen their shattered home land.

'They don't want war,' I had said in many outnumbered

political arguments. I had invested something of myself in the Soviet Union, and somehow I trusted it. *Callisto*'s voyage was not really going back into the past. It was prompted by curiosity about what the Russians who I had defended were really like now. It was also an act of faith for the future. I hoped the Russians would see it that way.

I sat watchfully in the cockpit as Ana steered. Soon we would be off Tyuva bay and to the rendezvous with the pilot. What happened after that would be out of my hands.

Alice called up from the chart table, 'We're about on position now,' and came up the ladder to look. Ana knocked back the throttle to neutral. It was five minutes to five o'clock, our estimated time of arrival. *Callisto* slowed and lay still. Now what? I wondered. With the mains'l set we could be seen from a long way off. Even with the movement of many vessels in the Kola Inlet we would show up clearly against the wooded shore. Murmansk lay fifteen miles away to the south still invisible. Ana's eyes were searching in that direction.

There was no sign of the pilot boat. 'Perhaps they've forgotten us,' she said. She looked around at the unbroken forest and the foreign ships. 'It feels a bit lonely. What shall we do if they don't come?'

'We could anchor,' I said, 'and wait.' My mind as usual was full of contingency plans. 'Perhaps we could call up one of the ships on the VHF and ask them to radio to the port authorities. Anyway let's not do anything for a bit.'

I didn't know what the Russians were like. Perhaps 1700 hours to them meant anytime in the evening. They might have thought we were a nuisance with our telexes and cables and weren't bothering very much. I fumbled in my pocket for my pipe and tobacco.

Supposing they didn't come? Long hours stretched ahead of me in nail biting anti-climax. We could anchor and drink endless cups of tea neglected and alone. I thought of the long hopeful passage from Bergen. Sandy and I would both feel that our flawed arrangements had let the others down. We didn't know any Russians – we had come here trusting in brief and tenuous communications. My attempts to light my pipe didn't seem to be working but it gave me something to do with my hands.

Suddenly Alice shouted, 'I can see a boat. It's coming towards us.'

We all looked in the direction she pointed. It was a big motor boat travelling fast with a white bone in its teeth. I could just see the red and white pilot flag at her yardarm. I looked at my watch: it was one minute to five. *Callisto* had sailed nearly two thousand miles towards Russia and now Russia was coming to meet her. The pilot boat was dead on schedule.

'I don't believe this,' Ana said. She was still holding the tiller and I could see the relief in her eyes.

'Out fenders, on the port side.' My mind suddenly concentrated on how you took a pilot on board. I had never done it before.

As the motor boat approached I could see that she was twice the size of *Callisto*. She would be used to going alongside merchant ships. I was fearful for our frail hull. I had the Russian words in my head for 'please stop your engine'. I needn't have bothered: the Russian seamen knew what they were doing. The pilot boat was slowing down. Her bow wave diminished. Fifty yards from us she went astern on her engines and lay still and unthreatening. Three men on her deck were waving and grinning.

'Take her alongside, Ana,' I said, 'it's just like going alongside a quay.' Ana moved the throttle lever to slow revs. 'The rest of you, down mains'l.'

With an audience of Russian sailors there was a slight swagger in the way the crew faultlessly lowered and furled the big sail.

Motoring slowly ahead Ana stopped the yacht with the fenders lightly touching the steel side of the pilot boat. The pilot carrying his briefcase and wearing a thin raincoat stepped lightly down onto our deck. We fended off, Ana put the motor in gear and we were clear. The pilot was young and confident but he looked uneasily at our tiller steering. He was used to the wheels of big ships. He shook his head and left Ana at the helm.

'Priamo,' he said hopefully and smiled. Ana looked at me.

'Straight on,' I translated.

Then he said, 'Naprava' – to starboard. We could manage just enough of the language.

In hesitant Russian I told him we had a draft of 1.5 metres and could motor at six knots. I said 'shiest' – six. I couldn't recall the Russian word for knots but he nodded. Knots are an international measure of speed.

The pilot stared ahead avoiding unseen shallows and other ships. We were just another professional job to him but surely such care and attention deserved a more important ship. I felt rather guilty. We had just come here for fun.

Ana said, 'Pass up an oilskin for Andrey.' They were already on first name terms. Lesley went below and fetched the pilot an oilskin jacket. His raincoat was more suitable for a warm wheelhouse than the exposed cockpit of a yacht. I was less worried about him, he was being looked after.

Motoring against the tide it would be hours before we reached Murmansk. I went below into the warm saloon; for the first time since 4th of June I was not in charge. Sandy had the contents of Andrey's briefcase spread on the table – customs and health declarations, twelve forms to fill in.

'It all worked,' she said raising her voice against the noise of the engine. 'They were on time, they really did want us to come.' She was laughing but there were tears glistening in her eyes. I had sailed the ship but she had made the administrative arrangements that made the cruise possible. It was a moment of triumph for her. I thought of all her telephone calls, her telexes, her letters asking for permission for a private yacht to enter Murmansk. I sat down beside her and put my arm round her shoulders. I could feel her trembling through her thick woollen jerseys. She had believed in the Russians.

She had a tear stained face and disordered fair hair. I felt a great tenderness towards her.

'It was a hell of a responsibility,' she said, wiping her eyes and laughing at herself. She handed back my handkerchief.

'Tell Lesley and Alice to stop sightseeing and come down to help me fill in these bloody forms. Tell everybody I want their passports.'

She was still clearing our path through the undergrowth of bureaucracy.

In the cockpit Andrey was looking more relaxed. He gave his orders calmly to Ashley who was now steering. We weren't a bulk carrier or a factory fishing ship but he was taking us just as seriously.

We were approaching a frigate of the Northern Fleet anchored in the channel. I could see missile launchers, guns and a mast, a Christmas tree of secret antennae. Her crew in sailor's uniform were working on deck. Out of the corner of my eye I noticed Ana unfastening the case of her camera. She saw my glance and hesitated, then turned to the pilot showing him her camera.

'Da,' he said with a grin. 'Okay.'

Ana photographed a major unit of the Soviet navy. The sailors on deck lined her guardrail to wave at the British yacht.

Ten minutes later Andrey altered course to clear the path of an outward bound merchant ship. She passed quite close and I could read her name in the Cyrillic alphabet, *Theodore Nette*. I knew that name. It was the title of a poem by a revolutionary poet. I addressed the pilot and chanced my Russian, 'Poetry' I said 'by Mayakovsky.' He nodded vigorously and spoke to me rapidly. I understood some of what he said. Mayakovsky had shot himself in 1930 because he could no longer live in Stalin's dictatorship. It was surprising, but it seemed wholly appropriate, that the first conversation I had ever had with a Russian was about poetry. Perhaps he was surprised too that an Englishman knew some Russian poetry.

I reflected on the poem. There was something ironic about it in the Soviet Union of 1990, already experiencing the rumblings of nationalism. Theodore Nette had been a communist hero of the Civil War. He was a Latvian and he had died outnumbered in a gun fight defending dispatches he was taking to Moscow by train.

> 'For that -
>   we're crucified
>   and bullets fly:
> that the world shall be
>   one human commonwealth,
> without any Russia
>   without any Latvia.'

We had not yet set foot on Russian soil yet I was already getting mixed up with its paradoxes and contradictory ideals.

At half past seven I took over steering. The laminated hardwood tiller felt comforting in my hand. I would keep an open mind about this country.

As I steered in response to the pilot's orders I felt calm. Flashes of sunshine lit low birch clad hills on the port side. Murmansk began to emerge between the trees sprawling along the Kola Inlet – lines of quays, ships and cranes. Behind them was a backcloth of high rise apartments in long terraces on the hills. When the sun caught the buildings they were white, blue and yellow in the clear arctic light. They looked like fairy palaces. I hadn't known what to expect. When I had been here last it had been a city ruined by bombs – just quays and a railhead. The sirens of freight trains had sounded across the snow as they started on their long journey south to Kandalaksha, Leningrad and Moscow loaded with the cargoes from the convoy. Here it still was, but all brave and new in its wild arctic setting. As more and more of it stretched before us along the shore I felt a sense of awe. Into my mind came lines from another poem.

'. . . Therefore I have sailed the seas and come
To the holy city of Byzantium.'

The city in the poem hadn't been a real one; it had been a metaphor, an idea. Murmansk was a real city and certainly not holy, but in the minds of many Russians, and yes, many British too, it was also an idea. *Callisto* had sailed real seas, too, not metaphorical ones. Nevertheless those lines from W. B. Yeats' great poem had sprung to mind. They would do to express my wonder and relief.

'Nyalyeva,' Andrey said. I altered course to port. It was nine o'clock. I was hemmed in by ships and quays. Beyond the green dome of the railway station great buildings shone in the low sun. There was an icebreaker in a floating dry dock. The Norwegian flag flew from the stern of a ferry ship. I gripped the tiller hard. We were in the city centre of a great port. I moved back the throttle and looked at Andrey. I wanted to go more slowly.

'Okay,' he said and pointed to a floating pontoon projecting from a quay. It seemed to be surrounded by the superstructures of ships, but there would be space for us. There were people standing on it.

I was back in charge, now I knew where we were going. Forget the strange sights around you, don't botch this.

'Fenders on the port side – mooring lines on deck.'

I put the engine in neutral lining *Callisto* up for the pontoon. The crew were all ready with mooring lines correctly cleated and led under the guard rails. Alice and Ashley were standing amidships with lines coiled in their hands.

Slow ahead, then astern on the motor, then neutral. The yacht lay stopped against the pontoon. Alice and Ashley jumped off and walked for'ard and aft to secure the moorings.

'Turn off the motor,' I said to Ana. *Callisto* had arrived.

The pilot took off the oilskin jacket and snapped the fastening of his briefcase. He had been concentrating for four hours. I thanked him for his good services. 'Skolka?' I asked.

He grinned and shook his head. There was nothing to pay.

He shook hands all round and stepped over the side.

I had thought the people on the pontoon were there to catch a ferry but they were waiting for us. We were wearing the yellow Q flag which indicated we were a foreign vessel needing customs clearance. Our first visitors were two very young officers in smart brown uniforms. They went below to the saloon looking serious. Customs clearance, however, was a brief formality. In a minute they were laughing and trying hard not to do so as my crew photographed them. It wasn't a bit like the sometimes grisly experience of clearing customs at Ramsgate after a passage from Boulogne.

When they left Alice lowered the Q flag and the yacht seemed to fill up with people. The first was Vladimir Zadorin, a young man speaking perfect English, agent of the Murmansk Shipping Company. Did we need anything? Food, diesel, propane, medical attention? Here was the Company's phone number and radio frequency. We could ask for any help we needed night or day. He was followed by Sergei Melinkov, assistant chairman of the City Soviet and Vassili Tonkih, chairman of the war Veterans Committee with his two colleagues Mikhail Kemerov and Nicholai Graznik. The saloon seemed very full. Everybody talked and Sergei translated. It didn't seem to matter that all we had to drink was tea. I don't remember what we talked about. We were given a programme of events and visits already arranged for us. There would be showers next morning followed by a meeting with Nikolai Berezhnoi, Mayor of Murmansk, at the Town Hall. It looked as if the next few days were going to be as challenging as sailing.

Vassili looked lean and tough, surely too young to be a war veteran. He wore a raffish black beret and medal ribbons. He subjected the women members of the crew to rapid Russian gallantries and massive charm. I could see them warming to him. There seemed to be an instant rapport between these soldiers of a long-ago war and my crew to whom it was only a story.

I sat back on the cushions exhaustedly. Listening to the

conversation I began to realise that *Callisto*'s voyage was not seen by the Russians as a slightly extended summer cruise but a mission of friendship from Britain. The yacht that had come so far to visit them was a symbol of goodwill and peace. She was evidence too of the new open frontiers. That first night in Russia I was quite close to tears.

They went at midnight. I waved goodbye from the cockpit. Before I went below to sleep I sat down for a moment and thought about *Callisto*. She lay quietly at her mooring dwarfed by the quays and ships of Murmansk.

She was trim and shining in the midnight sun. I ran my hand along the smooth glassfibre of her hull. She seemed to be at peace in Russia.

Bright sunshine lit the conference room in the modestly ornate Town Hall. There were pictures of Murmansk on the wood pan-elled walls and a portrait of Lenin. We were greeted warmly by Nikolai Berezhnoi the Chairman of the City Council. We were private people unsponsored and representing nobody but we were made to feel like honoured guests of the city. After hand shaking and introductions we sat down at a long table. Nikolai had with him his assistant, Sergei Melinkov, who we already knew and Galena, an interpreter. I was glad to see at the other end of the table Vassili and the ex-servicemen who had been with us last night. Natasha Galliayva, an English teacher from School 51, to whom we had spoken on the 'phone from England, was also there. She looked as pretty as her soft voice talking in English had suggested.

Nikolai Berezhnoi was tall with dark hair and thick eye brows. He looked as if he were in his early forties and had a mag-netic charm. As he talked about Murmansk I could sense the pride in this voice.

He pointed to a map on the wall. 'It's twenty five kilome-tres long and is still growing. We can't spread out to the east away from the Kola Inlet because of the hills. The hills aren't very high but the climate is more severe higher up.'

Indicating a photograph with his hand he said, 'This is the ferry port where your yacht lies. Southwards is the fishing port with the fish processing plants. To the north, as you saw coming in, is the commercial port. The Northern Fleet base is 12 Km north of the city at Severemursk.' He looked at me. 'You will remember it as Vaenga.'

My crew listened intently, their eyes moving from the Mayor speaking in Russian to Galena speaking in English.

I tried hard to concentrate. We had been wakened very early in the morning by Vassili who had taken us all to his flat. The heating system had managed six baths and his wife, Rosa, had prepared a splendid breakfast. He had got us all to the Town Hall on time. Murmansk had been just a blurred vision of sunny streets, lilac trees and trolley buses, but the crew of *Callisto* had been transformed. As I looked around the table I wondered who were these beautiful well dressed women wearing summer frocks? Surely they weren't the oilskin clad crew who had sailed the Atlantic and Barents Sea? Even Ashley was wearing a tie. What a marvellous improvement, I thought. I felt as proud of them as Nikolai was of his great city.

I think what impressed me most about the Mayor's talk was its admission of difficulties and its absence of propaganda. There were failures in house construction, the provision of energy to keep the city working in winter, the supply of food – nothing grew in the region – and the psychological problems of living through the long polar night. The City needed somewhere where people could walk along the shore of the Kola Inlet and enjoy the view but couldn't afford it.

'But it works,' he said, 'and it's the world's biggest city in the arctic.'

When he had finished I thanked him for his welcome and his talk.

'Nikolai Sergeievitch,' I said formally, 'I can remember what your city was like in the Great Patriotic War. It had been almost destroyed. You have totally rebuilt it.'

Nikolai said, 'Our fathers and grandfathers defended it for four years against the fascist armies. The Government made us a Hero City like Leningrad and Moscow.' He paused and looked at me. 'You represent a country that helped us, we feel a deep gratitude.' I knew that he meant it.

The war veteran Mikhail Kemerov was sitting beside Vassili. I could see silent tears running down his face. Perhaps he was remembering a time when all seemed lost for Russia and the convoys came.

We walked out into the sunlit street. The heat shimmered. I was grateful for the transparent shade of the birch trees. My crew walked ahead surrounded by students from School 51. As we had left the Town Hall Natasha Galliayva had introduced us to some of her senior pupils waiting for us in the foyer.

'They want to practise their English,' she had said, 'and they will show you round, help you to get currency, and take you shopping.' They had greeted us with laughter and a lot of hand-shaking.

I walked by myself. There were too many new impressions and half of me was still with *Callisto* in the empty sea. I had not adjusted to the crowds, the traffic and the heat. I ought to have been chatting to my crew and the students. Instead I lagged behind thinking of Mikhail's tears. Now that we had left him and his friends I felt about two generations older than everybody else. It was alright being the skipper of a modern yacht in another country but it wasn't so much fun being a visitor from another time. I narrowed my eyes against the dazzle of the light and felt lonely.

'Why do you walk alone?' A young girl had caught me up with light footsteps and was walking beside me. There was gentle concern in her question. She had long dark hair and a troubled expression and was, I discovered later, seventeen years old. At that moment I thought she was the most beautiful girl I had ever seen. We stopped walking. She looked at me with big enquiring eyes.

'I am Natasha Vanyushkina from the school and I think we should talk.'

I was dumbly collecting my thoughts. I was about to say something about the weather when she asked a question.

'What does it feel like coming back to Murmansk?'

As an Englishman I find it difficult to describe my feeling about important things, especially in a sudden encounter. She waited for my reply looking up at me intently. She really wanted to know.

'It's absolutely marvellous,' I said, 'but I'm a bit over-whelmed by our welcome.' She nodded.

'What was Murmansk like when you were here with the convoys?'

'Not so good,' I said and laughed and told her an impression of my one day ashore.

'What do you feel about the Russians you have met so far?'

I was beginning to get the hang of this kind of conversation.

'They are exactly like the people in the novels of Turgenev, Dostoevsky and Tolstoy.'

Natasha's face lit up. I hadn't meant it to be a compliment but to hear an Englishman equating the Russian people of today with their own great literature must have been heart warming.

We walked slowly back to the yacht talking about books. I was not feeling lonely any more. Natasha's reading of English literature was more extensive than most English people of her age. I was glad that I could keep up with her in my knowledge of the classics of Russia.

We crossed the railway lines by the high footbridge. Natasha said, 'I've learnt today that our two countries which are so far away share a common culture.'

From the bridge I could see the ferry quays with *Callisto* moored to the pontoon; beyond that the ships at anchor in the blue harbour; then the forest tundra on the western shore. It was a foreign land but connected to Britain by books and ships.

'I'm beginning to feel at home here,' I said. Natasha looked pleased.

'I'll have to go now,' she said. 'I'll come to the yacht later. You may need an interpreter and I want to talk more with you and also with your brave crew.'

We had only known each other for half an hour but we were firm friends. In England it would have taken three months and about five hundred cups of tea.

In early July the lilac flowers were coming out. Mountain ash and birch trees line every street and fill the squares of the city. The grass grows tall and unmown. The forest tundra runs through the streets. Beyond the city limits the same small trees stretch in unbroken forest for hundreds of miles: the home of reindeer herdsmen, wolves and bears.

I had become a tourist. The yacht was full of young people talking English and Russian and drinking tea. I had taken off my tie and jacket and stuffed my guide book in my hip pocket. I went ashore by myself to see Murmansk.

It was less than fifteen minutes walk to the city centre. The Lenin Prospect could be the main street of any big town in Europe. It is wide and flanked by six and seven storey buildings. They have vaguely classical facades of brightly painted stucco. The street runs north and south; I walked on the shady side. The streets that intersect the Lenin Prospect at right angles end in the green hills in one direction and the blue waters of the harbour on the other. In its brief summer there was a feeling of vitality in the air. The streets were thronging with people, many of them carrying flowers, flown in from the south and sold at pavement stalls. Pink and blue flags were flying for the annual Fishermen's Festival. There were not many children; most have gone for their long holidays in the south: part of the life style of the arctic. As elsewhere in Russia there was not much to buy in the shops but after weeks in Norway it was nice to know that we could at least afford what there was.

Constitution Square is at the north end of the Lenin

Prospect: trolley buses, trees, wild grass and streets radiating in all directions. It is dominated by the only really high building – the sixteen storey Hotel Arctica. I rather liked it, a tall plain tower marking the city centre and glittering in the sun.

On that first afternoon I didn't walk very far: I was still tired. The air was invigorating but it was hot in the sunshine. I was content just to get the feel of the place.

Murmansk is built where no city ought to be. It owes its position to two accidents of geography. One is the superb natural harbour of the Kola Inlet and the other is that it is ice free in winter. The Gulf Stream that washes the coast of Britain and Norway extends a finger into the Barents Sea. The Baltic ports like Leningrad 700 miles to the south all freeze in the winter. Murmansk, far more than Peter the Great's city, is Russia's window to the west – open winter and summer. For all that, it is still bitterly cold in winter as I remembered from my previous visit but far worse than the cold is the darkness. The polar night lasts for fifty two days: from 20th November to 16th January the sun does not rise at all. Not many people could stand it. The busy streets I walked through were full of the people who could. They lived in a great isolated city on the frontier in the arctic wilderness of the Kola peninsula, as far from Moscow as they were from the Shetland Islands. As my short walk had shown me they did it too with some style; Murmansk did not look like a frontier town.

I idled for a few minutes by the broad entrance steps of the Arctica watching the sparse traffic, the many people strolling in Constitution Square and the bright flags for the Festival. At intervals Volvo buses would discharge parties of Norwegians to check in at the city's only international hotel. Small boys hopefully tried to sell them badges which said 'Murmansk – hero city'. They weren't beggars, but free market operators. Later I bought a badge for myself: it was very good value for the money asked.

It was time to return to the yacht. I walked slowly down the hill towards the railway and the ferry terminal. Flower stalls and ice cream booths were bright colours in the shade of the trees.

Beyond the green dome of the station were the cranes and masts of ships and the blue water of the Kola Inlet. Away from the central square I was the only tourist. There was a feeling of relaxed festivity in the sunny afternoon but it was entirely a Russian occasion.

As I crossed the railway by the long footbridge I reflected on the short history of Murmansk. The railway had been built through marshes and forests and was completed in 1916 during the First World War. It linked the newly constructed port to Petrograd and the Russian railway system. Thereafter it had been used to deliver British and French armaments to the Russian army. In 1917 it had a population of 30,000. For a while it had been occupied by the British during the war of intervention that followed the Russian Revolution. This had been one of Britain's more inglorious and illegal military operations and her forces had been driven out by a combination of the new Red Army and lack of enthusiasm by the British people for the fight against the new republic. Between the wars Murmansk was developed into one of Russia's biggest ports and the centre of the Atlantic and arctic fisheries. It had also become an important naval base. In the Second World War it was once again of major strategic importance. The German armies advancing from Finland had tried to capture it marching along the coast. They had got to within eighty kilometres in 1941 but the Russian defences held firm. The city, however, was ruined by bombing. The tenacious defence of the hero-city had been matched by the fight of the Royal Navy. It had brought in the convoys and went on doing so year after year in a dogged and never ending campaign. As far as the Russians were concerned this had a hundred times made amends for the intervention in the First World War.

I had enjoyed seeing the sights but when I got back to the yacht it was apparent that she was one of them. There was a continual procession of visitors. Our arrival had been reported in the papers and with her tall mast and red ensign *Callisto* looked unusual. The crew were at work making tea, shaking hands, and showing people around. There was no sense of invasion. Our visitors stood on the pontoon waiting to be invited on board holding flowers, or small tourist flags as presents for the yacht.

Looking around they would say in surprise, 'You have come all this way to see us in this small ship!' and then, 'We hear your captain was with the convoys.'

Katia drank a glass of Georgian tea admiring the comfort of the saloon. She was like many of the women here – slim and well dressed. Her husband was a fisherman.

'How much does it cost?' she asked in her uncertain English. I did a quick sum and was alarmed by the result.

'Half a million roubles.'

It is easy enough to go sailing in the Soviet Union but all yachts are owned by clubs. There is no individual ownership of such expensive equipment. Suddenly I remembered my partner, Roy Sowden, who shares the cost of the yacht.

'She's owned by a co-operative,' I said. Katia nodded understandingly.

Natasha Vanyushkina and one or two of her friends were acting as interpreters on deck. When she came briefly down into the saloon I thanked her for her help.

'I hope you don't mind so many visitors,' she said. 'Your arrival here means so much to them. Most of them have never met English people before and Ashley and the girls are being so kind.' She sat quietly for a moment at the saloon table. It was a chance for me to add to my quick impressions of Murmansk. I had not yet been here twenty four hours.

'What's it like living here, Natasha?'

I had heard how dissatisfied the Russians were with their own country. She thought for a minute before answering. She said slowly, 'I travel a lot. I go with my parents to the south each year and I know Leningrad quite well. I have spent some time in Copenhagen which is a fine city.' She paused and smiled. 'I am always glad to get back to Murmansk. I wouldn't want to live anywhere else.'

In the evening *Callisto*'s crew went to see the Gorki ballet which was visiting the town. Natasha Galliayva, the teacher from School 51, had arranged good seats at short notice. I elected to stay on board. Architecture, ships, books and people filled my mind: there didn't seem room for ballet. I watched the normally agile girls stepping gingerly off the yacht in skirts and high heels.

Loudspeakers on the quay announced the arrival of ferries. *Callisto* rocked gently in their wash. Sometimes there was music. I sat quietly in the saloon littered with hurriedly discarded clothes enjoying being by myself. It wouldn't last long I thought; the others would soon be back from the ballet probably bringing their new Russian friends. Nobody seemed to need much sleep in the never ending summer daylight.

The tour of the city started quite early in the morning. Vassili, Nicholai and Mikhail were already in the mini bus when we boarded it by the Hotel Arctica. Galena, the interpreter from the City Council, was in charge and Natasha Galliayva assisted her. I sat next to Vassili. He was wearing his black beret and not bothering with interpreters. He had made up his mind that I could understand Russian so he gave me his commentary on the buildings and monuments we saw in his own words. Because of his gestures and facial expressions as well as his frequent repetitions surprisingly I understood quite a lot of what he said. He seemed to believe that language could not possibly separate men who had fought together in the Great Patriotic War. He had made me into an honorary Russian.

As the streets and squares of the city opened before us I found that I recognised nothing. I had walked around the town on the evening of 21 March 1945 with the heightened perception of a sailor in from the sea. I remembered everything about that visit but nothing I saw from the bus corresponded to this memory.

The city had been in ruins but surely something would have been familiar today. Had I really been here before? Was this the same city I remembered? Then I had an alarming thought – perhaps the twenty one year old sailor had not really been me at all.

As I gazed out of the window of the mini bus hoping to recognise a building or a street I realised I was searching for my self. I stopped listening to Galena and Vassili. I felt a tightening in my chest. Who was I?

On the north side of the city centre the road signs pointed to Severemorsk. That was the base of the Soviet Northern Fleet which had once been called Vaenga. To the south of that was Rosta where the British destroyers and corvettes had laid along-side the quays. Perhaps that name had gone too, but I must have come this way before. The bus turned sharply left as the road crossed the railway line. Something caught my attention. I recog-nised the level crossing. The city of memory and the real city came together at a point where road and rail intersected. I felt a surge of relief: I really had been here and the young sailor really had been me. Like reading a page of a long lost diary I instantly recalled the scene.

On that afternoon's shore leave from the ship Ken Buckler and I had got down here from the Ford lorry that had given us a lift from Rosta. It had been bitterly cold on the open platform of the speeding lorry and perhaps the relief of stopping here had etched the level crossing on my memory.

We had explored the city in the gathering darkness. Snow was piled in great heaps on the pavements. There were many empty spaces where there had once been buildings. Those that remained were badly damaged. The people in the streets had all been in a hurry as if they were trying to get out of the cold. Occasionally a lorry passed throwing up fountains of snow.

We had ended up at the Intourist Club. There was an armed sentry outside. It was full of cigarette smoke and American and British seamen – mainly from the merchant ships. There were also pretty girls who were interpreters and waitresses. They weren't the sort of girls that you could pick up but they would play chess and tell you the history of Murmansk. Ken and I settled for vodka and Russian tea. It was all we wanted after the cold streets.

After the third glass Ken had said, 'They'll be waiting for

us outside, you know.' He was looking at me with worried eyes fumbling with his vodka glass. He was suspicious of foreigners, especially socialist foreigners.

'Of course they won't be,' I said. 'They seem all very friendly.'

He gave me a steady look. 'Not the Russians, Henry. I mean the German U-boats. They can stay at sea for months. They know we've got to come out. They'll just hang around outside the Kola Inlet. By this time they must know that our asdic is perfectly useless.'

I hadn't wanted to think about the convoy home. I took a gulp of vodka. The Intourist Club looked rather insubstantial. In my imagination the warm room was full of the thundering of depth charges and the long lines of ships. That vision had rather spoilt my one evening in Murmansk. Thankfully the memory faded and I was back in today's world.

Galena was saying, 'These are new apartment blocks. They are not very well built but much better than the older ones built soon after the war. It is hard to build in this climate.'

I could listen to her with interest now. I knew where I was and above all, who I was. The skipper of *Callisto* who had sailed to Murmansk was still the young seaman who had anxiously explored the city forty five years before. I hadn't changed all that much but it was reassuring to meet the young man again. I felt a strengthening of my own identity.

I listened to Galena. Everything about Murmansk was fine by me. I even began asking Vassili questions in Russian.

The ice breakers are the showpieces of Murmansk. Natasha Galliayva took me to see the *Rassia* which was being refitted. The chauffeur driven car threaded its way between crates of equipment and bumped over the railway lines on the quayside. The *Rassia* was a very large ship; her white superstructure hung over us like a ten storey block of flats. I was taken for a tour of the ship. An officer showed me the searchlight controls on the bridge. He explained, 'We work in the polar night. We see the white bears. They are not really white but cream coloured. In the searchlights they show up clearly against the ice.'

Afterwards we had tea and cognac with the captain. 'Ice is strong in compression but weak in tension. We drive up onto it and break it downwards.' He described how the ice breakers kept the sea lanes open along the Siberian coast. When he heard that our home port was Whitby he said, 'Ah, James Cook, the greatest English sailor.' He paused, perhaps reflecting that the British hero was Nelson. 'Cook was a man of peace.'

He treated me as an equal and called me 'captain' because my small yacht had also sailed in the Arctic Ocean

I liked this great lonely ship and I liked her skipper. When we said goodbye on the gangway he kissed me on the cheek.

As we walked back to the car Natasha said, 'I think Anatoli is a very nice man.' She smiled at me. 'He liked you, too. He found you . . .' and she stopped. 'There isn't an English word. The word in Russian is simpatichniy.'

On our second day in harbour Alla Sharapova, another English teacher, arranged a party for us in her flat. She had visited the yacht several times, always accompanied by a friendly group of students. Now she wanted the crew of *Callisto* to meet more of her friends and relatives. The apartment was small and lacked certain amenities but the critical eye of an architect was instantly overwhelmed by the sense of occasion. This was the famous Russian hospitality I had read about. We sat round low tables drinking vodka and homemade cranberry water and eating salads, cold meat, and smoked fish. I particularly liked the crab salad with egg, cucumber and tomato. The main dish was 'asiatic' consisting of meat and rice cooked by Alla's nephew, Vladimir. He was a fisherman but cooking was his hobby. Murmansk may be poor, I thought, and the shops empty, but we didn't eat like this in *Callisto*, nor, I thought regretfully, did I at home.

We didn't drink a lot. We drank toasts in vodka. Nobody

knocked back whole glassfulls; that was pre-Gorbachov. The President's disastrous failure to have vodka banned at least achieved something: we took modest sips. A toast required a speech. We toasted Murmansk, *Callisto*, peace between nations and each other.

There was singing too. Zoya had a strong soprano voice and she sang some beautiful Ukrainian songs. I was grateful for my neice, Alice, who could sing Scottish folk songs equally well. Conversations were about family, friends and world affairs. I had not yet met a Russian who made small talk. A Russian party is for people to get to know each other, exchange ideas and share feelings. Somehow it is serious as well as immensely entertaining. I remember the slightly startled expression on Alice's face when I heard Alla ask her, 'What do you feel about God in England?' The crew of *Callisto* felt privileged to share in such an evening.

The memorial to the dead of the Second World War is a huge statue of a soldier. He stands on a hill where once was sited one of the main anti-aircraft batteries that defended the city. His stone eyes stared across the Kola Inlet to the old front line. Natasha Galliayva, Galena, Vassili and Mikhail had brought me to see it. We had also been joined by C. N. Polosov, Secretary of the Veterans Committee. Visiting war memorials is not something the British do very much but Alice and Sandy accompanied me. Alice perhaps remembered that her father had been wounded in the fighting in Normandy and Sandy had come out of a sense of solidarity. The statue of the soldier was too grim and too big but he had been humanised: everybody called him, rather guiltily, by the pet name of Aloysha. More impressive than the statue were the guns they left behind; their muzzles still pointing to the western sky from where the enemy bombers came. It was as if the gunlayers had just stood down. The Kola Inlet was a band of silver under a light grey sky. All the docks and ships of Murmansk were spread out below us. The eternal flame flickered in the wind. Vassili must have been here many times with foreign visitors but he was standing still and not talking for once, lost in thought. He was a man of the generation born between 1920 and 1925. Unbelievably only three percent of that generation had come back from the fighting. I thought of the sunken British ships and dead sailors on the bed of the Barents Sea – just one tiny part of the tragedy of Russian history. I looked at Vassili's grave face and, for all the awfulness of the Russian convoys, felt that I came from a lucky land.

'The best part was being welcomed by the captain of one of your destroyers.' The Tass correspondent scribbled as Natasha translated. He had asked me about *Callisto*'s voyage. We were sitting on a bench in a small grassy park after visiting the war memorial. There was a statue of St. Cyril who invented the Russian alphabet. Natasha explained to him why we had come. I kept recognising the word 'convoy'. The correspondent nodded understandingly. She must have told him my profession because his next question was 'What do you think of the architecture here?' and he grinned. Russian housing had been badly criticised in architectural magazines for its ruthless standardisation and poor workmanship.

'Your architects had a difficult problem,' I said cautiously. 'Murmansk was vital to the Soviet Union. You needed homes for people. Reasonably good buildings on time are better than perfect ones too late. They had to use factory production methods to rebuild the city. The apartment blocks could be better, but your architects solved the problem that you set them. Murmansk is a success story for your country.' As Natasha translated the Russian looked at me smiling. I had evaded the question and paid them a compliment too. In fact I believed what I said; the first task of architecture is to solve social problems not aesthetic ones. He persisted, 'But what about the look of the city?'

I pointed around to the small birch and mountain ash trees in the park. 'You planted and cared for your trees,' I said. 'Murmansk is a green city. It was the best architectural decision that you made.' He wrote it down in his note book. Sandy and Alice were also questioned and photographed. They described how in Britain women sailed as much as men and were often better at it. I thought they laid it on a bit thick.

The early morning train to Leningrad was waiting as we walking along the platform. The five members of my crew had decided to go home by rail via Leningrad and see something of that city. The railfare in British money for the 700 miles was less than seven pounds. I would be staying on the yacht to await Roy Sowden's arrival in Murmansk. In the meantime, accompanied by our Russian friends, we were seeing them off. The dark green railway coaches looked comfortable; an important consideration since the journey would last twenty-seven hours. They were carrying heavy bags and Alice, in addition, was hefting a balalaika she had unwisely bought. I didn't envy them. I didn't need to see Leningrad. Everyone told me how beautiful it was but I was content with the city I had sailed into; it could stand for all of Russia.

The crew eventually found their reserved compartments. They looked tired and overwhelmed by the friendship and warmth of their reception in Murmansk. After a farewell dinner at a restaurant the previous evening talking had gone on all night in the yacht. It seemed ages ago, not just four days, that they had been sailing *Callisto*.

Alice's parting words were, 'Where are we sailing to next year?'

Ana took my hand and said, 'I hope you will be alright here by yourself.'

The train pulled out. It was sad to see them go. I walked slowly back to the yacht. She seemed strangely empty without the others. I made some tea and sat drinking it. I felt exhausted. Then I heard voices on the pontoon.

'Henry, Henry, we have brought some friends who want to meet you. Can we come on board?'

It is impossible to feel lonely in Russia.

Chapter Thirteen

Roy Sowden and his crew arrived on the 22 July. The Murmansk Shipping Company car had met them at the airport. They were big and confident and *Callisto* rocked as they came on board. It was early in the morning but I was up and had the kettle on. They were the first English I had seen for eleven days. I was glad they had come but they seemed to overwhelm me. I had been living by myself in the yacht. I had had many visitors but they had been invited guests. The new crew and their heavy bags seemed to fill the saloon. I didn't know where to put myself.

After brief introductions Roy turned his attention to the yacht. 'Where's the radar reflector?'

'We took it down, Roy, there's no night here'

'Can I see the repair you made to the genoa?'

We unfurled the sail revealing the stitches I put in at Tromso.

'Pass up some adhesive tape,' Roy said. 'The repair needs reinforcing. How much fuel have you got left?'

I said, 'The tank's nearly full; we topped up with diesel at

Vardo and only motored for a few hours.'

Roy got a torch and shone it on the transparent pipe in the cockpit locker that shows the level in the tank. 'It's empty,' he said crossly.

I was going to dispute this when something inside me told me to say nothing. I wasn't going to win any arguments with Roy on this particular morning. I went ashore to find the shipping company's agent who offered to send round a fuel barge. When I got back to the yacht Roy was staring at the Decca Navigator.

'It's not properly calibrated,' he said and started pressing buttons.

'We haven't been using it,' I said mildly 'It isn't much good around here'.

'It's spot on now,' Roy said as the display showed the correct latitude and longitude for Murmansk. He made me feel like an unbeliever in the presence of an electronic god. He then, for his own satisfaction, pressed the buttons that would display the degree of accuracy. I looked over his shoulder. The green lights said brutally 'degree of error ten miles'. He looked at it silently for a moment; the god hadn't come up with the goods. He turned round slowly and seemed to see me for the first time.

'It looks as if we are going to have to use your kind of navigation.'

I didn't say anything. He said, 'I'm going to turn in now. I need some sleep, but I'll fix up the radar reflector first.' I felt relieved; two of his crew, David Auld and Stewart Boyd, had already got their heads down in the fore peak. Roy being difficult with me had made me feel like a Russian. The Russians got most things right. Every thing important in Murmansk worked. Planes and pilot boats arrived on time, people met you when they said they would, the great port ran like clockwork. The Russians didn't believe this. Through their eyes all they could see was empty shops, incompetence and lucky improvisation. I had worked quite hard to have *Callisto* ready for her long voyage home and I knew she was on the top line. I had not even defended myself:

perhaps I had caught from the Russians a lack of self confidence.

Roy started rummaging in the cockpit lockers and I went below to the saloon. Don Stentiford, the third member of his crew, was washing up the coffee cups. He was thoroughly at ease in the yacht.

'You seem pissed off, Henry,' he said, giving me a searching look. 'Don't bother about Roy.'

He is a tough security officer from Portland harbour, an experienced sailor owning his own yacht but enjoys sailing with Roy. He is one of those rare, and very popular yachtsmen, who is quite happy not to be skipper. He is a first class cook and likes looking after the other members of the crew, including Roy.

He carefully wiped the mugs and put them neatly away.

'Ship's in good order,' he said and lit a cigarette. The smoke curled up through the hatch. He saw me looking at it and produced a relaxed smile. We both knew that Roy hated smoking below deck. Don was very fond of Roy but this didn't extend to letting himself be bossed around, in any case the ship's cook had special privileges.

'You know Roy as well as I do,' he said sitting down at the table. 'He's got to sail out into the Barents Sea in a day or two. He wants everything to be a hundred per cent. He worries like anything before sailing. That's why he never gets into trouble. I'm afraid he's working it off on you.'

He grinned at me sympathetically. 'As a matter of fact, he's very impressed with you, Henry. Somebody a few weeks ago asked him if you were strong enough to get *Callisto* to Murmansk. He told them you weren't and nor was your crew but you were very determined. You'd make it.'

He flicked the ash of his cigarette into the illicit ash tray.

'The other thing is he's tired. It's a long flight from London. He was photographing the Kremlin in Moscow at four o'clock this morning. We all need sleep.'

Don stubbed out his fag. 'I'm turning in now.'

A couple of minutes later Roy came down the ladder. The

radar reflector was once again at the yardarm. He lay down on the starboard saloon berth and pulled his sleeping bag over his head to keep out the daylight. It was only 9.30 and the sun was shining from a clear blue sky. I took a book and went up into the cockpit to guard the sleeping Englishmen from any Russian friends who might turn up to see the new arrivals.

My conversation with Don Stentiford had cheered me up. He was – what was the Russian word ? – sympatichniy.

I sat in the cockpit feeling the warmth of the sun and thought about going home. I was no longer in charge of the yacht.

It was going to be a wrench leaving Murmansk: I had been very happy here minding *Callisto*.

Almost every day Vassili and Natasha Galliayva had taken me out in the afternoon to visit museums and ships. We had driven into the forest tundra – and I had marvelled at the trees that went on forever. Natasha had taken me to the apartments of her friends and relatives where there was always good food, books and views of the Kola Inlet. Above all there was a loving friendship for the strange Englishman with his halting Russian. Vassili and his wife Rosa made me feel perfectly at home in their beautiful flat. Vassili and I had sat on the balcony looking down on the harbour talking and smoking – Rosa, like Roy, had rules about smoking indoors.

Natasha Varyushkina had joined me in the yacht and talked about her hopes for the future – her own and the future of her bewildered country. The quality of life in Murmansk seemed to me to be very high. It couldn't be judged just by the lack of things to buy.

I had discussed the matter with the skipper of the factory fishing ship, Kola Zaliv. 'You are all too apologetic,' I said to him. 'A lot of things here are as good as anything in the West.'

He laughed. His ship sailed the oceans of the world. 'I often wonder about that myself,' he said. 'I think it is because we have all had too much propaganda; seventy years of telling ourselves how wonderful we are in the Soviet Union. Now everybody knows the truth they have all gone to the other extreme; everything is awful.' He had seemed very proud of his great ship.

In the evenings I had dined at the restaurant at the ferry terminal. Natasha Galliayva had introduced me to Irina. 'She will look after you,' she said. Irina made sure I got the food I liked – soup, smoked sprats and tomato salad. Sometimes when she was not too busy she would sit with me.

'It isn't good to eat alone,' she said in Russian. She would help me with the language until I could manage simple conversations. She was a beautiful young woman and I could gaze into her large soft eyes and wonder about all those pictures of fat ladies wearing shawls that appeared in the British press.

When Irina wasn't there it was still impossible to eat alone. Complete strangers would invite you to join their tables. I dined with shipyard workers and sailors and on one hilarious occasion with the Kola Inlet Pilots. There was a piano accordion and many toasts. It was nice to see Andrey, the pilot who brought us in. Dining was delightfully un-English.

Irina had also introduced me to the crews of the two small yachts owned by the Murmansk Shipping Company. Her husband was one of the crew. I never found out which he was because she radiated her warmth and friendship to all of them.

Alexander Smolienko had come to see me in the yacht every day. He was an agent of the Murmansk Shipping Company and had been given the task of making sure the British yacht had all it needed. The company owned a hundred merchant ships and four nuclear powered ice breakers – one of the biggest ship owners in the world. It still found time to care for its small visitor. Alexander was slight and alert and spoke English with difficulty. He made up for this by his knowledge of the needs of yachtsmen. He was one of the qualified skippers who sailed the yachts that Irina had shown me. He was president of the Arctic Sailing Club. It wasn't much of a club but a brave hope for the future, a promise that one day Russia was going to parallel its huge merchant fleet with participation in the world of amateur sailing.

Alexander said, 'I'm sorry we haven't got better facilities for yachts just yet. For instance, there is no water laid on. You have to get it in containers and there is not much in the shops. Tell British yachtsmen though that we will always be glad to see them.' He had looked rather depressed.

I said with a grin, 'Russia is already often mentioned in our yachting magazines, usually when one of your ships rescues a British yachtsman in trouble.'

He never stayed long to chat; he had many duties.

I sat in the sunny cockpit and wondered what it would be like going home. Perhaps it would be lonely back in England.

I wanted Roy to sleep as long as possible but at noon I noticed a tall familiar figure approaching the pontoon. It was Nicholai Berezhnoi, Mayor of Murmansk, with his wife and small son. He would have known that the new English captain had arrived. If you are skipper of a small yacht and the leading citizen of one of the world's busiest ports comes to see you you have to put on some sort of performance.

I went below. 'Wake up, Roy,' I said. 'We've got visitors.' Roy was instantly alert as if there had been an emergency at sea. 'It's the Mayor,' I said. Roy just had time to comb his hair and came up into the dazzling light of the cockpit. As principal of one of Britain's biggest and most successful community colleges he was well used to putting on a performance. 'Zdrastvuytye', he said to Nicholai who stood smiling on the pontoon. It was the only Russian word he knew. There was hand shaking all round but the Mayor didn't seem to want to come on board. No doubt he guessed the crew were below in exhausted sleep.

He started talking to Roy in Russian. There were other people collecting on the pontoon. I looked round hopefully for an interpreter but there was nobody who I recognised. I was going to have to do it. To begin with it wasn't too difficult; I managed the conventional greetings. Then it got harder as Nicholai began to ask Roy questions. By this time the Mayor was surrounded by about twenty people, most of them school children who seemed to be enjoying the encounter. As I groped for English words to translate Nicholai's questions they started making suggestions. They had all learnt English at school, why not help the Mayor and the incompetent English sailor? Roy and Nicholai were soon conversing effectively by courtesy of twenty eager children each throwing in a word in English or Russian. Roy is a dedicated teacher and these helpers were like the pupils in his own school and here was a Mayor happy to defer to their greater knowledge. He couldn't have had a nicer welcome to Murmansk.

When they had gone Roy sat down in the cockpit. He had had nearly three hours sleep and his mood had changed completely. The tension had gone out of his eyes and he looked around at the exciting confusion of ships and lilac trees in the bright sun.

'What a super country,' he said. 'We had a marvellous flight here. We had time at Moscow to see Red Square. The planes were on time. Everything worked. Then your friends sent a car to meet us. And now the Mayor and those kids.'

It didn't seem to be the same Roy who had stepped aboard four hours ago looking for trouble.

He went on, 'We seem to have been fed a lot of lies about the Soviet Union by too many Cold War journalists.'

Don joined us in the cockpit.

'I've just put the kettle on,' he said. At that moment the fuel barge came alongside. In a minute the diesel oil was gurgling into our tank. In another minute it overflowed.

Roy said, 'It was nearly full.'

Don said, 'Henry told you it was nearly full. Norwegian and Russian diesel is colourless – not pink as in Britain, so you couldn't see the level in the transparent pipe.'

'Why didn't Henry tell me that?'

Don said gently, 'You didn't give him much chance.' He gave me a wink and we all laughed. The man on the fuel barge fended off refusing to accept any payment for his 3 gallons.

Roy said, with his irritatingly charming smile, 'After nearly

2000 miles there doesn't seem to be a single defect in the boat.'
It was the nearest thing I was going to get to an apology.

'Don't throw the baby out with the bathwater,' Roy said and I
wondered how that would translate into Russian. 'You've got a
lot of things right – don't start imitating the West.' The party at
Galena's flat was well into a political discussion before even the
first toast.

Alla, the English teacher, Natasha Varyushkina and their
friend Mick had arrived at the yacht in the afternoon and shaken
hands with Roy and his crew.

Alla said, 'We have arranged a party for you at my friend
Galena's apartment. She is a teacher too, and we would like to
talk about education.' Alla had been delighted to learn from me
that the new captain ran a progressive community college. I had
given him quite a build up. Roy had looked pleased. Like the
flight from Moscow and the welcome from the Mayor, Russia
was turning out better than he had expected. Roy, Don and I had
been glad to accept the invitation, Stuart and David had preferred
a quiet evening walking around the city.

Alla must have successfully translated babies and bathwater. She said, 'We want to know what you think is better here than
in the West,' and I could see the other guests waiting for Roy's
reply. Natasha, who was helping Galena lay the table, paused to
listen. There is usually only one conversation at such a party.
They were looking at this tall Englishman intently. Murmansk,
like the rest of Russia, was searching for a new identity. The rigid
control by the Communist Party had gone. What to put in its
place? All ideas were examined carefully. Here was a foreigner
who said he actually liked the place.

Roy said, 'I've only been here a short time but I'll just men-
tion one thing – you are better educated.' He looked around the
room smiling. Natasha Varyushkina and at least two others were
teenagers who had only just left school. The Russians looked as
if the thought had never occurred to them. Perhaps there were

208

ways of measuring a country's success other than by what was in the shops. The small glasses were filled with vodka.

Roy was asked a lot of questions about his college in Nottinghamshire. Most of the guests at the party were teachers and students. They wanted to know how English education worked.

Suddenly he said, 'Why don't you come over and see?'

There was silence for a few moments but I could see a smile beginning on Alla's face. Roy went on, 'I'm sure my pupils' parents would put up your students. They could meet English children and see the country too. They would do us a lot of good. You would have to get visas and air fares but there would be no other expenses.'

Everybody looked pleased. What a wonderful idea – an exchange of students in secondary schools crossing all the frontiers of geography and history between Murmansk and distant Nottinghamshire. The Russians loved such dreams.

Roy addressed himself to Alla, 'Let's work out the details tomorrow.'

I suppose I was the only person in that room who knew it would happen. I knew Roy. Most people have dreams. Roy had dreams but he made them come true. It hadn't been just an interesting idea thrown out at a party, it was an achievable project. Roy's political experience and management skills would see to that. I thought if Mikhail Kemerov, the war veteran, were with us there would have been tears in his eyes. The convoys were still running.

We left after midnight. The three of us walked back to the yacht through the quiet streets. The low sun cast the long shadow of the Hotel Arctica across Constitution Square.

'What marvellous friends you've made here, Henry,' Don said. 'Russia's hope for the future?' He looked at Roy questioningly.

'I don't think so,' Roy said sadly. 'There's a narrow path between reform and reaction. They're alright for the moment with Gorbachov but when he goes the country will be run by the entrepreneurs, spivs and wideboys. Henry's friends are too soft and lack confidence. It'll be the ruthless people who don't mind walking over other folk that will come to the top.'

Roy is not a cynic but he is realistic. I hoped he was wrong on this occasion. I could see him grinning. He said as we walked down towards the harbour, 'That's the way it is in Britain.'

Callisto would be sailing in half an hour. It was the evening of 24th July and it was overcast and grey. Roy wanted to get south before August. He looked confident preparing for sea but his eyes showed the tension that skippers feel before a long passage.

'Stewart, single up to bow and stern line,' he said. He set the engine throttle. 'Start the motor, Don.' The motor rumbled in neutral at low revs. There were still things to be done before leaving.

Alexander Smolyenko came on board. He brought with him the weather map from the Murmansk Shipping Company. Roy studied it on the saloon table. The isobars were well spread out – not too much wind but it was from the north. Alexander translated, 'Visibility moderate to poor. Fog patches.'

'Sod it,' said Roy and he grinned, 'we can manage that, though.'

I wanted to settle our debts. 'How much do we owe you, Alexander?' I asked.

He looked uncomfortable, 'Nothing,' he said.

I read off my list, 'Harbour dues, pilotage, cars, propane gas, diesel.'

'I am afraid there is no charge for these things. You are guests. Perhaps we are old fashioned.'

Roy caught my eye. 'Come on deck,' he said.

I followed Alexander up the ladder. There was a crowd of people on the ferry quay and the pontoon. They had come to see *Callisto* off. I seemed to recognise them all. Roy went aft and untied the red ensign.

'Okay, Henry?'

I nodded, we had a spare. Roy raised his voice above the sound of the engine.

'Alexander,' he said, 'we would like to present this flag to you as representative of the Murmansk Shipping Company and as the President of the Arctic Sailing Club. It is just a small token of our gratitude for all your help.'

You didn't have ceremonies like this in Britain but it was just right in Murmansk. I could see our friends on the quay looking pleased and Alexander held the flag up for all to see. The national flag is an essential feature on a foreign going ship and this one had been flying all the way to Russia. Cameras flashed, including our own.

The pilot came on board. Somebody gave Roy and each member of his crew a red rose.

'Goodbye, dosvidanya, goodbye.'

I stepped onto the pontoon with my sailing bags. The last lines were cast off. Roy took the tiller, reversed away from the pontoon, turned through 90 degrees and headed north. I watched brave *Callisto* threading her way between the moored ships, diminishing into the greyness, until I lost sight of her. I turned away.

A company car took me to the Hotel Arctica where they had reserved a room for me. It would take a day or two to arrange my passage home. I wanted to sleep. I did not seem to have had a minute to myself since leaving Bergen. Responsibility for my crews had developed into the even greater responsibility of responding to the warmth and enthusiasm of the Russians. Finally, I had the anxiety of preparing the yacht for my partner's long voyage. Back at the hotel I slept for a long time.

I left Murmansk as I had come, by sea, boarding the Norwegian catamaran for her regular evening voyage to Kirkenes, the Norwegian frontier town. She was a superb modern ship, fast and clean. I knew most of the crew by sight. They came each morning to Murmansk with day trippers and as the catama-

211

ran lay all day on the other side of the pontoon they were familiar faces. Being Norwegian and English we had, of course, not said a word, just smiled at each other, but some of them had been with the Russians waving to *Callisto* when she left. I had said all my goodbyes when I was at the hotel and had meant to slip away quietly. Nevertheless my friends came to see me off. As the catamaran pulled away I waved to them from the open quarterdeck. I wanted to get back to Britain but my heart wasn't in it. There seemed to be more love in Murmansk. I was clutching a book seventeen year old Natasha had given me. When I went into the saloon I opened it and read again what she had written on the flyleaf.

'Dear Henry,

I hope you'll remember Murmansk – I mean the new Murmansk which has been built after the war (because you knew the old town). We, the inhabitants of Murmansk remember your exploit and I'll remember you . . .'

It was written under a photograph of herself looking at me with a grave smile.

After a few minutes I felt alright and went to the big windows on the starboard side feeling the vibration of the gas turbine engines going slowly. Murmansk was sliding astern – cranes, quays, ships and the apartment blocks, their colours now faded in the cloudy evening twilight. Aloysha surrounded by his guns stood on his hill staring over us to the Finnish frontier. I was insulated from it. In the bright lights and air conditioning I was physically already in another country, yet my thoughts were with Murmansk. It had been so hard to get to and now so easy to leave. Murmansk was past tragedy and uncertain hope. It was rough and dramatic in its wild setting. It was a huge success shadowed by anxiety. I could see the ice breaker *Rassia* and the thin railway that ran to Severemorsk and the trees now dying away as we went

212

north. Murmansk had gone to my heart.

I turned away from the window. The stewardesses were serving a light meal. I could hear the engines slowing down to drop the pilot. A minute later we picked up speed. The cups and plates rattled, the catamaran was making twenty knots towards the Barents Sea. We would be at Kirkenes in three hours. It wasn't my sort of cruising but there was something exhilarating about such power and speed. The Novolok light was on the port beam flashing in the twilight. It seemed to be saying, 'Goodbye, British sailor, goodbye again.' We began to feel the waves of the open sea. I lay down on a soft sofa with my head on a pile of blankets. The sea wasn't rough but at this sort of speed the pitching was quite violent: I wasn't going to be seasick at this stage – lying down seemed a wise precaution. I relaxed comfortably with time to think. Somebody else was in charge.

I had done all this before in another ship heading for the Barents Sea homeward bound. I closed my eyes. The vibration of the engines and the ship steering directly into the waves produced a sense of total recall. I was leaving Murmansk on 23 March 1945.

Chapter Fourteen

We were to sail for home in the evening, three days after entering harbour. All day the merchant ships of the return convoy RA65 had been assembling and anchoring in the Kola Inlet to the south of us. Many of the ships were light, floating high in the water showing rusty red hulls above their usual waterlines but some were heavily laden with cargoes for Britain. The Russians were doing their best to pay for the munitions they received. We were now tied up alongside a cruiser and a destroyer. We had steam up and were ready for sea. The sun set in a clear sky, cold and immaculate.

At 9.30, the loudspeakers said, 'D'you hear there? D'you hear there?' and then the Skipper's voice came on.

'This is the Captain speaking.'

The messdeck became suddenly very quiet. I listened with leaden expectancy.

'We slip in forty minutes,' he said. 'We are going to be very offensive but we have to be defensive too because we may be attacked like *Lapwing* was. Coming up we were lucky; we were not sighted. Now I expect the Blohm and Voss reconnaissance planes will be sent out. It's up to every rating to be alive to his job.'

He spoke a couple more minutes in the same bleak and unencouraging way. I was glad when he stopped. He had got us into harbour safely and I had confidence in his skill. If anyone could get us out through the waiting U-boats, he could but I didn't want to hear him talking about it. I looked around the messdeck. The seamen were expressionlessly going through routines – changing into clean clothes, putting on life-belts, tidying away playing cards and ludo, finding ways of getting through the forty minutes before we were needed to get the ship under way. Outside, I could hear engines of ships and the rattling of capstans and anchor cables. I got out my diary and tried to write.

I wrote, 'I am not afraid now . . .' and couldn't get any further. It was a lie. I was in fact more frightened than I had ever been. I stared at the paper and decided to take fear head on. If you imagined the worst, perhaps it wouldn't happen. I tried to envisage the U-boats out there between the minefields below the surface of the sea in the arctic night. All they had to do was wait. The convoy was restricted to the narrow swept channel. They would be able to watch through their periscopes the ships' outlines against the night sky coming into their sights. I thought of their torpedoes running invisibly towards us. U-boats were very patient and they would be waiting for us like wolves. I didn't write these thoughts in my diary.

I wrote, ' I'm not afraid now . . .'

As I struggled to resolve the contradiction of what I had written and what I was thinking, I heard a new sound. Above the background hum of generators and air fans I heard the sound of sobbing. It was something that I had never encountered before in the ship. I looked up and saw that the youngest ordinary seaman in No. 6 mess was crying. He was a huddled figure at the forward end of the mess table wearing his overalls and his seaman's cap on the back of his head. He was crying into his knuckles as he rested his elbows on the table. His action station was below the waterline in the magazine. I knew the magazine quite well. The four inch gun shells and cartridges clinked eerily as the ship rolled. There were a lot of ladders to climb and small hatchways to go through if you wanted to get out in a hurry. You were down there with your thoughts out of the sight of men. Nobody else was showing such obvious signs of fear. All the seamen in the mess were older. Many of them had been at sea longer and, more important, none of them would be in the magazine surrounded by high explosives. I remembered what John Brooksbank had said when we were still in the Clyde about helping the young ordinary seamen. This lad needed help badly and I couldn't do anything about it because I could only just about cope with my own fear. I had no fortitude left over to help a crying boy. Then I saw Jim Pickthall only a few months older than he was, go over to him. He put his hand on his shaking shoulder and I heard him say in his gentle Lancashire voice, 'Stokers are worse off than you down in stokehold.'

It was not much and it was not true but it was enough. The young seaman looked round at him with an empty tear stained face. He stopped sobbing and wiped his eyes with Jim's hand-kerchief. Then he smiled. It had been some sort of crisis for him and for the rest of us too and Jim had moved in and dealt with it. This was the Jim Pickthall who only a few days before had said in the wheelhouse, '. . . ordinary seamen are supposed to know fuck all.'

There were a lot of things Jim Pickthall didn't know but he knew how to follow his heart. I wished I could have done what he did.

At 10 o'clock, the American merchant ship anchored near-by began to get in her cable. A few minutes later, the bosun's mate came round piping, 'Hands to stations for leaving harbour. Special sea-duty men close up.'

It had been a bad forty minutes. Out on the fo'c'sle in the dark I could see the faint glimmer of snow along the shore of the

216

Kola Inlet and the green, red and white navigating lights of the ships coming on and beginning to move. A voice from the bridge shouted, 'Single up,' and we hauled in the long wires. Then, 'Let go aft, let go for'ard.'

The crew of the destroyer alongside cast off our remaining mooring lines and we heaved them in cold from the water. We stowed fenders and coiled wires as the ship began to head north down the Kola Inlet – another Russian convoy was on the way back to Britain. The corvettes led out and one by one the merchant ships fell into line astern. Twenty five merchant vessels and almost as many warships – a huge fleet – left Russia in the night without any fuss at all, with only the sound of their slowly revving engines disturbing the silence of the forest and the snow-fields.

I thought, 'Goodbye, Murmansk, goodbye poor bloody, beaten up, brave Russia,' and then all my thoughts were about myself and how I would fare when the convoy encountered the picket line of the U-boats outside the safety of the Kola Inlet. Perhaps I was exaggerating the danger but, nonetheless, I had a clear perception that if we could get safely through the next few hours, I could live thereafter on borrowed time. In a way, it was a fairly positive idea.

We went out of harbour, closed up to action stations, expecting trouble and looking for it. All hatches and water-tight doors were closed. Men on the bridge and the after Oerlikon platform searched the dark horizons with binoculars. The radar scanner rotating on the mast searched through the night. The asdic impulses hunted ahead and around the ship. Hands were ready at depth-charge fuses and four inch gun shells. A hundred men listened and looked and waited.

I didn't want a fight. In the action plot cabinet, the Navigating Officer and Ron Teece were quiet and grey in the dim red lights and the glow of instruments. They seemed lost in thought. There was nothing to say. Tonight seemed like a re-run of the action three days ago but this time in the dark and with only the fear and not the excitement. Outside on the bridge, it was just possible to see three other Castle class corvettes of the 7th Escort Group. They were dark shapes against the slightly lighter sky and their bow waves were palely phosphorescent. They were starting to pitch in the sea as we began to clear the land.

Back in the plot, a few minutes later, we heard the first depth-charges. These hadn't been fired by the close escort corvettes. They sounded quite a long way off. There was a look of interest on the faces of my two companions. Something was happening. The explosion seemed to be once again a continuous barrage.

We were altering course a little. I could hear the orders from the bridge to the wheelhouse. The Cox'n was at the wheel. I had briefly watched him steering as I came through the wheelhouse to the bridge. His acknowledgements of steering orders sounded much more crisply efficient than mine. They befitted a young man who was the senior rating in the ship and on his way up in his chosen profession. He was wearing a Russian fur hat with ear flaps. This looked rather incongruous in the wheelhouse of a corvette and a bit theatrical.

Time seemed to drag but the depth charging was sounding further away. By 2 o'clock I was finding it difficult to keep awake. The dim lights and the pinging of the asdic transmissions had a soporific effect. There was nothing to do so I combatted sleep with mental arithmetic. We had cast off about four hours ago. Assuming convoy speed of nine knots, then we were thirty six miles off the coast. Some of the time, however, was spent in the Kola Inlet so, say, twenty five miles. If it had been daylight we would not have seen the coast at that distance. We must surely already be clear of the minefields and the restrictions of the swept channel. We were still at action stations but there was now no sound of depth-charges. Either the barrage had stopped or we were too far away to hear it. I began to entertain a hope that somehow we were not going to be attacked, at least not by the U-boats we knew were on patrol outside the Kola Inlet. The

Navigator and Teece were looking more relaxed and were lighting each others' cigarettes.

At a quarter to three, the ship's loudspeakers clicked into life, 'Secure action stations, White Watch to cruising stations.'

It was over. There had been no attack. We were far out at sea. Only surfaced U-boats could out-run us and we could deal with them. I ought to have been overwhelmed with relief but I seemed to have used up all my feelings in the last few days. All I felt as I stumbled stiffly out of the plot was exhaustion. On the bridge, look-outs, signalmen, Oerlikon gunners and officers were changing places as the White Watch took over. The rest of us were free to go below. I lingered briefly on the bridge. In the east it was already getting light. There was little wind but a medium size swell was running – a sure indication of a storm somewhere and the ship was beginning to roll. As I turned in in No. 6 Mess, I wondered why there had been no attack. Perhaps the distant depth-charges had been some kind of deception or perhaps we had just been lucky. In the meantime, as the ordinary cruising routine of the ship took over, I experienced a great sense of anti-climax. All that fear before sailing and we had got away without a fight. I was glad about anti-climaxes.

How had this come about? There were nine U-boats waiting for us but they were waiting in the wrong place. It was a long time before I found out why this was so. Unknown to the enemy a new channel had been swept in the minefields and the Vice-Admiral decided RA65 should use it. He sent four destroyers along the old channels dropping depth charges as a ruse to deceive the U-boats. It was the distant noise of these that I had heard in the action plot. By the time the U-boat skippers realised what had happened it was too late. There was no chance of repeating their success of three days before.

'Come on, you've had your time.'

I was awakened at 7 o'clock. I hadn't had my time, only three and a half hours. I felt bad tempered. Steering in the forenoon watch was hard work. The wind was now quite strong and we were rolling fairly heavily. It was difficult to steer a straight course. Loose gear which had accumulated in the calm weather and in harbour slid from side to side on the wheelhouse deck. Through the partially open portside door, I could see waves climbing up and receding and snow kept coming in. The convoy was invisible behind snow storms. This was encouraging because we were not far from the Luftwaffe air bases. If we could not see ourselves, it was most unlikely that we should be located by reconnaissance planes.

We were on the way home but the eight days it would take us to get there stood before me like a barrier. If the weather was calm like it had been on the outward trip, it would not be too uncomfortable but I didn't like the way the wind was increasing. The look-outs, gunners and watch keeping officers were already looking cold and wet and miserable. I had experienced Russian convoy weather in the arctic in my previous ship; it had not been much fun. It looked as if the experience was about to be repeated.

MacLaughlan was sitting at the wheelhouse table eating a bacon roll. He had spread a piece of newspaper on the table and was spitting bits of bacon rind onto it. They lay there like casualties. When he had finished, he wiped his mouth carefully and screwed up the newspaper. He had a bad sty on his eye and this made half of his face look old and corpse-like. If he hadn't been one of the few regular sailors on board, I should have felt sorry for him. He went off to read the Walker log and report to the bridge.

After the watch was over I went out on the quarterdeck to look at the rising sea. My diary entry that afternoon described it,

'I watch the ship diving down, bow steep below, ensign bar tight in the wind, then bow climbing up, stern dropping below me. And so it goes on. Spray drives from for'ard in white clouds, hissing along the decks, wetting me.'

I also noted, rather cruelly, that I had been glad to see the only man who disliked me, the able seaman with the missing front tooth, being seasick over the bulwarks.

I was right about the wind. When I took the wheel at 4 o'clock next morning, it was blowing a full gale. The inclinometer on the wheel standard indicated that we were rolling 45 degrees each way. This is about the slope of an ordinary house roof. It meant that at the end of each roll, it would have been as easy to stand on the wall of the wheelhouse as on the deck. One problem was to steer something like an approximately straight course; the other was to stay at the wheel at all. The wheelhouse rotated around me through 90 degrees every thirty seconds and the four hours I was going to have to steer would test me to the limit of my strength and concentration. My legs were tired with keeping in place and my arm muscles ached as I spun the wheel in anticipation of the next sea. Sometimes it was all I could do to hold on to the wheel and to hell with the ship's course. It was some comfort that it was just as bad for the officers and the other people on the bridge and they had, in addition, to put up with the deafening violence of the wind. I soon began to feel sick. I had got over sea sickness long before so I was not going to need the bucket but the human body was not supposed to be treated like this. There had to be some ill effect. The wheelhouse clock seemed to go very slowly. In these conditions I was not able to daydream about poetry, girls or the end of the war; I just had to steer as well as I could. The dawn twilight that showed under the light screens never became daylight. When Taff Jones relieved me at 8 o'clock I was dog tired.

Down in the mess, nothing was secure. The tea fanny slid off the table in an excessive roll, crashing against my leg. I jumped clear and the roll the opposite way caused the washing up water to capsize. Tea and dirty water raced from side to side of the deck in a muddy tide. Little islands of cigarette packets, biscuits, boots and books stood out in it. A few cups were broken. Rice from an upended tin scattered over it all. I stood in the mess holding on to the hammock rails in a state of exhausted dismay with the water washing over my shoes. Breakfast was out of the question and anyway the tea was sluicing about on the deck. Most of the men had reported for work at 8 o'clock so I set wearily about the task of helping Simmonds to restore order. He said, 'There's no need to scrub out today, just wipe up the mess. That'll be good enough in this weather.' Later he said, 'People only see you when you go ashore in blue suits all clean; they ought to see us now!'

At 9 o'clock, wearing sea-boots, sheepskin and oilskins I went to the upper deck to join the off watch seamen. There was no need to ask what needed to be done. In the full light of day, I could see the ship was a mass of ice. The spray coming onto us as we ploughed into the big seas now froze instantly. I could hardly see the fo'c'sle. It looked like dirty wedding cake and horizontal icicles hung from the guardrails. The ice covered upper deck was a lethal hazard. Moving about on such a violently bucking steel deck was dangerous enough at the best of times; the slippery ice sheeting made the risk of going overboard far greater. Seamen were chipping away with ice picks and steam hoses. I joined them but you couldn't stand it for very long. The ice you chipped off was blown into your face by the wind and was added to by more spray that froze on you. People would have to go below for a while to thaw out. It was a pretty awful job but ice clearing was a task that seamen worked at with a will. We had heard stories about what happened to ships that got iced up. They turned over with the weight of the ice on the upper deck and superstructure. Jimmy and the Buffer didn't need to shout at us. Before I had been to the arctic, I had thought of ice as something beautiful and transparent, glittering in the low winter sun. This ice was quite different. It was grey saltwater ice, opaque and rock-like. This ship was encrusted. The only thing that was not frozen was the sea itself. The waves were very big and very far apart. Their crests seemed to shut out a lot of the sky the way the hills did when you were in a valley. As they broke, the wind blew their tops off. Wind and ice and violent seas – this was Russian convoy weather. It was this that fed the fearful legend.

That forenoon passed in a blur of misery. I didn't believe in God but I cursed him every time the spray hit me. We had had one enemy to deal with – the Germans – now God was turning it on for us and the worst of it was, that he could keep at it longer than they could. I was not looking forward to the next few days.

When I went below for dinner, I had had enough; four hours steering in the morning watch, cleaning up the messdeck with Simmonds then chipping ice in the forenoon. I swallowed my rum in one gulp and ate my bully beef and bread and butter which was all that was on offer. Then I went to sleep for three hours, insulated from the worst of the rolling by my hammock. The crashing of the seas and the rattling of loose gear didn't disturb me. Indeed they shielded me from the noise of the BBC Forces programme coming from the messdeck loudspeaker and the sound of people cursing.

I had a marvellous dream. There were two kinds of dreams – nice ones and nightmares. The nightmares were all the same; they were always about going to sleep at the wheel and allowing the ship to go miles off course. They always woke me up to find myself not in the wheelhouse but in my hammock. In fact I never did go to sleep at the wheel but I must have been near to it sometimes, hence the recurring nightmare. It was always a relief to find that it had only been a dream but I lost a lot of sleep. In some ways, the nice dreams were worse because you were awakened to the nightmare reality of the ship herself. The particular dream that I had this afternoon was about Bear Island which was quite appropriate because it was probably the nearest land. I had gone ashore and found, instead of a frozen coast, a pleasant harbour with fishermen sitting on the quay in the sunshine mending their nets. I walked past them and they looked up and smiled but didn't say anything and I had a strong feeling that they had been expecting me and that I had come home at last. When I awakened at a quarter past three for the first dog watch and encountered again the violence and noise of the ship, I experienced a sense of loss – my home had gone.

I steered through the midnight to 4 o'clock middle watch on 26th March. I was glad it was dark and I couldn't see the waves. Since the strength of the wind and the size of the seas very much affected my standard of living, I had taken every opportunity to read about them when I had the chance to look at the books in the chart room. I guessed the wind was now blowing Force 10 on the Beaufort Scale, 44 to 55 knots velocity-storm force. The Beaufort Scale gave recognisably different ranges of wind speeds. The definition for Force 10 was 'very high waves with long overhanging crests. The rolling foam in great patches is thrown in dense white streaks along the direction of the wind. On the whole the waves take on a white appearance. The tumbling of the sea becomes heavy and shock like. Height of waves 24 – 40 ft.' This described what I had seen.

It took me a while to get the hang of steering in these wild conditions. You couldn't steer the course directly because the ship's head was swinging through 30 degrees. The course was supposed to be 223 degrees True. Such a precise course couldn't have been set in the Flag Ship, *Campania*. The escort carriers had been almost invisible in the spray. They were tilting and gyrating almost as badly as we were. Perhaps the Convoy Commodore in his slightly steadier leading merchant ship had worked this one out. The best I could do was to make 223 the mean course but the last digit made the mental arithmetic hard. The red numbers on the giro compass repeater simply flashed in a blur as the waves hit us. I tried desperately to contain the swing between 208 and 238.

The officer of the watch had evidently been staring at his compass on the bridge unbelievingly. I heard him say down the voice pipe, 'Can't you do better than this, quartermaster?'

The correct answer to this question, which was not really a question, should have been, 'Aye, aye, sir,' but I didn't give it.

I was doing my best and I was pretty sure that nobody could steer a better course. I shouted angrily back up the voice pipe, 'No, I bloody well can't, sir.'

There was silence above. I was not sure who the officer of
the watch was. It was hard to recognise voices in the racket of the
wind and sea. I knew it was not the First Lieutenant, however,
because if it had been, I should have had an immediate response.
It would have been on the lines of, 'Yes, you bloody well can,
Henry, and if you can't do it, I'll show you how to drive this sodding ship myself.'

As the seconds ticked past, I imagined being put on a
charge for insubordination. I didn't care. As far as I could see,
nobody could devise a worse punishment than that which I was
already being subjected to – steering a wildly pitching and rolling
corvette in the arctic night in a Force 10 storm.

When the officer of the watch spoke again, he was quite
nice. He said, 'Okay, quartermaster, do your best. Try and keep
the mean course as near as you can.'

'Aye, aye, sir,' I said, slightly relieved.

I was working myself to the limits of my strength at the
wheel and the officer of the watch was trying to keep the ship in
her right position in zero visibility and trying to dodge some of
the spray as well. We were both, I reflected, in the same shit.

Taff Jones took over at 4 o'clock. Dawn was beginning to
break. There was just enough light to see the nearest waves. The
ship seemed to be threading her way through mountain passes.
As I went below I knew that I could look forward to three hours
sleep then chipping ice in the forenoon on the upper deck and
then in the afternoon, steering. Everybody who had written about
war had stressed the danger, the fear and the blood. Nobody had
said anything about it being such brutally hard work.

Not working was not much better. I was off duty in the two
evening dog watches. The seamen's messdeck had by this time
become squalid even by our standards. We were endlessly wiping
up things and putting things away, establishing some semblance
of order. The ship would hit a specially big wave – we called
them milestones – and everything again would be dislodged and
spilt and men not holding on would go flying. Seamen coming

from the bridge and the upper deck dripped pools of water and snow. The mess smelt of sweat, oilskins and toast. The glare of the bare electric lightbulbs shone on the dirty brown cortiscene covered deck and the white tired faces. Eating was the worst thing. First you had to clear the mess table of discarded oilskins and arctic clothing, then you rolled down the oil-cloth on the deal table. George Seeley's hammock knocked against my back as I tried to cut bread and all the cups slid together like skaters from side to side of the table. At one point, one of the tables, regarded as a fixed item in our world, itself became unseated from its base, tipping tea onto the men sitting on the inboard benches. The problem of actually eating diminished into insignificance when compared with the chaos of dirty dishes, greasy washing up water and refuse which eating entailed. Every object not actually bolted down or held in your hand was potentially a dangerous missile.

On the 27th March, four days out of Murmansk we were past Bear Island and steering south and west. The mountains of ice on the upper deck were beginning to melt but the wind and waves were just as violent. I was glad about the ice and only had a slight regret that we could never carry the stuff back to Glasgow. It would have been nice to have tied up in Govan Dock in the middle of the town so all the girls could have seen it.

One other thing cheered us up that day. The BBC news was good. When I came down to the mess for dinner, somebody said, 'Patton's in Frankfurt, Montgomery's captured Dortmund. Not much longer now boys – no more Russian convoys.'

It was only half believed but a spark of hope flickered that there could be an end to this brutish life. What would peace be like? None of us had experienced it in adult life. We had been children before the war. I remembered the frightening rubbery smell of my first gas mask when I was fourteen. My only concept of peace-time was that it would surely mean sleeping in a proper bed all night and every night.

The other thing that cheered us up was the knowledge that in spite of the gale, the convoy was going south minus 4 degrees of latitude a day. The visibility had been a bit better in the forenoon and I had had a look at the other ships. The freighters were rolling heavily and a Flower class corvette was labouring ahead of us taking solid seas on her fo'c'sle. Beyond her, far ahead, I could sometimes see some of the leading fleet destroyers on the southern horizon. The two carriers were spray covered rectangles among the merchant ships and I could distinguish the cruiser. Against the irregular chaos of the breaking seas, it all looked orderly and competent. It seemed to have an air of success.

Having had the U-boats to contend with and then four days of storm, we now started fighting each other. Ken Buckler had his other eye blacked. This time it was done by a torpedoman in No. 5 Mess. I asked Ken what he had done to promote this assault.

"Laying down the law as usual," he said, smiling miserably. "I told him to take his filthy gear off the table while I was eating."

The torpedoman had a tiny head and a huge horse-like body. Gordon Powell commented to me afterwards, "If Ken used his fists, they wouldn't keep hitting him."

Then in the afternoon two able seamen, Allen and Knocker White, had a fight on the quarterdeck which was now almost free of ice. It was something to do with wetting the tea. It was a proper fight.

Joking in the bathroom, men said, "Don't say anything against 6 Mess or they'll trim your lamps."

I discussed the fighting with Len Tilley. We were having one of our conversations about the building industry.

I said, "Why do most fights happen when it's rough? Is it because people get even more fed up with each other than usual or is it because they feel safe from the enemy?"

"Neither," said Len Tilley. "It's because they can't really hurt each other. With the bloody ship rolling its gut out, it's difficult to get in a really hard punch but you can still have a good go and it relieves your feelings."

I said, "Well nobody wants to fight me."

I expected Len Tilley to say something like, "They all like you" or "You've got a kind face."

Instead he said, "I'm not surprised, you're six foot bloody two!"

In the evening, unbelievably, the sea got even rougher. Evidence of this was that the gash can started sliding from side to side of the mess. You had to jump clear – it was pretty heavy. No. 5 Mess's washing up water capsized and there were shouts of, 'Get scrubbing out, Shep.' But nobody did anything about it and it added to the swirling tide that sloshed from one mess to the other.

Simmonds shouted, 'Right lads, come and get it, supper on the table.'

There was an almighty roll and everything, including Simmonds, went flying and half the lightbulbs went out. Simmonds wearily hauled himself up, gripping the table. He surveyed the debris, his face ashen with anger. He said, 'Right lads, supper on the fucking deck.'

A few minutes later, the bosun's mate came round piping the routine order, 'Clear up messdecks and flats for rounds.'

Everybody shouted abuse at him and there was great satisfaction when his boots slipped on the remains of our supper and he went flying out of sight into No.5 Mess.

That was the worst the sea did to us and two days later the wind had dropped and the sky cleared. We were heading southwards, approaching the Faeroe Isles over a cold blue sea and there was even some sunshine. My spirits rose. We were well on the way home.

At 12.30 I relieved Tony Baynon at the wheel for the last time. It was the second of April and the convoy was entering the Firth of Clyde. We had closed up to action stations once when enemy air-

228

craft had been sighted and for a while the sky was lit with the bright arcs of tracer. The planes hadn't attacked and that was the last we saw of the enemy.

Tony was standing feet apart wearing grey flannel trousers, his dark blue seaman's jersey, his cap on the back of his head and his big hands on the spokes of the wheel. We had increased speed during the forenoon to 150 revs, about 14 knots. We were running home. Usually when Tony handed over the wheel he went below straight away; this time he seemed to be inclined to linger in the wheelhouse. He went over to the open door on the port side. MacLaughlan had gone on his rounds of the upper deck and the off watch look-outs were chatting with the bosun's mate on the starboard side. Tony gazed out and then he said, turning towards me, 'I can see the Mull of Kintyre lighthouse on the headland. There are high cliffs. It all looks just the same.'

His face, turned towards me was shadowed against the bright light of the doorway. I had not talked to Tony very much during the trip although I relieved him every time I went on watch. He was in 5 Mess and when I went there on the occasions when neither of us were steering, he was usually deep in a book with his weight on his left arm, his head lowered and his hair falling over his eyes. I had not wanted to disturb him. Now he was saying, 'Do you remember when we were here last time; I think I envied the people in Kintyre?'

'Yes,' I said, my eyes on the compass. I thought of all the miles we had sailed since then.

'Well, I don't think I do any more. I was scared then and I'm not now but there's more to it than that. I feel I've had a chance to learn things. Most people don't get this sort of opportunity.'

He was silent. I glanced away from the compass. Tony was momentarily lost in thought. He was looking at the coast.

'What have you learnt, Tony?' I asked.

He turned and said slowly, 'When we started this trip I had mixed feelings about the crew. I liked some of them; others irritated me. Now I like people better.'

He grinned at me, 'Perhaps going to Russia has made me more tolerant. The ship worked alright when things got difficult. Maybe, I've grown up a bit.'

'Were you frightened?' I asked.

Tony said, 'This is my third ship but the shoot-out we had on the Russian coast scared me rather. With the war nearly over, it seemed a silly time to die.'

He paused and gave me a sharp look, 'Something else frightened me nearly as much though,' he said. 'I was afraid of putting the wheel the wrong way. It would have been pretty easy to do; I was tired most of the time. It could have been nasty with all those ships around.'

I thought of the way he always looked so confident; his steady hands on the spokes of the wheel, his alert eyes on the compass. It had all looked so easy.

The voice pipe said, 'Steer 160.'

'Steer 160, sir.'

We were altering course for the Clyde. Tony said, 'Well, I'll leave you to it.'

When the look-outs changed, young Scott came down from the bridge. He said, 'You can see Ailsa Craig on the starboard side, Henry.'

Through the wheelhouse door I could see our corvettes under their white ribbons of smoke outlined against the misty coast of Kintyre.

Dusk was falling as we passed through the harbour boom. The ships of the convoy were slowly and tiredly steaming in line ahead. I could see the big rusty hulls of the merchant ships close alongside. From the quarterdeck they looked no different from any other ships but these ships were home from Murmansk. All around us were the green fields, the red ploughed earth, the woods and the white houses scattered along the shores. We had sailed in spring and it was still spring.

Soon the convoy would lose its identity, the ships going their various ways becoming separate units. Our gramophone was sounding through the loudspeakers. It was playing The Marriage of Figaro.

I had a surge of tired exaltation. We were home, we had done it. In the mess John Brooksbank said, 'This is the moment I have been waiting for for weeks.'

He was taking off his life jacket. I noticed that his eyes had rings round them. None of us I suppose had had enough sleep. He seemed to want to share this moment with others.

'I bet the Russians are glad we got all that stuff to them. It must be helping them already.'

Len Tilley was making a pile of the letters he had written each day to his wife. They were numbered on the envelopes so that she would open them in the right order. He would give them to the signalman who would post them at the earliest opportunity. His wife would not have had a letter for nearly a month. When he had finished, he turned to me and said, 'The Skipper looked dead weary this afternoon. He did bloody well I thought. I don't think he enjoys this life any more than we do. Lucky to have him.'

Even the man with the missing tooth was in a good mood. He said to me, 'You didn't fuck up the steering this time, Henry.'

His grin showed his nasty mouth.

We went alongside the oiler to fill up our fuel tanks. I was on the fo'c'sle and I could see the Skipper on the bridge. When we were tied up I saw his head lowered to the wheelhouse voice pipe. He would be saying, 'Finished with main engines.'

The mail came aboard from the oiler and silence descended on the ship as everyone not involved in oiling read their letters.

My mail consisted mainly of copies of the *Architects Journal* and the *New Statesman*.

When I had read my few personal letters I went up to the upper deck and leant on the bulwarks. The harbour looked quiet

231

and smooth in the fading light. Greenock was close on our port side and on the far shore the lights were beginning to prick out in Helensburgh.

Out in the Atlantic I had thought about the Clyde as the 'land of lost content' in A. E. Houseman's poem.

> 'Into my heart an air that kills
> From yon far country blows:
> What are those blue remembered hills,
> What spires, what farms are those?'

We had come home. Lancaster Castle lay still and safe in her familiar anchorage. We were one of the lucky ships in the lottery of war. We had lost two merchant ships and our Senior Officer's sloop. Because of them my gladness was shadowed by grief – almost guilt. The death of 158 men in HMS Lapwing was a relatively small statistic in the bloody record of the Russian convoys. Standing there by myself watching the shore lights coming on it didn't seem like a statistic. It felt like a personal loss. The sadness would fade as it always did but I would still remember them. Perhaps a small part of me would remain up there off the high white coast of Russia.

Chapter Fifteen

The bus driver said, 'I'm afraid you have to pay in Norwegian currency.' I was still ten Kroner short of the fare from the hotel in Kirkenes to the airport. I fumbled in all my pockets as the other passengers paid and left the bus. I had paid my air fare to Heathrow with travellers cheques without really looking at the high cost of travel in Norway. I had thought I had plenty of Kroner for a short bus journey and a few cups of coffee as well. I had offered to pay in sterling, write a cheque, use a credit card. No good, and the driver was looking impatient wanting to get back to Kirkenes. I had already handed over all the coins I had, now I was short of about one pound, which is about what the whole fare would have been in England. I think it was the first time I had actually run out of money. I had run out of ideas too. The driver and I stared at each other for long seconds both nailed to the honesty and financial probity of Norway. It was an impasse and as far as I could see it could go on forever. It was broken by the return of one of the passengers, a small fair haired boy. He handed one ten Kroner piece to the bus driver and disappeared before I could thank him. The bus driver looked relieved and drove off glad to see the back of me. I found the boy in the air terminal building and thanked him for his kind help. He nodded but didn't smile. I got the impression that it was a routine act for twelve year olds to bail out indigent foreigners.

Kirkenes airport at 9.30 in the morning is the grimmest place in the world. It is on a plateau with bare treeless tundra stretching in all directions. I thought I could see the sea in the north but it was spotting with rain, and low clouds hid the horizon. I had left Russia late last night in the catamaran: it seemed inconceivable that I would be in London this evening.

It was warm in the departure lounge but even wearing two jerseys and a padded jacket I shivered as I crossed the apron to the waiting plane.

We flew west through impenetrable cloud. I hoped the skipper of the aeroplane had better navigational aids than my Decca. I worried about flying in aeroplanes.

The sky cleared as we approached the west coast of Norway. Through my window I could see once again the sunlight on the snowy mountains and the blue fjords. My journey from the arctic to England was like a fast rewind of the film of *Callisto*'s voyage north. As the plane banked I could see beautiful Tromso, linked by the long bridges, it's harbour a shining blue pool. Beyond, and all around, were the low green islands and the channels and fjords of the inner leads.

I wasn't at the airport long. The plane took off for the long flight to Oslo. It was now full of passengers reading newspapers. I gazed through the window. At the height we were flying I wasn't involved in Norway. There was nothing I could recognise; it wasn't the same coast that had troubled and fascinated me for so many weeks. The stewardess served coffee. 'I'm afraid I haven't any Norwegian money,' I said cautiously.

She smiled, 'Nothing to pay.'

The good coffee reminded me of the bus station in Harstad and Le Mirage in Tromso. Would I see Kate again? Sailing to

Murmansk had been an achievement but I was tired of achieving things. Kate had seemed fond of me because I was what I was, not what I did but she wanted honest communication not bullshit. I thought sadly that I had lost her somewhere between Bergen and Tromso.

I drained my coffee cup and wished the rules of Norwegian internal air lines permitted me to light my pipe. There seemed to be an emptiness at the end of the journey.

Oslo in the afternoon felt tropical under a cloudless sky. I was wearing far too many clothes. Taking off jerseys in the terminal added to the weight of my baggage which made me sweat even more as I humped it to the departure gate.

I had to catch the plane to Stavanger and I boarded the wrong one. I only realised this after take off and saw that we were flying south west along the coast with the sea on our port side. Stavanger would surely have meant a flight path west over the mountains. There is something slightly alarming in finding yourself encapsulated in a splendidly efficient aeroplane going in the wrong direction. It was particularly so in this case because I was going to miss the evening flight from Stavanger to London.

Don't panic, I thought. This must happen quite often. I couldn't, however, recall it happening to any of my friends who flew successfully all over the place in aeroplanes.

The wisest thing seemed to be to hand the problem over to the management. One of the stewardesses serving coffee seemed to have a kind face. When she reached me I said, 'When you've got a moment could you give me some advice?'

'I'll be with you in a few minutes,' she said.

Through the window the coast was green and golden in the sun. The sea was blue and sparkling. Wherever we were going would be very beautiful.

The stewardess sat down in the empty seat beside me. She looked at me enquiringly.

'I think I'm on the wrong plane,' I said.

She didn't look surprised. Perhaps I was right; people often got on the wrong planes and she was quite used to it. In answer to her question I said, 'I'm trying to get to Stavanger to catch the flight to Heathrow.'

She looked at me sympathetically. I felt much better about it now I had told somebody.

'I'm afraid you are on the wrong plane,' she said. 'You ought to be on the flight that goes direct from Oslo to Stavanger. We're going to Christiansand and going on to Stavanger afterwards. I'm afraid you will miss the connection to London.'

I must have looked despondent because she gave me an encouraging smile. 'Leave it with me,' she said, 'I'll go and see the captain.'

I felt rather feeble. I had sailed 1500 miles along the coast of Norway without bothering anybody: now I was being a nuisance. It didn't really matter missing the flight to London; nobody was expecting me. I could book in at a hotel and fly to London in the morning but now I was on the way home I wanted desperately to get there. A night alone in Stavanger would have seemed like a failed ending to the trip.

The plane was beginning its descent to Christiansand when the stewardess returned.

'The captain has fixed it,' she said. 'You'll be alright. He's radioed ahead to Stavanger and the London plane will wait for you.'

I couldn't believe my ears. 'You can't do that,' I protested. 'You can't hold up an international flight for one passenger.'

She laughed hearing the alarm in my voice, 'No problem, it'll only be a ten minute delay.'

She left me with a kind smile promising to thank the captain. I felt a sense of relief and gratitude. What did it cost per minute to keep a four engined jet SAS airliner standing idle on the tarmac? The stewardess had left me with the feeling that such things were normal.

At Stavanger a stewardess from the London flight met me and hustled me smoothly through customs into the waiting plane.

Norway was giving VIP treatment to an Englishman who had got in a muddle!

Heathrow was hot and feverish. It was night time. As I waited for the bus to central London I wondered at the darkness. I hadn't seen any night since the ferry crossing from Newcastle on 2nd June. It was now 27th July – high summer in England. Between the glare of the lights I could see stars overhead – Vega, Deneb, Altair. There hadn't been any in Norway or Russia: the thought registered in my mind, in a dull sort of way, as a good mark for England.

The bus went no further than Euston Station. I had to get to St. Pancras to catch the last train to Nottingham. There were no taxis. I walked between stations. It was only a short distance but my bags were heavy. I had to keep putting them down to wipe the sweat out of my eyes. The train left just before midnight. It was empty and cool. I had checked carefully that it was the right train. It ran through fields and woods under the starlight. England was a dark sleeping land. I looked at my watch. We would be home at one thirty: good going, I thought inappropriately, Nottingham was over two degrees of latitude north of London.

The taxi dropped me outside my house. In the street lights the front garden looked overgrown and neglected, the windows stared at me emptily. It was difficult opening the front door; I had to push aside a pile of letters and junk mail. I switched on all the lights feeling like a stranger; the house didn't seem anything to do with me. I sat down in an armchair in the living room feeling exhausted. In thirty six hours I had travelled in three countries in a catamaran and three different planes, through three time zones, from the arctic tundra to a hot summer's night. This morning I had been walking in the cold rain of Kirkenes. All the same I didn't want to sleep. I fetched myself a glass of whisky and water. The living room with its book lined walls, pictures and the dark garden through the window, looked as if it belonged to someone else. I caught sight of myself in the big mirror over the mantelpiece and was startled by what I saw. I had only had a small mirror on the yacht. This big mirror was reflecting a thin face.

I had been thin enough when I was last in this room; now I had lost about a stone. Perhaps it hadn't all been as easy as I had pretended to myself. I sat back in my chair and took a gulp of the whisky.

I suppose I ought to have felt a sense of achievement. I had sailed a yacht to Murmansk, I had overcome each obstacle in my path. The voyage had been a success. Instead I felt flat. I wished there was someone to talk to so that I could say, 'Yes, we had a super trip but I'm glad to be home.'

I took another sip of whisky and lit my pipe. I thought about Roy and *Callisto* up somewhere in the arctic heading south. I thought about my friends in Murmansk. Natasha Vanyushkina had asked me to write to her; perhaps tomorrow or the next day I would send her a letter describing my journey home. It would make her laugh. The thought cheered me up.

Thinking of letters reminded me of the mail littered over the hall floor. I went out and kicked it around gently with my foot. Picking up the hand written envelopes and postcards I returned to the living room. The clock said a quarter to three. Surely bedtime, I thought, but it didn't matter. I could lie in tomorrow, nobody knew of my return. I felt uncurious about the letters and cards and put them on my work table.

The traffic noise had stopped; it was very quiet. My living room was beginning to look more familiar.

I looked at the pictures on the walls one by one. They were all of HMS *Lancaster Castle* and her crew. The first was a watercolour of the ship at anchor in the Clyde. Her light grey hull was reflected in the still harbour water and beyond her were the hills of Renfrew. The second drawing was of the ship in dry dock in Gibraltar under a cobalt blue sky. I remembered that it had taken me more than two hours to do and it was extremely accurate. A lot of the ships company and dockyard people had stood in silence and watched me as I sat on the dock wall working on it.

238

There is a kind of magic in the way pencil and ink and water colour can transform a flat sheet of paper into the living reality of a ship. It always seemed to collect a crowd. The third picture wasn't so good. It was the framed official photograph of the ship taken soon after she had been commissioned in Tobermory. It made her black and grey and inert. It was surely less accurate than my two drawings. The picture on the opposite wall was, however, my favourite. I got up and went over to look at it closely. In a big frame there were six quick sketches of sailors in the mess deck who I had drawn when they weren't looking. They were playing cribbage or writing letters. I could only identify some of them. Leading torpedoman Higginbottom was sewing. Simmonds was sitting by himself looking fed up, John Brooksbank was relaxing on a bench looking at something in the distance, and Len Tilley sat hunched over the mess table writing the daily letter to his wife. They had been there for years but I had been a long time away from them and now they had come alive. The house wasn't completely empty.

'Hey, you,' I said to them. 'Do you remember the Russian convoys? D'you remember Murmansk? I've just come back from there. You'll think I'm an idiot but I sailed there for fun in a yacht. I thought about you all quite a lot, though.'

I felt a bit self-conscious talking to a picture but somehow it made me feel less lonely. I could sleep now.

Before turning off the lights I glanced at the pile of unopened letters; I would read them tomorrow. A postcard caught my eye – a picture of Nottingham Castle. Who would send a picture of Nottingham Castle to me? I turned it curiously over; it hadn't got a stamp, it had been delivered by hand. I read, 'Thank you for all your letters. I've missed you. Please ring me as soon as you get back.' It was signed 'Kate'.

I felt a sharp feeling of joy; my letters hadn't been written into thin air. Think about that tomorrow I decided cautiously but I could see myself grinning in the mirror.

When I switched off the lights to go upstairs the room filled with faint daylight. There was a lightening of the sky over the city – it was the first dawn I had seen for a long time.

Postscript

Callisto arrived back at Whitby on 24th August. She had made a good passage. Roy told me the story over lunch in the White Post – a pub halfway between Nottingham and his home near Retford. He looked tired but elated. He had had an engine failure and was delayed at Honningsvag, just east of North Cape, for four days waiting for spares. Otherwise all had gone well.

'She's in good order,' he said, 'ready to sail immediately.'

He handed me the log book of the cruise.

'It's all in there,' he said.

In the evening I read through the log book. Ships' logs are boring documents – rows of figures for courses steered, barometric pressure, wind velocity and direction but there is a remarks column and you can often read between the lines of the scribbled entries. There were two that caught my eye. The first was written soon after *Callisto* had left Murmansk. It said,

'Murmansk towards Vardo 24 July 1800 hours.
Five roses thrown into the water in memory of Henry's friends who perished here.'

The second was made only five days before whilst the yacht was crossing the North Sea. *Callisto* had been called on the VHF by a ship who had detected her on radar. She was asked to alter course. This would show on the radar screen and the ship would know that both radio and radar were in contact with the same vessel. Roy had written in the log:

'Bergen towards UK. 22 August 2330 hours.
Test to identify radar contact with Russian seismic survey vessel

was ordered (270 degrees to clear cable in our path). The Russians on the bridge wanted the story about Murmansk. Their words on the VHF were 'Welcome home, sailor, we're from Murmansk too'.'

Somehow these two hurried remarks in Roy's handwriting could stand for *Callisto*'s voyage.